WHITMAN COLLEGE LIBRARY

WITHDRAWN BY WHITMAN COLLEGE LIBRARY

$2395
Good
ex-lib
3/12 EW A
philosophy

JOHN LOCKE

A LETTER CONCERNING TOLERATION
in focus

John Locke's defence of religious toleration, and his insistence on the separate roles of Church and State, have been of fundamental importance in the theoretical and practical development of liberalism. However, the *Letter* has received comparatively little attention from Locke scholars and philosophers, and critical articles are few and often inaccessible. This new edition aims to remedy the situation by bringing together the text of the *Letter* (in the original translation by William Popple) with some new essays and a selection of important earlier critical articles.

The editors' introduction sets the *Letter* in the wider context of Locke's political philosophy and traces the philosophical themes which run though it. The articles by Gough and Nicholson analyse the development of Locke's views on toleration before and after publication of the *Letter*, whilst those by Cranston, Kelly, Mendus and Waldron discuss the philosophical coherence of Locke's beliefs on toleration, and their relevance in the modern world.

The book will be of interest to students and specialists interested in political theory and the history of political thought, as well as to Locke scholars.

The editors: John Horton is Lecturer in Politics and Director of the Morrell Studies in Toleration at the University of York. Susan Mendus is Senior Lecturer in Politics at the University of York, and former Morrell Fellow in Toleration 1985–8.

D0165452

ROUTLEDGE PHILOSOPHERS IN FOCUS SERIES

General Editor: Stanley Tweyman

York University, Toronto

GÖDEL'S *THEOREM* IN FOCUS
Edited by S. G. Shanker

DAVID HUME: *DIALOGUES CONCERNING NATURAL
RELIGION* IN FOCUS
Edited by Stanley Tweyman

J. S. MILL: *ON LIBERTY* IN FOCUS
Edited by John Gray and G. W. Smith

CIVIL DISOBEDIENCE IN FOCUS
Edited by Hugo Adam Bedau

WHITMAN COLLEGE LIBRARY
WITHDRAWN BY
WHITMAN COLLEGE LIBRARY

JOHN LOCKE

A LETTER CONCERNING TOLERATION

in
focus

*Edited by John Horton and
Susan Mendus*

London and New York

BR
1610
'L823
1991

First published 1991
by Routledge
11 New Fetter Lane, London EC4P 4EE

Simultaneously published in the USA and Canada
by Routledge
a division of Routledge, Chapman and Hall, Inc.
29 West 35th Street, New York, NY 10001

The collection as a whole © 1991 Routledge; 'The development of
Locke's belief in toleration' © Oxford University Press;
'Locke: toleration and the rationality of persecution'
© Cambridge University Press; other essays © respective authors

Set in 10/12pt Bembo
Printed in Great Britain by Redwood Press Ltd

All rights reserved. No part of this book may be reprinted or
reproduced or utilized in any form or by any electronic,
mechanical, or other means, now known or hereafter
invented, including photocopying and recording, or in any
information storage or retrieval system, without permission in
writing from the publishers.

British Library Cataloguing in Publication Data
Locke, John *1632–1704*
John Locke, 'A letter concerning toleration' in focus. – (Routledge
philosophers in focus).
1. Christian church. Relations with state
I. Title   II. Horton, John. III. Mendus, Susan.
IV. [Epistola de tolerantia. *English*]
322.1

Library of Congress Cataloging in Publication Data
John Locke, A letter concerning toleration in focus / edited by
John Horton and Susan Mendus.
p.   cm. – (Routledge philosophers in focus series)
Includes translation of: Epistola de tolerantia.
Includes bibliographical references and index.
1. Religious tolerance – History – 17th century.   2. Locke, John,
1632–1704. Epistola de tolerantia.   I. Horton, John (John P.)
II. Mendus, Susan.   III. Locke, John, 1632–1704. Epistola de
tolerantia. English. 1991.   IV. Title: A letter concerning toleration in
focus.   V. Series.
BR1610.L823   1991
261.7'2 – dc20   91–48663

ISBN 0 415 02205 3
ISBN 0 415 06082 6 pbk

PENROSE MEMORIAL LIBRARY
RECEIVED

APR 14 1992

WHITMAN COLLEGE LIBRARY
ACQUISITIONS DEP'T

CONTENTS

v

PENROSE MEMORIAL LIBRARY
WHITMAN COLLEGE
WALLA WALLA, WASHINGTON 99362

ACKNOWLEDGEMENTS

The editors wish to acknowledge their gratitude to the trustees of the C. and J. B. Morrell Trust which since 1981 has generously supported a programme of studies concerned with the philosophical and theoretical aspects of toleration in the Department of Politics of the University of York and of which this volume is a product. We are also very grateful for their helpful advice and comments to our colleagues David Edwards and Peter Nicholson, and to the latter particularly for preparing the bibliography. Our thanks are also due to Jean Darley and Jackie Morgan for their efficient preparation of the manuscript.

'The development of Locke's belief in toleration' © Oxford University Press 1973 is reprinted from J. W. Gough, *John Locke's Political Philosophy* (2nd edn 1973) by permission of Oxford University Press; 'Locke: toleration and the rationality of persecution' © Cambridge University Press 1988 is reprinted from Susan Mendus (ed.), *Justifying Toleration: Conceptual and Historical Perspectives* (1988) by permission of Cambridge University Press; and 'John Locke and the case for toleration' © Maurice Cranston 1986, is reprinted from Susan Mendus and David Edwards (eds), *On Toleration* (Oxford University Press 1987) by permission of the author.

John Horton
Susan Mendus

LOCKE AND TOLERATION

Susan Mendus and John Horton

John Locke was born in Somerset in 1632 and died in Essex in 1704. His family circumstances were modest; his father was an attorney and clerk to local Justices of the Peace; and both his parents came from a Puritan trading background. He was educated at Westminster School and then Christ Church, Oxford, where religious toleration was already a topic of long-standing controversy. The early part of his life was spent in relative obscurity and it was not until 1689, with the publication of *An Essay Concerning Human Understanding*, that he achieved recognition as a great philosopher, though he played an increasingly significant role in national politics from 1667 through his association with the Earl of Shaftesbury. Even today, Locke's philosophical fame rests almost entirely on two works: the *Essay*, and the *Two Treatises on Government*.

The Latin *Epistola de Tolerantia* (*A Letter Concerning Toleration*), anonymously published, also in 1689, has received comparatively little attention from philosophers and Locke scholars and has sometimes been thought to contain virtually nothing of philosophical interest. Why should this be so? One reason is that the *Letter* was written in response to the specific circumstances pertaining in England during the latter part of the seventeenth century. Locke was deeply influenced by his Puritan background and as close friend of the politician and statesman Lord Shaftesbury he was closely involved with the religious and constitutional events of his day. During the seventeenth century religious discord was commonplace, and controversies about religion were highly charged political issues. More specifically, those who advocated toleration in opposition were unlikely to display it when in power, nor did they adopt consistent views about who should and who should not be granted

1

toleration. Reflecting on the events of the later seventeenth century, Locke's translator, William Popple, writes:

> Our government has not only been partial in matters of religion, but those also who have suffered under that partiality, and have therefore endeavoured by their writings to vindicate their own rights and liberties, have for the most part done it upon narrow principles, suited only to the interests of their own sects. This narrowness of spirit on all sides has undoubtedly been the principal occasion of our miseries and confusions.[1]

Locke's *Letter* was thus presented, in its own day, as a response to state intolerance – a diagnosis of the prevailing political ills of seventeenth-century England and Europe, and a proposed remedy for those ills. By the mid–eighteenth century circumstances had eased considerably, the immediate practical significance of the *Letter* had diminished and its wider relevance, as a philosophical text outlining universal principles of toleration, was largely neglected.

A second reason for the comparative neglect of the *Letter* is that it is a quite specific defence of *religious* toleration, and says little about the justification of toleration generally. In modern society problems of toleration arise most often in connection with political, racial or sexual matters, or with freedom of speech and of opinion more generally. Yet on these questions Locke is silent. He provides no general defence of the value of toleration, but only a specific and limited defence of religious toleration. Third, and connectedly, the *Letter* was written in and for an age when Christian belief was the norm rather than the exception, and when few were willing to admit to atheism. Although Locke speaks fleetingly of the toleration of non-Christians, his defence is primarily aimed at securing toleration for different varieties of Christian believers, though even here his arguments would not extend toleration to Catholics, on the grounds that they owed allegiance to a foreign power, the Pope, and were therefore a threat to civil order. Similarly atheists were not to be tolerated since they did not acknowledge divine sanction and hence were not to be trusted. Yet in modern society the toleration of atheists is barely a problem at all, and Locke's assumption of Christian belief can no longer be sustained. Thus, if we require a more general defence of toleration and if, unlike Locke, we do not assume the truth of Christianity, both the relevance and validity of his arguments appear to be threatened. In brief, the scope of the *Letter* is thought to be too narrow, the circumstances too specific and the assumptions no longer commonly accepted as true.

Our aim in presenting this collection is to indicate that the *Letter* deserves serious consideration as both a philosophical and an historical text. Although written at a time when religious belief was the norm, and religious persecution an ever-present threat, the *Letter* also occupies an important place in Locke's political philosophy. It helps us to understand the coherence of his views about the proper limits of state intervention, the duties of the magistrate and the rights of citizens. Moreover, Locke himself saw his task as a very wide, even universal one – to 'inquire how far the duty of toleration extends, and what is required from everyone by it'.[2] Although his arguments do indeed presuppose the religious belief of his audience, and are written against the background of his personal acquaintance and sympathy with those who suffered religious persecution, they are nevertheless not confined to the specific, but are also arguments from principle and of wider interest. Indeed, it was a theoretical defence of toleration which Shaftesbury felt to be imperative, and which prompted him to invite Locke to write the *Letter*. Commenting on the status of Locke's *Letter* Richard Ashcraft has recently written:

> *The Letter on Toleration* is an interesting document because, as a contribution to the political debate on toleration, it represents an attempt both to occupy the higher ground of principles and at the same time to rake up the most basic antipopery prejudices and fears that shaped the popular response to James' policies.[3]

Our aims, therefore, are twofold: to set the *Letter* in its historical context, and to examine the philosophical significance of Locke's arguments and their role in his political thought. We will begin by outlining briefly the circumstances in which the *Letter* was written. We will then introduce the philosophical problems which are discussed in detail in the accompanying essays. Finally, we shall say a few words about the translation presented here.

RELIGION AND POLITICS IN THE SEVENTEENTH CENTURY

In order fully to understand the reasons which prompted Locke to write the *Letter* it is necessary to explain both the place of religion in seventeenth-century Europe, and the place of religion in Locke's own life. For our purposes the story begins in 1648, when the Peace of Westphalia finally put an end to the Thirty Years' War in Europe. Exhausted by long and bitter religious struggles, the nations of Europe were anxious to preserve peace and to avoid the turmoil which had characterized the preceding years. Religious toleration increased throughout Europe, and solutions to problems of religion and religious toleration were sought within rather than between states.

However, in France, the conclusion of the Thirty Years' War coincided with the reign of Louis XIV, who came of age in 1659 and established absolute rule in his own person. In 1685 he revoked the Edict of Nantes which had allowed a degree of religious toleration to Protestants and, supported by the French church, embarked upon ruthless persecution of the Huguenots. In his contribution to this volume Maurice Cranston notes:

> I think it is not generally remembered today how cruel and barbarous was the repression of the Huguenots in France in 1685. Protestants who refused to convert, under orders of Louis XIV, were beaten, pillaged, dragooned, their children were taken from them; men were sent to the galleys or driven into exile. . . . Locke does not refer to France by name: everybody knew what was happening there, and we can hardly doubt that those events did much to undermine the allegiance of the English people to James II, and smoothed the way for the Revolution of 1688. [4]

A Letter on Toleration is thus a European text as much as an English one: although religious battles were fought within rather than between nations, Locke and his readers would have been in no doubt about what was happening in France, nor would they have failed to see the potentially dangerous implications which those events might have for England. This is a significant factor, for in England too religious discord was widespread and Locke himself, through his friendship with the Earl of Shaftesbury, was often close to the centre of political controversies which had their root in religious conviction.

Locke met the Earl of Shaftesbury (then Lord Ashley) in 1666. A close friendship developed between them, and through Shaftesbury Locke became involved in highly controversial and often dangerous political activities. When they first met, Shaftesbury was an influential figure at the court of Charles II with whom he appeared to share a commitment to religious toleration. However, by the 1670s Shaftesbury's relationship with the king had been transformed for a variety of complex political reasons. Their increasing estrangement also revealed that their shared concern for toleration was more apparent than real, for while Charles favoured toleration for Catholics, Shaftesbury was primarily interested in toleration for Protestants. Thereafter the currents of politics took the two men further apart: from being a collaborator Shaftesbury became an open enemy of the king.

During the Exclusion Crisis Shaftesbury led a national political movement against the crown. He attempted to place restraints upon the power of the king, to strengthen the role of the elected members of the House of Commons and to prevent the Catholic James II from succeeding to the throne. As John Dunn has put it, 'it was a bitter and dangerous struggle in which the line between exercising legally recognised political rights and committing high treason was always difficult to draw. . . . By 1682, if not before, Shaftesbury and Locke were gambling with their lives'.[5] Shaftesbury, anticipating his arrest for treason, fled to Holland late in 1682 and within a short time died. Locke, implicated in Shaftesbury's seditious activities, was also forced to seek asylum in Holland where he remained until 1689, by which time the Protestant William of Orange had succeeded to the English throne, and the political climate in England was altogether more congenial to him.

It was against this background, and during his period of exile, that Locke prepared the text of *A Letter Concerning Toleration*. According to Le Clerc, the *Letter* was written in Amsterdam between the first days of November and the second half of December of 1685. While Locke was in exile he made many friends among French Protestant refugees, who were also seeking asylum in Holland after the revocation of the Edict of Nantes. French Huguenots, like English dissenters, had suffered a reversal of their fortunes during the seventeenth century. In 1598 the Edict of Nantes had granted them a degree of religious toleration, but was always a rather precarious suspension of hostilities. In 1685 the Edict was revoked and Protestant pastors were compelled to renounce their calling, or die.

Thus, in both Britain and Europe, religious dissenters were in a constant state of uncertainty: the religious liberty and toleration granted by the Declaration of Indulgence and the Edict of Nantes were no more than temporary respites. By 1685 Protestantism had suffered a severe reverse in France and seemed to be dangerously menaced throughout Britain. Both Protestantism and toleration appeared to be under threat in the Christendom that stretched from Hungary to the New World of America. Some commentators have argued that this period of exile set the seal on a great change in Locke's ideas on toleration which had occurred under the influence of Shaftesbury and his own bitter experience of the consequences of persecution and intolerance; an authoritarian in his early, conservative days, he became committed to toleration only later, when his liberalism was fully developed.

The development of Locke's theory of toleration is examined in several of the essays presented here: J. W. Gough's seminal essay discusses the relationship between *A Letter Concerning Toleration* and Locke's earlier writings, and Gough contends that the main arguments of the *Letter* are consistent with Locke's earlier works and, moreover, that they are an important plank of his political theory generally. Paul Kelly similarly argues that the philosophical perspective which informs the *Letter* is largely consistent with Locke's earlier, and seemingly more conservative, writings. By contrast, Maurice Cranston claims that the early Locke was an authoritarian and a man of the Right, whose views changed markedly in later life. Each of these essays considers the political and religious circumstances in which Locke wrote, and discusses the extent to which changing circumstances themselves accounted for changes in Locke's prescriptions concerning toleration.

THE PHILOSOPHICAL ARGUMENTS OF THE *LETTER*

The magnitude of the political and religious events of the seventeenth century has often eclipsed the philosophical significance of Locke's *Letter* and has also served to detract attention from its theoretical basis. However, far from obviating the need for a philosophical defence of toleration, the events of seventeenth-century Britain and Europe emphasized its importance. As has been noted above it was a *theoretical* defence of toleration which Shaftesbury urged Locke to write – a defence which would rise above mere special pleading or thinly disguised self-interest and which would have wide and general application. In a world in which, as Cromwell had put it, 'everyone desires to have liberty, but none will give it' the need for a philosophical defence was urgent. Thus, whatever the success of Locke's arguments, they are, as Maurice Cranston notes, the arguments of a philosopher, not merely the arguments of a religiously heterodox seventeenth-century exile concerned to fight his own corner.

The essays presented here identify three main philosophical themes in Locke's *Letter*. Jeremy Waldron construes the argument as one which is essentially concerned with religious toleration and with the alleged irrationality of attempting to employ coercive means to induce religious belief. Paul Kelly draws upon the whole corpus of Locke's writings and suggests that, taken together, these constitute an attempt on Locke's part to reconcile liberty of conscience with the necessary authority of the state. Susan Mendus defends Locke's emphasis on the obligations of would-be-persecutors, and relates this more generally to modern justifications of toleration. The three themes dovetail into a general discussion of the proper limits of state intervention and authority. Of course, opinions differ as to how successful Locke's argument actually is: Waldron is critical of the 'fatal attraction' of ethical rationalism for Locke, and contends that it is this which led him to believe that 'if only we can show that intolerance is irrational we may be excused from the messy business of indicating the reasons why it is *wrong*'.[6] Mendus and Kelly, on the other hand, interpret the *Letter* as an attempt to indicate the necessity of a legal framework within which social toleration may develop: 'the basic framework of law will provide the conditions of ordered social interaction, but within that framework of law political problems have to be resolved which require more than an appeal to abstract principle'.[7]

This quotation from Kelly draws attention to one very significant way in which Locke's *Letter* provides more than a merely pragmatic, seventeenth-century defence of specifically religious toleration. In the history of political philosophy Locke is often recognized as the father of liberalism. His *Two Treatises of Government*, with their emphasis on the social contract and individual rights, do most to justify his claim to this title. However, *A Letter Concerning Toleration* also introduces important liberal themes such as the proper role and jurisdiction of the magistrate (the state), and the necessity of government neutrality in certain areas. Two questions are central here: How are we to decide what is the proper area of government intervention? and What constitutes government neutrality? Waldron indicates ways in which the *Letter* contains an implied theory of the state. For Locke, the state is to be defined not in terms of its functions, but in terms of the characteristic means at its disposal: 'rods and axes', 'force and blood', 'fire and the sword' are the legitimate means by which the state operates. Moreover, these serve both to justify and to set limits to state toleration, for the coercive means available to the state are simply inappropriate in religious matters, whereas they are legitimately employed in order to ensure civil peace.

There is, as both Gough and Kelly point out, a crucial distinction between necessary and indifferent matters underpinning Locke's argument for toleration, and indeed underpinning his political philosophy as a whole. This distinction

> determines the boundaries to the civil magistrate's sphere of influence, but within that realm it does not prescribe the particular policies which will secure the civil interests of his subjects. This practical question can only be answered, like all political questions, by an uneasy compromise between principle, experience and understanding of human nature.[8]

The role of the necessary–indifferent distinction in determining the boundaries of state intervention draws attention to similar questions in modern liberal discussions of toleration. While liberal societies are characterized by their commitment to toleration, they must also explain the limits of toleration, and give an account of why unlimited toleration is not justifiable. Locke's insistence on the necessary–indifferent distinction serves to ground his account of toleration, while his characterization of the state in terms of the means at its disposal sets limits to toleration. Modern political philosophy, by contrast, is less clear about the role of the state and this, as Maurice Cranston points out, gives rise to inconsistencies in modern liberal theory.

As indicated earlier Locke's defence of toleration has not gone unchallenged either in his day or ours. However, while for most modern critics, such as Waldron, Locke's arguments are considered too weak and limited to support the extensive toleration now thought necessary and desirable, his contemporary critics had rather different worries. The concern of one commentator, Thomas Long, is clearly indicated in the title of his reply to Locke, *The 'Letter for Toleration' Deciphered and the Absurdity and Impiety of an Absolute Truth Demonstrated*. A far more important response, however, was *The Argument of the 'Letter Concerning Toleration' Briefly Considered and Answered* by Jonas Proast, an Oxford chaplain, whom, unlike

Long, Locke did not feel he could ignore. The vagaries of the protracted and prolix exchanges between Locke and Proast are discussed in the essay by Peter Nicholson. As he shows, though the merits of the dispute hardly justified its extravagant length (Locke wrote three further 'letters', the *Third Letter* being a very sizeable book) it does raise matters of some substance. Proast was a more astute critic than has commonly been appreciated and he succeeded in forcing Locke to refine and clarify some of his arguments and, in particular, pushed him into taking a more sceptical attitude towards religious knowledge. Though of primarily historical interest the debate between Locke and Proast is not without significance for a modern audience.

A Letter Concerning Toleration is both a philosophical text and an historical one: written from profound personal and vicarious experience of state persecution it also attempts to provide an argument of universal relevance with 'as much relevance to the problems of toleration in England today as of three hundred years ago'.[9]

A NOTE ON THE TRANSLATION

We have adopted here the most famous, and probably the most controversial, translation of Locke's *Letter* – that by William Popple. As has been noted already the *Letter* was first published anonymously in Latin in 1689. Before the year was out it had been translated by Popple and published in English with an introductory address 'To the Reader' by Popple himself. Locke always claimed that the translation had been made 'without my privity' and Maurice Cranston claims, in his contribution to this volume, that there are features of Popple's translation which are simply over-enthusiastic and at variance with Locke's views. Cranston notes:

> There is one especially striking phrase in Popple's preface: 'Absolute liberty, just and true liberty, equal and impartial liberty, is the thing we stand in need of.' This was Popple's demand. It was not Locke's. Locke wanted toleration, not 'absolute liberty'.[10]

Thus, some have claimed that Popple's translation is unreliable: Locke was a moderate and a liberal; Popple a zealot and a radical, who hoped to find support for his radicalism in Locke's more judicious text.

So far as the literal accuracy of Popple's translation is concerned there is undeniably some justification for this charge and Popple's prose is sometimes significantly more colourful than that of Locke. For this reason there is certainly a place for a more scrupulously exact modern translation such as that by J. W. Gough. However, we have used Popple's translation for two reasons: first, it is the only translation by a contemporary of Locke, and one who had first-hand experience of the controversies of the day. Second, there are grounds for believing that although made 'without my privity' Popple's translation was nevertheless approved by Locke.

Thus, Richard Ashcraft has argued that

Locke's notation 'without my privity' means that the translation was carried out without active participation. It does not mean without his knowledge, since Locke clearly knew of the translation; nor, on the other hand, does it mean without his approval . . . given the opportunity to make any changes in meaning in Popple's translation where the latter had not faithfully reproduced his own intended meaning, Locke chose not to do so. On the contrary, he defended that translation at great length in his replies to Proast.[11]

Furthermore, the claim that Locke was opposed to Popple's radicalism is a contentious one, for some critics have suggested that Locke was in fact more radical than we, in the twentieth century, are disposed to allow. Thus Ashcraft argues with considerable plausibility that, far from being a moderate, Locke was more of a radical on the matter of toleration.

The debate about Locke's radicalism clearly connects with the earlier debate about the extent to which his views changed between the 1660s and the 1680s, and about the consistency of his earlier and later writings. Whatever the truth of that matter, Popple's translation is itself an important historical document providing a unique insight into the nature of the seventeenth-century debate on toleration, and enabling us to understand more clearly the terms in which that debate was conducted.

NOTES

1 'To the Reader'. Popple's introductory address to his translation of Locke's *Letter*. See below, p. 12.
2 See below p. 22.

3 Richard Ashcraft, *Revolutionary Politics and Locke's Two Treatises of Government* (Princeton 1986), p. 498.
4 See below p. 82.
5 John Dunn, *Locke* (Oxford 1984), p. 9.
6 See below p. 120.
7 See below p. 144.
8 See below p. 144.
9 See below p. 92.
10 See below p. 85.
11 Richard Ashcraft, op cit., pp. 498–9 n. 127.

A LETTER CONCERNING TOLERATION

TO THE READER

The ensuing Letter concerning Toleration, first printed in Latin this very year, in Holland, has already been translated both into Dutch and French. So general and speedy an approbation may therefore bespeak its favourable reception in England. I think indeed there is no nation under heaven, in which so much has already been said upon that subject as ours. But yet certainly there is no people that stand in more need of having something further both said and done amongst them, in this point, than we do.

Our government has not only been partial in matters of religion, but those also who have suffered under that partiality, and have therefore endeavoured by their writings to vindicate their own rights and liberties, have for the most part done it upon narrow principles, suited only to the interests of their own sects.

This narrowness of spirit on all sides has undoubtedly been the principal occasion of our miseries and confusions. But whatever have been the occasions, it is now high time to seek for a thorough cure. We have need of more generous remedies than what have yet been made use of in our distemper. It is neither declarations of indulgence, nor acts of comprehension, such as have yet been practised or projected amongst us, that can do the work. The first will but palliate, the second increase our evil.

Absolute liberty, just and true liberty, equal and impartial liberty, is the thing that we stand in need of. Now, though this has indeed been much talked of, I doubt it has not been much understood; I am sure not at all practised, either by our governors towards the people in general, or by any dissenting parties of the people towards one another.

12

I cannot, therefore, but hope that this discourse, which treats of that subject, however briefly, yet more exactly than any we have yet seen, demonstrating both the equitableness and practicableness of the thing, will be esteemed highly seasonable by all men who have souls large enough to prefer the true interest of the public, before that of a party.

It is for the use of such as are already so spirited, or to inspire that spirit into those that are not, that I have translated it into our language. But the thing itself is so short, that it will not bear a longer preface. I leave it, therefore, to the consideration of my countrymen; and heartily wish they may make the use of it that it appears to be designed for.

William Popple

HONOURED SIR,

Since you are pleased to inquire what are my thoughts about the mutual toleration of Christians in their different professions of religion, I must needs answer you freely, that I esteem that toleration to be the chief characteristical mark of the true church. For whatsoever some people boast of the antiquity of places and names, or of the pomp of their outward worship; others, of the reformation of their discipline; all, of the orthodoxy of their faith, for every one is orthodox to himself: these things, and all others of this nature, are much rather marks of men's striving for power and empire over one another, than of the church of Christ. Let anyone have ever so true a claim to all these things, yet if he be destitute of charity, meekness, and goodwill in general towards all mankind, even to those that are not Christians, he is certainly yet short of being a true Christian himself. 'The kings of the Gentiles exercise lordship over them', said our Saviour to his disciples, 'but ye shall not be so', Luke xxii. 25, 26. The business of true religion is quite another thing. It is not instituted in order to the erecting an external pomp, nor to the obtaining of ecclesiastical dominion, nor to the exercising of compulsive force; but to the regulating of men's lives according to the rules of virtue and piety. Whosoever will list himself under the banner of Christ, must, in the first place, and above all things, make war upon his own lusts and vices. It is in vain for any man to usurp the name of Christian, without holiness of life, purity of manners, and benignity and meekness of spirit. 'Let every one that nameth the name of Christ depart from iniquity', 2 Tim. ii. 19. 'Thou, when thou art converted, strengthen thy brethren', said our Lord to Peter, Luke xxii. 32. It would indeed be very hard for one that appears careless about his own salvation, to persuade me that he were extremely concerned for mine. For it is impossible that those should sincerely and heartily apply themselves to make other people Christians, who have not really embraced the Christian religion in their own hearts. If the Gospel and the apostle may be credited, no man can be a Christian without charity, and without that faith which works, not by force, but by love. Now I appeal to the consciences of those that persecute, torment, destroy, and kill other men upon pretence of religion, whether they do it out of friendship and kindness towards them, or no: and I shall then indeed, and not till then, believe they do so, when I shall see those fiery zealots correcting, in the same manner, their friends and familiar acquaintance, for the manifest sins they commit against the precepts of the Gospel; when I

14

shall see them prosecute with fire and sword the members of their own communion that are tainted with enormous vices, and without amendment are in danger of eternal perdition; and when I shall see them thus express their love and desire of the salvation of their souls by the infliction of torments, and exercise of all manner of cruelties. For if it be out of a principle of charity, as they pretend, and love to men's souls, that they deprive them of their estates, maim them with corporal punishments, starve and torment them in noisome prisons, and in the end even take away their lives; I say, if all this be done merely to make men Christians, and procure their salvation, why then do they suffer 'whoredom, fraud, malice, and such like enormities', which, according to the apostle, Rom. i. manifestly relish of heathenish corruption, to predominate so much and abound amongst their flocks and people? These, and such like things, are certainly more contrary to the glory of God, to the purity of the church, and to the salvation of souls, than any conscientious dissent from ecclesiastical decision, or separation from public worship, whilst accompanied with innocence of life. Why then does this burning zeal for God, for the church, and for the salvation of souls; burning, I say, literally with fire and faggot; pass by those moral vices and wickednesses, without any chastisement, which are acknowledged by all men to be diametrically opposite to the profession of Christianity, and bend all its nerves either to the introducing of ceremonies, or to the establishment of opinions, which for the most part are about nice and intricate matters, that exceed the capacity of ordinary understandings? Which of the parties contending about these things is in the right, which of them is guilty of schism, or heresy, whether those that domineer or those that suffer, will then at last be manifest, when the cause of their separation comes to be judged of. He certainly that follows Christ, embraces his doctrine, and bears his yoke, though he forsake both father and mother, separate from the public assemblies and ceremonies of his country, or whomsoever, or whatsoever else he relinquishes, will not then be judged an heretic.

Now, though the divisions that are amongst sects should be allowed to be ever so obstructive of the salvation of souls, yet, nevertheless, 'adultery, fornication, uncleanness, lasciviousness, idolatry, and such like things, cannot be denied to be works of the flesh'; concerning which the apostle has expressly declared, that 'they who do them shall not inherit the kingdom of God', Gal. v. 21. Whosoever, therefore, is sincerely solicitous about the kingdom of

15

God, and thinks it his duty to endeavour the enlargement of it amongst men, ought to apply himself with no less care and industry to the rooting out of these immoralities, than to the extirpation of sects. But if any one do otherwise, and, whilst he is cruel and implacable towards those that differ from him in opinion, he be indulgent to such iniquities and immoralities as are unbecoming the name of a Christian, let such a one talk ever so much of the church, he plainly demonstrates by his actions, that it is another kingdom he aims at, and not the advancement of the kingdom of God.

That any man should think fit to cause another man, whose salvation he heartily desires, to expire in torments, and that even in an unconverted estate, would, I confess, seem very strange to me, and, I think, to any other also. But nobody, surely, will ever believe that such a carriage can proceed from charity, love, or goodwill. If any one maintain that men ought to be compelled by fire and sword to profess certain doctrines, and conform to this or that exterior worship, without any regard had unto their morals; if any one endeavour to convert those that are erroneous unto the faith, by forcing them to profess things that they do not believe, and allowing them to practise things that the Gospel does not permit; it cannot be doubted, indeed, that such a one is desirous to have a numerous assembly joined in the same profession with himself; but that he principally intends by those means to compose a truly Christian church, is altogether incredible. It is not therefore to be wondered at, if those who do not really contend for the advancement of the true religion, and of the church of Christ, make use of arms that do not belong to the Christian warfare. If, like the Captain of our salvation, they sincerely desired the good of souls, they would tread in the steps and follow the perfect example of the Prince of Peace, who sent out his soldiers to the subduing of nations, and gathering them into his church, not armed with the sword, or other instruments of force, but prepared with the Gospel of peace, and with the exemplary holiness of their conversation. This was his method. Though if infidels were to be converted by force, if those that are either blind or obstinate were to be drawn off from their errors by armed soldiers, we know very well that it was much more easy for him to do it with armies of heavenly legions, than for any one of the church, how potent soever, with all his dragoons.

The toleration of those that differ from others in matters of religion, is so agreeable to the Gospel of Jesus Christ, and to the genuine reason of mankind, that it seems monstrous for men to be so blind, as not to perceive the necessity and advantage of it, in so clear a light. I will not here tax the pride and ambition of some, the passion and uncharitable zeal of others. These are faults from which human affairs can perhaps scarce ever be perfectly freed; but yet such as nobody will bear the plain imputation of, without covering them with some specious colour; and so pretend to commendation, whilst they are carried away by their own irregular passions. But, however, that some may not colour their spirit of persecution and unchristian cruelty with a pretence of care of the public weal, and observation of the laws, and that others, under pretence of religion, may not seek impunity for their libertinism and licentiousness; in a word, that none may impose either upon himself or others, by the pretences of loyalty and obedience to the prince, or of tenderness and sincerity in the worship of God; I esteem it above all things necessary to distinguish exactly the business of civil government from that of religion, and to settle the just bounds that lie between the one and the other. If this be not done, there can be no end put to the controversies that will be always arising between those that have, or at least pretend to have, on the one side, a concernment for the interest of men's souls, and, on the other side, a care of the commonwealth.

The commonwealth seems to me to be a society of men constituted only for the procuring, preserving, and advancing their own civil interests.

Civil interest I call life, liberty, health, and indolence of body; and the possession of outward things, such as money, land, houses, furniture, and the like.

It is the duty of the civil magistrate, by the impartial execution of equal laws, to secure unto all the people in general, and to every one of his subjects in particular, the just possession of these things belonging to this life. If any one presume to violate the laws of public justice and equity, established for the preservation of these things, his presumption is to be checked by the fear of punishment, consisting in the deprivation or diminution of those civil interests, or goods, which otherwise he might and ought to enjoy. But seeing no man does willingly suffer himself to be punished by the deprivation of any part of his goods, and much less of his liberty or life, therefore is the magistrate armed with the force and strength of all his subjects, in order to the punishment of those that violate any other man's rights.

Now that the whole jurisdiction of the magistrate reaches only to these civil concernments; and that all civil power, right, and dominion, is bounded and confined to the only care of promoting these things; and that it neither can nor ought in any manner to be extended to the salvation of souls; these following considerations seem unto me abundantly to demonstrate.

First, Because the care of souls is not committed to the civil magistrate, any more than to other men. It is not committed unto him, I say, by God; because it appears not that God has ever given any such authority to one man over another, as to compel any one to his religion. Nor can any such power be vested in the magistrate by the consent of the people; because no man can so far abandon the care of his own salvation as blindly to leave it to the choice of any other, whether prince or subject, to prescribe to him what faith or worship he shall embrace. For no man can, if he would, conform his faith to the dictates of another. All the life and power of true religion consists in the inward and full persuasion of the mind; and faith is not faith without believing. Whatever profession we make, to whatever outward worship we conform, if we are not fully satisfied in our own mind that the one is true, and the other well-pleasing unto God, such profession and such practice, far from being any furtherance, are indeed great obstacles to our salvation. For in this manner, instead of expiating other sins by the exercise of religion, I say, in offering thus unto God Almighty such a worship as we esteem to be displeasing unto him, we add unto the number of our other sins, those also of hypocrisy, and contempt of his Divine Majesty.

In the second place. The care of souls cannot belong to the civil magistrate, because his power consists only in outward force: but true and saving religion consists in the inward persuasion of the mind, without which nothing can be acceptable to God. And such is the nature of the understanding, that it cannot be compelled to the belief of any thing by outward force. Confiscation of estate, imprisonment, torments, nothing of that nature can have any such efficacy as to make men change the inward judgment that they have framed of things.

It may indeed be alleged that the magistrate may make use of arguments, and thereby draw the heterodox into the way of truth, and procure their salvation. I grant it; but this is common to him with other men. In teaching, instructing, and redressing the erroneous by reason, he may certainly do what becomes any good man to do. Magistracy does not oblige him to put off either humanity or Christianity. But it is one thing to persuade, another to command; one thing to press with arguments, another with penalties. This the civil power alone has a right to do; to the other, good-will is authority enough. Every man has commission to admonish, exhort, convince another of error, and by reasoning to draw him into truth: but to give laws, receive obedience, and compel with the sword, belongs to none but the magistrate. And upon this ground I affirm, that the magistrate's power extends not to the establishing of any articles of faith, or forms of worship, by the force of his laws. For laws are of no force at all without penalties, and penalties in this case are absolutely impertinent; because they are not proper to convince the mind. Neither the profession of any articles of faith, nor the conformity to any outward form of worship, as has been already said, can be available to the salvation of souls, unless the truth of the one, and the acceptableness of the other unto God, be thoroughly believed by those that so profess and practise. But penalties are no ways capable to produce such belief. It is only light and evidence that can work a change in men's opinions; and that light can in no manner proceed from corporal sufferings, or any other outward penalties.

In the third place. The care of the salvation of men's souls cannot belong to the magistrate; because, though the rigour of laws and the force of penalties were capable to convince and change men's minds, yet would not that help at all to the salvation of their souls. For, there being but one truth, one way to heaven; what hopes is there that more men would be led into it, if they had no other rule to follow but the religion of the court, and were put under a necessity to quit the light of their own reason, to oppose the dictates of their own consciences, and blindly to resign up themselves to the will of their governors, and to the religion, which either ignorance, ambition, or superstition had chanced to establish in the countries where they were born? In the variety and contradiction of opinions in religion, wherein the princes of the world are as much divided as in their secular interests, the narrow way would be much straitened; one country alone would be in the right, and all the rest of the world put under an obligation of following their princes in the ways that lead to destruction: and that which heightens the absurdity, and very ill suits the notion of a Deity, men would owe their eternal happiness or misery to the places of their nativity.

These considerations, to omit many others that might have been urged to the same purpose, seem unto me sufficient to conclude, that all the power of civil government relates only to men's civil interests, is confined to the care of the things of this world, and hath nothing to do with the world to come.

Let us now consider what a church is. A church then I take to be a voluntary society of men, joining themselves together of their own accord, in order to the public worshipping of God, in such a manner as they judge acceptable to him, and effectual to the salvation of their souls.

I say, it is a free and voluntary society. Nobody is born a member of any church; otherwise the religion of parents would descend unto children, by the same right of inheritance as their temporal estates, and every one would hold his faith by the same tenure he does his lands; than which nothing can be imagined more absurd. Thus therefore that matter stands. No man by nature is bound unto any particular church or sect, but every one joins himself voluntarily to that society in which he believes he has found that profession and worship which is truly acceptable to God. The hopes of salvation, as it was the only cause of his entrance into that communion, so it can be the only reason of his stay there. For if afterwards he discover any thing either erroneous in the doctrine, or incongruous in the worship of that society to which he has joined himself, why should it not be as free for him to go out as it was to enter? No member of a religious society can be tied with any other bonds but what proceed from the certain expectation of eternal life. A church then is a society of members voluntarily uniting to this end.

It follows now that we consider what is the power of this church, and unto what laws it is subject.

Forasmuch as no society, how free soever, or upon whatsoever slight occasion instituted, (whether of philosophers for learning, of merchants for commerce, or of men of leisure for mutual conversation and discourse) no church or company, I say, can in the least subsist and hold together, but will presently dissolve and break to pieces, unless it be regulated by some laws, and the members all consent to observe some order. Place and time of meeting must be agreed on; rules for admitting and excluding members must be established; distinction of officers, and putting things into a regular course, and such like, cannot be omitted. But since the joining together of several members into this church-society, as has already been demonstrated, is absolutely free and spontaneous, it necessarily follows, that the right of making its laws can belong to none but the society itself, or at least, which is the same thing, to those whom the society by common consent has authorized thereunto.

Some perhaps may object, that no such society can be said to be a true church, unless it have in it a bishop, or presbyter, with ruling authority derived from the very apostles, and continued down unto the present time by an uninterrupted succession.

To these I answer. In the first place, Let them show me the edict by which Christ has imposed that law upon his church. And let not any man think me impertinent, if, in a thing of this consequence, I require that the terms of that edict be very express and positive, – For the promise he has made us, that 'wheresoever two or three are gathered together in his name, he will be in the midst of them' Matth. xviii. 20, seems to imply the contrary. Whether such an assembly want any thing necessary to a true church, pray do you consider. Certain I am, that nothing can be there wanting unto the salvation of souls, which is sufficient for our purpose.

Next, pray observe how great have always been the divisions amongst even those who lay so much stress upon the divine institution, and continued succession of a certain order of rulers in the church. Now their very dissension unavoidably puts us upon a necessity of deliberating, and consequently allows a liberty of choosing that, which upon consideration we prefer.

And, in the last place, I consent that these men have a ruler of their church, established by such a long series of succession as they judge necessary, provided I may have liberty at the same time to join myself to that society, in which I am persuaded those things are to be found which are necessary to the salvation of my soul. In this manner ecclesiastical liberty will be preserved on all sides, and no man will have a legislator imposed upon him, but whom himself has chosen.

But since men are so solicitous about the true church, I would only ask them here by the way, if it be not more agreeable to the church of Christ to make the conditions of her communion consist in such things, and such things only, as the Holy Spirit has in the holy Scriptures declared, in express words, to be necessary to salvation? I ask, I say, whether this be not more agreeable to the church of Christ, than for men to impose their own inventions and interpretations upon others, as if they were of divine authority; and to establish by ecclesiastical laws, as absolutely necessary to the profession of Christianity, such things as the holy Scriptures do either not mention, or at least not expressly command? Whosoever requires those things in order to ecclesiastical communion, which Christ does not require in order to life eternal, he may perhaps indeed constitute a society accommodated to his own opinion, and his own advantage; but how that can be called the church of Christ, which is established upon laws that are not his, and which excludes such persons from its communion as he will one day receive into the kingdom of heaven, I understand not. But this being not a proper place to inquire into the marks of the true church, I will only mind those that contend so earnestly for the decrees of their own society, and that cry out continually the CHURCH, the CHURCH, with as much noise, and perhaps upon the same principle, as the Ephesian silver-smiths did for their Diana; this, I say, I desire to mind them of, that the Gospel frequently declares, that the true disciples of Christ must suffer persecution; but that the church of Christ should persecute others, and force others by fire and sword to embrace her faith and doctrine, I could never yet find in any of the books of the New Testament.

The end of a religious society, as has already been said, is the public worship of God, and by means thereof the acquisition of eternal life. All discipline ought therefore to tend to that end, and all ecclesiastical laws to be thereunto confined. Nothing ought, nor can be transacted in this society, relating to the possession of civil and worldly goods. No force is here to be made use of, upon any occasion whatsoever: for force belongs wholly to the civil magistrate, and the possession of all outward goods is subject to his jurisdiction.

But it may be asked, by what means then shall ecclesiastical laws be established, if they must be thus destitute of all compulsive power? I answer they must be established by means suitable to the nature of such things, whereof the external profession and observation, if not proceeding from a thorough conviction and approbation of the mind, is altogether useless and unprofitable. The arms by which the members of this society are to be kept within their duty, are exhortations, admonitions, and advice. If by these means the offenders will not be reclaimed, and the erroneous convinced, there remains nothing farther to be done, but that such stubborn and obstinate persons, who give no ground to hope for their reformation, should be cast out and separated from the society. This is the last and utmost force of ecclesiastical authority: no other punishment can thereby be inflicted, than that the relation ceasing between the body and the member which is cut off, the person so condemned ceases to be a part of that church.

These things being thus determined, let us inquire, in the next place, how far the duty of toleration extends, and what is required from every one by it.

At first, I hold, that no church is bound by the duty of toleration to retain any such person in her bosom, as after admonition continues obstinately to offend against the laws of the society. For these being the condition of communion, and the bond of society, if the breach of them were permitted without any animadversion, the society would immediately be thereby dissolved. But nevertheless, in all such cases care is to be taken that the sentence of excommunication, and the execution thereof, carry with it no rough usage, of word or action, whereby the ejected person may any ways be damnified in body or estate. For all force, as has often been said, belongs only to the magistrate, nor ought any private persons, at any time, to use force; unless it be in self-defence against unjust violence. Excommunication neither does nor can deprive the excommunicated person of any of those civil goods that he formerly possessed. All those things belong to the civil government, and are under the magistrate's protection. The whole force of excommunication consists only in this, that the resolution of the society in that respect being declared, the union that was between the body and some member, comes thereby to be dissolved; and that relation ceasing, the participation of some certain things, which the society communicated to its members, and unto which no man has any civil right, comes also to cease. For there is no civil injury done unto the excommunicated person, by the church minister's refusing him that bread and wine, in the celebration of the Lord's supper, which was not bought with his, but other men's money.

Secondly: No private person has any right in any manner to prejudice another person in his civil enjoyments, because he is of another church or religion. All the rights and franchises that belong to him as a man, or as a denison, are inviolably to be preserved to him. These are not the business of religion. No violence nor injury is to be offered him, whether he be Christian or pagan. Nay, we must not content ourselves with the narrow measures of bare justice: charity, bounty, and liberality must be added to it. This the Gospel enjoins, this reason directs, and this that natural fellowship we are born into requires of us. If any man err from the right way, it is his own misfortune, not injury to thee: nor therefore art thou to punish him in the things of this life, because thou supposest he will be miserable in that which is to come.

What I say concerning the mutual toleration of private persons differing from one another in religion, I understand also of particular churches; which stand as it were in the same relation to each other as private persons among themselves; nor has any one of them any manner of jurisdiction over any other, no, not even when the civil magistrate, as it sometimes happens, comes to be of this or the other communion. For the civil government can give no new right to the church, nor the church to the civil government. So that whether the magistrate join himself to any church, or separate from it, the church remains always as it was before, a free and voluntary society. It neither acquires the power of the sword by the magistrate's coming to it, nor does it lose the right of instruction and excommunication by his going from it. This is the fundamental and immutable right of a spontaneous society, that it has to remove any of its members who transgress the rules of its institution: but it cannot, by the accession of any new members, acquire any right of jurisdiction over those that are not joined with it. And therefore peace, equity, and friendship, are always mutually to be observed by particular churches, in the same manner as by private persons, without any pretence of superiority or jurisdiction over one another.

That the thing may be made yet clearer by an example; let us suppose two churches, the one of Arminians, the other of Calvinists, residing in the city of Constantinople. Will any one say, that either of these churches has right to deprive the members of the other of their estates and liberty, as we see practised elsewhere, because of their differing from it in some doctrines or ceremonies; whilst the Turks in the meanwhile silently stand by, and laugh to see with what inhuman cruelty Christians thus rage against Christians? But if one of these churches hath this power of treating the other ill, I ask which of them it is to whom that power belongs, and by what right? It will be answered, undoubtedly, that it is the orthodox church which has the right of authority over the erroneous or heretical. This is, in great and specious words, to say just nothing at all. For every church is orthodox to itself; to others, erroneous or heretical. Whatsoever any church believes, it believes to be true; and the contrary thereupon it pronounces to be error. So that the controversy between these churches about the truth of their doctrines, and the purity of their worship, is on both sides equal; nor is there any judge, either at Constantinople, or elsewhere upon earth, by whose sentence it can be determined. The decision of that question belongs only to the Supreme Judge of all men, to whom also alone belongs the punishment of the erroneous. In the meanwhile, let those men consider how heinously they sin, who, adding injustice, if not to their error, yet certainly to their pride, do rashly and arrogantly take upon them

to misuse the servants of another master, who are not at all accountable to them.

Nay, further: if it could be manifest which of these two dissenting
churches were in the right way, there would not accrue thereby unto
the orthodox any right of destroying the other. For churches have
neither any jurisdiction in worldly matters, nor are fire and sword
any proper instruments wherewith to convince men's minds of
error, and inform them of the truth. Let us suppose, nevertheless,
that the civil magistrate is inclined to favour one of them, and to put
his sword into their hands, that, by his consent, they might chastise
the dissenters as they pleased. Will any man say, that any right can be
derived unto a Christian church, over its brethren, from a Turkish
emperor? An infidel, who has himself no authority to punish Christians for the articles of their faith, cannot confer such an authority
upon any society of Christians, nor give unto them a right which he
has not himself. This would be the case at Constantinople. And the
reason for the thing is the same in any Christian kingdom. The civil
power is the same in every place: nor can that power, in the hands of
a Christian prince, confer any greater authority upon the church,
than in the hands of a heathen; which is to say, just none at all.

Nevertheless, it is worthy to be observed, and lamented, that the
most violent of these defenders of the truth, the opposers of error,
the exclaimers against schism, do hardly ever let loose this their zeal
for God, with which they are so warmed and inflamed, unless where
they have the civil magistrate on their side. But so soon as ever court
favour has given them the better end of the staff, and they begin to
feel themselves the stronger; then presently peace and charity are to
be laid aside: otherwise they are religiously to be observed. Where
they have not the power to carry on persecution, and to become
masters, there they desire to live upon fair terms, and preach up
toleration. When they are not strengthened with the civil power,
then they can bear most patiently, and unmovedly, the contagion of
idolatry, superstition, and heresy, in their neighbourhood; of which,
on other occasions, the interest of religion makes them to be
extremely apprehensive. They do not forwardly attack those errors
which are in fashion at court, or are countenanced by the government. Here they can be content to spare their arguments: which
yet, with their leave, is the only right method of propagating truth;
which has no such way of prevailing, as when strong arguments
and good reason are joined with the softness of civility and good
usage.

Nobody therefore, in fine, neither single persons, nor churches, nay, nor even commonwealths, have any just title to invade the civil rights and worldly goods of each other, upon pretence of religion. Those that are of another opinion, would do well to consider with themselves how pernicious a seed of discord and war, how powerful a provocation to endless hatreds, rapines, and slaughters, they thereby furnish unto mankind. No peace and security, no, not so much as common friendship, can ever be established or preserved amongst men, so long as this opinion prevails, 'that dominion is founded in grace, and that religion is to be propagated by force of arms'.

In the third place: Let us see what the duty of toleration requires from those who are distinguished from the rest of mankind, from the laity, as they please to call us, by some ecclesiastical character and office: whether they be bishops, priests, presbyters, ministers, or however else dignified or distinguished. It is not my business to inquire here into the original of the power or dignity of the clergy. This only I say, that whencesoever their authority be sprung, since it is ecclesiastical, it ought to be confined within the bounds of the church, nor can it in any manner be extended to civil affairs; because the church itself is a thing absolutely separate and distinct from the commonwealth. The boundaries on both sides are fixed and immoveable. He jumbles heaven and earth together, the things most remote and opposite, who mixes these societies, which are, in their original, end, business, and in every thing, perfectly distinct, and infinitely different from each other. No man therefore, with whatsoever ecclesiastical office he be dignified, can deprive another man, that is not of his church and faith, either of liberty, or of any part of his worldly goods, upon the account of that difference which is between them in religion. For whatsoever is not lawful to the whole church cannot, by any ecclesiastical right, become lawful to any of its members.

But this is not all. It is not enough that ecclesiastical men abstain from violence and rapine, and all manner of persecution. He that pretends to be a successor of the apostles, and takes upon him the office of teaching, is obliged also to admonish his hearers of the duties of peace and good-will towards all men; as well towards the erroneous as the orthodox; towards those that differ from them in faith and worship, as well as towards those that agree with them therein: and he ought industriously to exhort all men, whether private persons or magistrates, if any such there be in his church, to charity, meekness, and toleration; and diligently endeavour to allay and temper all that heat, and unreasonable averseness of mind, which either any man's fiery zeal for his own sect, or the craft of others, has kindled against dissenters. I will not undertake to represent how happy and how great would be the fruit, both in church and state, if the pulpits every where sounded with this doctrine of peace and toleration; lest I should seem to reflect too severely upon those men whose dignity I desire not to detract from, nor would have it diminished either by others or themselves. But this I say, that thus it ought to be. And if any one that professes himself to be a minister of the word of God, a preacher of the Gospel of peace, teach otherwise; he either understands not, or neglects the business of his calling, and shall one day give account thereof unto the Prince of Peace. If Christians are to be admonished that they abstain from all manner of revenge, even after repeated provocations and multiplied injuries; how much more ought they who suffer nothing, who have had no harm done them, to forbear violence, and abstain from all manner of ill usage towards those from whom they have received none! This caution and temper they ought certainly to use towards those who mind only their own business, and are solicitous for nothing but that, whatever men think of them, they may worship God in that manner which they are persuaded is acceptable to him, and in which they have the strongest hopes of eternal salvation. In private domestic affairs, in the management of estates, in the conservation of bodily health, every man may consider what suits his own conveniency, and follow what course he likes best. No man complains of the ill management of his neighbour's affairs. No man is angry with another for an error committed in sowing his land, or in marrying his daughter. Nobody corrects a spendthrift for consuming his substance in taverns. Let any man pull down, or build, or make whatsoever expenses he pleases, nobody murmurs, nobody controls him; he has his liberty. But if any man do not frequent the church, if he do not there conform his behaviour exactly to the accustomed ceremonies, or if he brings not his children to be initiated in the sacred mysteries of this or the other congregation; this immediately causes an uproar, and the neighbourhood is filled with noise and clamour. Every one is ready to be the avenger of so great a crime. And the zealots hardly have patience to refrain from violence and rapine, so long till the cause be heard, and the poor man be, according to form, condemned to the loss of liberty, goods, or life. Oh that our ecclesiastical orators, of every sect, would apply

27

themselves, with all the strength of argument that they are able, to the confounding of men's errors! But let them spare their persons. Let them not supply their want of reasons with the instruments of force, which belong to another jurisdiction, and do ill become a churchman's hands. Let them not call in the magistrate's authority to the aid of their eloquence or learning; lest perhaps, whilst they pretend only love for the truth, this their intemperate zeal, breathing nothing but fire and sword, betray their ambition, and show that what they desire is temporal dominion. For it will be very difficult to persuade men of sense, that he, who with dry eyes, and satisfaction of mind, can deliver his brother unto the executioner, to be burnt alive, does sincerely and heartily concern himself to save that brother from the flames of hell in the world to come.

In the last place. Let us now consider what is the magistrate's duty in the business of toleration: which is certainly very considerable.

We have already proved, that the care of souls does not belong to the magistrate: not a magisterial care, I mean, if I may so call it, which consists in prescribing by laws, and compelling by punishments. But a charitable care, which consists in teaching, admonishing, and persuading, cannot be denied unto any man. The care therefore of every man's soul belongs unto himself, and is to be left unto himself. But what if he neglect the care of his soul? I answer, what if he neglect the care of his health, or of his estate; which things are nearlier related to the government of the magistrate than the other? Will the magistrate provide by an express law, that such an one shall not become poor or sick? Laws provide, as much as is possible, that the goods and health of subjects be not injured by the fraud or violence of others; they do not guard them from the negligence or ill husbandry of the possessors themselves. No man can be forced to be rich or healthful, whether he will or no. Nay, God himself will not save men against their wills. Let us suppose, however, that some prince were desirous to force his subjects to accumulate riches, or to preserve the health and strength of their bodies. Shall it be provided by law, that they must consult none but Roman physicians, and shall every one be bound to live according to their prescriptions? What, shall no potion, no broth be taken, but what is prepared either in the Vatican, suppose, or in a Geneva shop? Or to make these subjects rich, shall they all be obliged by law to become merchants, or musicians? Or, shall every one turn victualler, or smith, because there are some that maintain their families plentifully, and grow rich in those professions? But it may be said, there are a thousand ways to wealth, but one only way to heaven. It is well said indeed, especially by those that plead for compelling men into this or the other way; for if there were several ways that lead thither, there would not be so much as a pretence left for compulsion. But now, if I be marching on with my utmost vigour, in that way which, according to the sacred geography, leads straight to Jerusalem; why am I beaten and ill used by others, because, perhaps, I wear not buskins; because my hair is not the right cut; because, perhaps, I have not been dipt in the right fashion; because I eat flesh upon the road, or some other food which agrees with my stomach; because I avoid certain by-ways, which seem unto me to lead into briars or precipices; because, amongst the several paths that are in the same road, I choose that to walk in which seems to be the straightest and cleanest; because I avoid to keep company with some travellers that are less grave, and others that are more sour than they ought to be; or in fine, because I follow a guide that either is, or is not, clothed in white, and crowned with a mitre? Certainly, if we consider right, we shall find that for the most part they are such frivolous things as these, that, without any prejudice to religion or the salvation of souls, if not accompanied with superstition or hypocrisy, might either be observed or omitted; I say, they are such like things as these, which breed implacable enmities among Christian brethren, who are all agreed in the substantial and truly fundamental part of religion.

But let us grant unto these zealots, who condemn all things that are not of their mode, that from these circumstances arise different ends. What shall we conclude from thence? There is only one of these which is the true way of eternal happiness. But, in this great variety of ways that men follow, it is still doubted which is this right one. Now, neither the care of the commonwealth, nor the right of enacting laws, does discover this way that leads to heaven more certainly to the magistrate, than every private man's search and study discovers it unto himself. I have a weak body, sunk under a languishing disease, for which I suppose there is only one remedy, but that unknown: does it therefore belong unto the magistrate to prescribe me a remedy because there is but one, and because it is unknown? Because there is but one way for me to escape death, will it therefore be safe for me to do whatsoever the magistrate ordains? Those things that every man ought sincerely to inquire into himself, and by meditation, study, search, and his own endeavours, attain the knowledge of, cannot be looked upon as the peculiar profession of any one sort of men. Princes, indeed, are born superior unto other men in power, but in nature equal. Neither the right, nor the art of ruling, does necessarily carry along with it the certain knowledge of other things; and least of all of the true religion; for if it were so, how could it come to pass that the lords of the earth should differ so vastly as they do in religious matters? But let us grant that it is probable the way to eternal life may be better known by a prince than by his subjects; or, at least, that in this incertitude of things, the safest and most commodious way for private persons is to follow his dictates. You will say, what then? If he should bid you follow merchandize for your livelihood, would you decline that course, for fear it should not succeed? I answer, I would turn merchant upon the prince's command, because in case I should have ill success in trade, he is abundantly able to make up my loss some other way. If it be true, as he pretends, that he desires I should thrive and grow rich, he can set me up again when unsuccessful voyages have broke me. But this is not the case in the things that regard the life to come. If there I take a wrong course, if in that respect I am once undone, it is not in the magistrate's power to repair my loss, to ease my suffering, or to restore me in any measure, much less entirely, to a good estate. What security can be given for the kingdom of heaven?

Perhaps some will say, that they do not suppose this infallible judgment, that all men are bound to follow in the affairs of religion, to be in the civil magistrate, but in the church. What the church has determined, that the civil magistrate orders to be observed; and he provides by his authority, that nobody shall either act or believe, in the business of religion, otherwise than the church teaches; so that the judgment of those things is in the church. The magistrate himself yields obedience thereunto, and requires the like obedience from others. I answer, Who sees not how frequently the name of the church, which was so venerable in the time of the apostles, has been made use of to throw dust in people's eyes, in following ages? But, however, in the present case it helps us not. The one only narrow way which leads to heaven is not better known to the magistrate than to private persons, and therefore I cannot safely take him for my guide, who may probably be as ignorant of the way as myself, and who certainly is less concerned for my salvation than I myself am. Amongst so many kings of the Jews, how many of them were there whom any Israelite, thus blindly following, had not fallen into idolatry, and thereby into destruction? Yet, nevertheless, you bid me be of good courage, and tell me that all is now safe and secure, because the magistrate does not now enjoin the observance of his own decrees in matters of religion, but only the decrees of the church. Of what church, I beseech you? Of that which certainly likes him best. As if he that compels me by laws and penalties to enter into this or the other church, did not interpose his own judgment in the matter. What difference is there whether he lead me himself, or deliver me over to be led by others? I depend both ways upon his will, and it is he that determines both ways of my eternal state. Would an Israelite, that had worshipped Baal upon the command of his king, have been in any better condition, because somebody had told him that the king ordered nothing in religion upon his own head, nor commanded any thing to be done by his subjects in divine worship, but what was approved by the counsel of priests, and declared to be of divine right by the doctors of the church? If the religion of any church become, therefore, true and saving, because the head of that sect, the prelates and priests, and those of that tribe, do all of them, with all their might, extol and praise it; what religion can ever be accounted erroneous, false, and destructive? I am doubtful concerning the doctrine of the Socinians, I am suspicious of the way of worship practised by the Papists or Lutherans; will it be ever a jot the safer for me to join either unto the one or the other of those churches, upon the magistrate's command, because he commands nothing in religion but by the authority and counsel of the doctors of that church?

But to speak the truth, we must acknowledge that the church, if a convention of clergymen, making canons, must be called by that name, is for the most part more apt to be influenced by the court, than the court by the church. How the church was under the vicissitude of orthodox and Arian emperors is very well known. Or if those things be too remote, our modern English history affords us fresher examples, in the reigns of Henry VIII, Edward VI, Mary, and Elizabeth, how easily and smoothly the clergy changed their decrees, their articles of faith, their form of worship, every thing, according to the inclination of those kings and queens. Yet were those kings and queens of such different minds, in points of religion, and enjoined thereupon such different things, that no man in his wits, I had almost said none but an atheist, will presume to say that any sincere and upright worshipper of God could, with a safe conscience, obey their several decrees. To conclude, it is the same thing whether a king that prescribes laws to another man's religion pretend to do it by his own judgment, or by the ecclesiastical authority and advice of others. The decisions of churchmen, whose differences and disputes are sufficiently known, cannot be any sounder or safer than his: nor can all their suffrages joined together add any new strength unto the civil power. Though this also must be taken notice of, that princes seldom have any regard to the suffrages of ecclesiastics that are not favourers of their own faith and way of worship.

But after all, the principal consideration, and which absolutely determines this controversy, is this: although the magistrate's opinion in religion be sound, and the way that he appoints be truly evangelical, yet if I be not thoroughly persuaded thereof in my own mind, there will be no safety for me in following it. No way whatsoever that I shall walk in against the dictates of my conscience, will ever bring me to the mansions of the blessed. I may grow rich by an art that I take not delight in; I may be cured of some disease by remedies that I have not faith in; but I cannot be saved by a religion that I distrust, and by a worship that I abhor. It is in vain for an unbeliever to take up the outward show of another man's profession. Faith only, and inward sincerity, are the things that procure acceptance with God. The most likely and most approved remedy can have no effect upon the patient, if his stomach reject it as soon as taken; and you will in vain cram a medicine down a sick man's throat, which his particular constitution will be sure to turn into poison. In a word, whatsoever may be doubtful in religion, yet this at least is certain, that no religion, which I believe not to be true, can be either true or profitable unto me. In vain, therefore, do princes compel their subjects to come into their church-communion, under pretence of saving their souls. If they believe, they will come of their own accord; if they believe not, their coming will nothing avail them. How great, soever, in fine, may be the pretence of good-will and charity, and concern for the salvation of men's souls, men cannot be forced to be saved whether they will or no; and therefore, when all is done, they must be left to their own consciences.

Having thus at length freed men from all dominion over one another in matters of religion, let us now consider what they are to do. All men know and acknowledge that God ought to be publicly worshipped. Why otherwise do they compel one another unto the public assemblies? Men, therefore, constituted in this liberty are to enter into some religious society, that they may meet together, not only for mutual edification, but to own to the world that they worship God, and offer unto his divine majesty such service as they themselves are not ashamed of, and such as they think not unworthy of him, nor unacceptable to him; and finally, that by the purity of doctrine, holiness of life, and decent form of worship, they may draw others unto the love of the true religion, and perform such other things in religion as cannot be done by each private man apart.

These religious societies I call churches: and these I say the magistrate ought to tolerate: for the business of these assemblies of the people is nothing but what is lawful for every man in particular to take care of; I mean the salvation of their souls: nor, in this case, is there any difference between the national church and other separated congregations.

But as in every church there are two things especially to be considered; the outward form and rites of worship, and the doctrines and articles of faith; these things must be handled each distinctly, that so the whole matter of toleration may the more clearly be understood.

Concerning outward worship, I say, in the first place, that the magistrate has no power to enforce by law, either in his own church, or much less in another, the use of any rites or ceremonies whatsoever in the worship of God. And this, not only because these churches are free societies, but because whatsoever is practised in the worship of God is only so far justifiable as it is believed by those that practise it to be acceptable unto him. – Whatsoever is not done with that assurance of faith, is neither well in itself, nor can it be acceptable to God. To impose such things, therefore, upon any people, contrary to their own judgment, is, in effect, to command them to offend God; which, considering that the end of all religion is to please him, and that liberty is essentially necessary to that end, appears to be absurd beyond expression.

But perhaps it may be concluded from hence, that I deny unto the magistrate all manner of power about indifferent things; which, if it be not granted, the whole subject matter of law-making is taken away. No, I readily grant that indifferent things, and perhaps none but such, are subject to the legislative power. But it does not therefore follow, that the magistrate may ordain whatsoever he pleases concerning any thing that is indifferent. The public good is the role and measure of all law-making. If a thing be not useful to the commonwealth, though it be ever so indifferent, it may not presently be established by law.

But further: Things ever so indifferent in their own nature, when they are brought into the church and worship of God, are removed out of the reach of the magistrate's jurisdiction, because in that use they have no connexion at all with civil affairs. The only business of the church is the salvation of souls: and it no ways concerns the commonwealth, or any member of it, that this or the other ceremony be there made use of. Neither the use, nor the omission, of any ceremonies in those religious assemblies does either advantage or prejudice the life, liberty, or estate, of any man. For example: Let it be granted, that the washing of an infant with water is in itself an indifferent thing: let it be granted also, that if the magistrate understand such washing to be profitable to the curing or preventing of any disease that children are subject unto, and esteem the matter weighty enough to be taken care of by a law, in that case he may order it to be done. But will any one, therefore, say, that the magistrate has the same right to ordain, by law, that all children shall be baptized by priests, in the sacred font, in order to the purification of their souls? The extreme difference of these two cases is visible to every one at first sight. Or let us apply the last case to the child of a Jew, and the thing will speak itself; for what hinders but a Christian magistrate may have subjects that are Jews? Now, if we acknowledge that such an injury may not be done unto a Jew, as to compel him, against his own opinion, to practise in his religion a thing that is in its nature indifferent, how can we maintain anything of this kind may be done to a Christian?

Again: Things in their own nature indifferent, cannot, by any human authority, be made any part of the worship of God, for this very reason, because they are indifferent. For since indifferent things are not capable by any virtue of their own, to propitiate the Deity, no human power of authority can confer on them so much dignity and excellency as to enable them to do it. In the common affairs of life, that use of indifferent things which God has not forbidden is free and lawful; and therefore in those things human authority has place. But it is not so in matters of religion. Things indifferent are not otherwise lawful in the worship of God than as they are instituted by God himself; and as he, by some positive command, has ordained them to be made a part of that worship which he will vouchsafe to accept of at the hands of poor sinful men. Nor when an incensed Deity shall ask us, 'Who has required these or such like things at your hands?' will it be enough to answer him, that the magistrate commanded them. If civil jurisdiction extended thus far, what might not lawfully be introduced into religion? What hodge-podge of ceremonies, what superstitious inventions, built upon the magistrate's authority, might not, against conscience, be imposed upon the worshippers of

God! For the greatest part of these ceremonies and superstitions consists in the religious use of such things as are in their own nature indifferent: nor are they sinful upon any other account, than because God is not the author of them. The sprinkling of water, and use of bread and wine, are both in their own nature, and in the ordinary occasions of life, altogether indifferent. Will any man, therefore, say that these things could have been introduced into religion, and made a part of divine worship, if not by divine institution? If any human authority or civil power could have done this, why might it not also enjoin the eating of fish, and drinking of ale, in the holy banquet, as a part of divine worship? Why not the sprinking of the blood of beasts in churches, and expiations by water or fire, and abundance more of this kind? But these things, how indifferent soever they be in common uses, when they come to be annexed unto divine worship, without divine authority, they are as abominable to God as the sacrifice of a dog. And why a dog so abominable? What difference is there between a dog and a goat, in respect of the divine nature, equally and infinitely distant from all affinity with matter; unless it be that God required the use of the one in his worship, and not of the other? We see, therefore, that indifferent things, how much soever they be under the power of the civil magistrate, yet cannot, upon that pretence, be introduced into religion, and imposed upon religious assemblies; because in the worship of God they wholly cease to be indifferent. He that worships God, does it with design to please him, and procure his favour: but that cannot be done by him, who, upon the command of another, offers unto God that which he knows will be displeasing to him, because not commanded by himself. This is not to please God, or appease his wrath, but willingly and knowingly to provoke him, by a manifest contempt; which is a thing absolutely repugnant to the nature and end of worship.

But it will here be asked, If nothing belonging to divine worship be left to human discretion, how is it then that churches themselves have the power of ordering anything about the time and place of worship, and the like? To this I answer; that in religious worship we must distinguish between what is part of the worship itself, and what is but a circumstance. That is a part of the worship which is believed to be appointed by God, and to be well pleasing to him; and therefore that is necessary. Circumstances are such things which, though in general they cannot be separated from worship, yet the particular instances or modifications of them are not determined; and therefore they are indifferent. Of this sort are the time and place of worship, the habit and posture of him that worships. These are circumstances, and perfectly indifferent, where God has not given any express command about them. For example; amongst the Jews, the time and place of their worship, and the habits of those that officiated in it, were not mere circumstances, but a part of the worship itself; in which, if anything were defective, or different from the institution, they could not hope that it would be accepted by God. But these, to Christians, under the liberty of the Gospel, are mere circumstances of worship which the prudence of every church may bring into such use as shall be judged most subservient to the end of order, decency, and edification. Though even under the Gospel also, those who believe the first, or the seventh day to be set apart by God, and consecrated still to his worship, to them that portion of time is not a simple circumstance, but a real part of divine worship, which can neither be changed nor neglected.

In the next place: As the magistrate has no power to impose, by his laws, the use of any rites and ceremonies in any church; so neither has he any power to forbid the use of such rites and ceremonies as are already received, approved, and practised by any church: because, if he did so, he would destroy the church itself; the end of whose institution is only to worship God with freedom, after its own manner.

You will say, by this rule, if some congregations should have a mind to sacrifice infants, or, as the primitive Christians were falsely accused, lustfully pollute themselves in promiscuous uncleanness, or practise any other such heinous enormities, is the magistrate obliged to tolerate them, because they are committed in a religious assembly? I answer, No. These things are not lawful in the ordinary course of life, nor in any private house; and, therefore, neither are they so in the worship of God, or in any religious meeting. But, indeed, if any people congregated upon account of religion, should be desirous to sacrifice a calf, I deny that that ought to be prohibited by a law. Meliboeus, whose calf it is, may lawfully kill his calf at home, and burn any part of it that he thinks fit: for no injury is thereby done to any one, no prejudice to another man's goods. And for the same reason he may kill his calf also in a religious meeting. Whether the doing so be well-pleasing to God or no, it is their part to consider that do it. The part of the magistrate is only to take care that the commonwealth receive no prejudice, and that there be no injury done to any man, either in life or estate. And thus what may be spent on a feast may be spent on a sacrifice. And if, peradventure, such were the state of things, that the interest of the commonwealth required all slaughter of beasts should be forborn for some while, in order to the increasing of the stock of cattle, that had been destroyed by some extraordinary murrain; who sees not that the magistrate, in such a case, may forbid all his subjects to kill any calves for any use whatsoever? Only it is to be observed, that in this case the law is not made about a religious, but a political matter: nor is the sacrifice, but the slaughter of calves thereby prohibited.

By this we see what difference there is between the church and the commonwealth. Whatsoever is lawful in the commonwealth, cannot be prohibited by the magistrate in the church. Whatsoever is permitted unto any of his subjects for their ordinary use, neither can nor ought to be forbidden by him to any sect of people for their religious uses. If any man may lawfully take bread or wine, either sitting or kneeling, in his own house, the law ought not to abridge him of the same liberty in his religious worship, though in the church the use of bread and wine be very different, and be there applied to the mysteries of faith, and rites of divine worship. But those things that are prejudicial to the commonweal of a people in their ordinary use, and are therefore forbidden by laws, those things ought not to be permitted to churches in their sacred rites. Only the magistrate ought always to be very careful that he do not misuse his authority, to the oppression of any church, under pretence of public good.

It may be said, What if a church be idolatrous, is that also to be tolerated by the magistrate? In answer, I ask, what power can be given to the magistrate for the suppression of an idolatrous church, which may not, in time and place, be made use of to the ruin of an orthodox one? For it must be remembered, that the civil power is the same every where, and the religion of every prince is orthodox to himself. If, therefore, such a power be granted unto the civil magistrate in spirituals, as that at Geneva, for example; he may extirpate, by violence and blood, the religion which is there reputed idolatrous; by the same rule, another magistrate, in some neighbouring country, may oppress the reformed religion; and, in India, the Christian. The civil power can either change every thing in religion, according to the prince's pleasure, or it can change nothing. If it be once permitted to introduce any thing into religion, by the means of laws and penalties, there can be no bounds put to it; but it will, in the same manner, be lawful to alter every thing, according to that rule of truth which the magistrate has framed unto himself. No man whatsoever ought therefore to be deprived of his terrestrial enjoyments, upon account of his religion. Not even Americans, subjected unto a Christian prince, are to be punished either in body or goods, for not embracing our faith and worship. If they are persuaded that they please God in observing the rites of their own country, and that they shall obtain happiness by that means, they are to be left unto God and themselves. Let us trace this matter to the bottom. Thus it is: an inconsiderable and weak number of Christians, destitute of every thing, arrive in a pagan country; these foreigners beseech the inhabitants, by the bowels of humanity, that they would succour them with the necessaries of life; those necessaries are given them, habitations are granted, and they all join together, and grow up into one body of people. The Christian religion by this means takes root in that country, and spreads itself; but does not suddenly grow the strongest. While things are in this condition, peace, friendship, faith, and equal justice, are preserved amongst them. At length the magistrate becomes a Christian, and by that means their party becomes the most powerful. Then immediately all compacts are to be broken, all civil rights to be violated, that idolatry may be extirpated: and unless these innocent pagans, strict observers of the rules of equity and the law of nature, and no ways offending against the laws of the society, I say unless they will forsake their ancient religion, and embrace a new and strange one, they are to be turned out of the lands and possessions of their forefathers, and perhaps deprived of life itself. Then at last it appears what zeal for the church, joined with the desire of dominion, is capable to produce: and how easily the pretence of religion, and of the care of souls, serves for a cloak to covetousness, rapine, and ambition.

Now, whosoever maintains that idolatry is to be rooted out of any place by laws, punishments, fire, and sword, may apply this story to himself: for the reason of the thing is equal, both in America and Europe. And neither pagans there, nor any dissenting Christians here, can with any right be deprived of their worldly goods by the predominating faction of a court–church; nor are any civil rights to be either changed or violated upon account of religion in one place more than another.

But idolatry, say some, is a sin, and therefore not to be tolerated. If they said it were therefore to be avoided, the inference were good. But it does not follow, that because it is a sin, it ought therefore to be punished by the magistrate. For it does not belong unto the magistrate to make use of his sword in punishing everything, indifferently, that he takes to be a sin against God. Covetousness, uncharitableness, idleness, and many other things are sins, by the consent of all men, which yet no man ever said were to be punished by the magistrate. The reason is, because they are not prejudicial to other men's rights, nor do they break the public peace of societies. Nay, even the sins of lying and perjury are nowhere punishable by laws; unless in certain cases, in which the real turpitude of the thing, and the offence against God, are not considered, but only the injury done unto men's neighbours, and to the commonwealth. And what if, in another country, to a Mahometan or a pagan prince, the Christian religion seem false and offensive to God; may not the Christians, for the same reason, and after the same manner, be extirpated there?

But it may be urged farther, that by the law of Moses idolaters were to be rooted out. True indeed, by the law of Moses; but that is not obligatory to us Christians. Nobody pretends that everything, generally, enjoined by the law of Moses, ought to be practised by Christians. But there is nothing more frivolous than the common distinction of moral, judicial, and ceremonial law, which men ordinarily make use of: for no positive law whatsoever can oblige any people but those to whom it is given. 'Hear, O Israel', sufficiently restrains the obligation of the law of Moses only to that people. And this consideration alone is answer enough unto those that urge the authority of the law of Moses, for the inflicting of capital punishments upon idolaters. But however I will examine this argument a little more particularly.

The case of idolaters, in respect of the Jewish commonwealth, falls under a double consideration. The first is of those, who, being initiated in the Mosaical rites, and made citizens of that commonwealth, did afterwards apostatize from the worship of the God of Israel. These were proceeded against as traitors and rebels, guilty of no less than high treason; for the commonwealth of the Jews, different in that from all others, was an absolute theocracy: nor was there, or could there be, any difference between that commonwealth and the church. The laws established there concerning the worship of one invisible Deity, were the civil laws of that people, and a part of their political government, in which God himself was the legislator. Now if any one can show me where there is a commonwealth, at this time, constituted upon that foundation, I will acknowledge that the ecclesiastical laws do there unavoidably become a part of the civil; and that the subjects of that government both may, and ought to be, kept in strict conformity with that church, by the civil power. But there is absolutely no such thing, under the Gospel, as a Christian commonwealth. There are, indeed, many cities and kingdoms that have embraced the faith of Christ; but they have retained their ancient forms of government, with which the law of Christ hath not at all meddled. He, indeed, hath taught men how, by faith and good works, they may attain eternal life. But he instituted no commonwealth; he prescribed unto his followers no new and peculiar form of government; nor put he the sword into any magistrate's hand, with commission to make use of it in forcing men to forsake their former religion, and receive his.

Secondly, Foreigners, and such as were strangers to the commonwealth of Israel, were not compelled by force to observe the rites of the Mosaical law: but, on the contrary, in the very same place where it is ordered that an Israelite that was an idolater should be put to death, there it is provided that strangers should not be 'vexed nor oppressed', Exod. xxii. 21. I confess that the seven nations that possessed the land which was promised to the Israelites were utterly to be cut off. But this was not singly because they were idolaters; for if that had been the reason, why were the Moabites and other nations to be spared? No; the reason is this: God being in a peculiar manner the King of the Jews, he could not suffer the adoration of any other deity, which was properly an act of high treason against himself, in the land of Canaan, which was his kingdom; for such a manifest revolt could no ways consist with his dominion, which was perfectly political, in that country. All idolatry was therefore to be rooted out of the bounds of his kingdom; because it was an acknowledgment of another God, that is to say, another king, against the laws of empire. The inhabitants were also to be driven out, that the entire possession of the land might be given to the Israelites. And for the like reason the Emims and the Horims were driven out of their countries by the children of Esau and Lot; and their lands, upon the same grounds, given by God to the invaders, Deut. ii. 12. But though all idolatry was thus rooted out of the land of Canaan, yet every idolater was not brought to execution. The whole family of Rahab, the whole nation of the Gibeonites, articled with Joshua, and were allowed by treaty; and there were many captives amongst the Jews, who were idolaters. David and Solomon subdued many countries without the confines of the Land of Promise, and carried their conquests as far as Euphrates. Amongst so many captives taken, of so many nations reduced under their obedience, we find not one man forced into the Jewish religion, and the worship of the true God, and punished for idolatry, though all of them were certainly guilty of it. If any one indeed, becoming a proselyte, desired to be made a denizen of their commonwealth, he was obliged to submit unto their laws; that is, to embrace their religion. But this he did willingly, on his own accord, not by constraint. He did not unwillingly submit, to show his obedience; but he sought and solicited for it, as a privilege; and as soon as he was admitted, he became subject to the laws of the commonwealth, by which all idolatry was forbidden within the borders of the land of Canaan. But that law, as I have said, did not reach to any of those regions, however subjected unto the Jews, that were situated without those bounds.

Thus far concerning outward worship. Let us now consider articles of faith.

The articles of religion are some of them practical, and some speculative. Now, though both sorts consist in the knowledge of truth, yet these terminate simply in the understanding, those influence the will and manners. Speculative opinions, therefore, and articles of faith, as they are called, which are required only to be believed, cannot be imposed on any church by the law of the land; for it is absurd that things should be enjoined by laws which are not in men's power to perform; and to believe this or that to be true does not depend upon our will. But of this enough has been said already. But, will some say, let men at least profess that they believe. A sweet religion, indeed, that obliges men to dissemble, and tell lies both to God, and man, for the salvation of their souls! If the magistrate thinks to save men thus, he seems to understand little of the way of salvation; and if he does it not in order to save them, why is he so solicitous about the articles of faith as to enact them by a law?

Further, The magistrate ought not to forbid the preaching or professing of any speculative opinions in any church, because they have no manner of relation to the civil rights of the subjects. If a Roman Catholic believe that to be really the body of Christ, which another man calls bread, he does no injury thereby to his neighbour. If a Jew does not believe the New Testament to be the word of God, he does not thereby alter any thing in men's civil rights. If a heathen doubt of both Testaments, he is not therefore to be punished as a pernicious citizen. The power of the magistrate, and the estates of the people, may be equally secure, whether any man believe these things or no. I readily grant that these opinions are false and absurd; but the business of laws is not to provide for the truth of opinions, but for the safety and security of the commonwealth, and of every particular man's goods and person. And so it ought to be; for truth certainly would do well enough, if she were once left to shift for herself. She seldom has received, and I fear never will receive, much assistance from the power of great men, to whom she is but rarely known, and more rarely welcome. She is not taught by laws, nor has she any need of force to procure her entrance into the minds of men. Errors indeed prevail by the assistance of foreign and borrowed succours. But if truth makes not her way into the understanding by her own light, she will be but the weaker for any borrowed force violence can add to her. Thus much for speculative opinions. Let us now proceed to the practical ones.

A good life, in which consists not the least part of religion and true piety, concerns also the civil government: and in it lies the safety both of men's souls and of the commonwealth. Moral actions belong therefore to the jurisdiction both of the outward and inward court; both of the civil and domestic governor; I mean, both of the magistrate and conscience. Here therefore is great danger, lest one of these jurisdictions intrench upon the other, and discord arise between the keeper of the public peace and the overseers of souls. But if what has been already said concerning the limits of both these governments be rightly considered, it will easily remove all difficulty in this matter.

Every man has an immortal soul, capable of eternal happiness or misery; whose happiness depending upon his believing and doing those things in this life, which are necessary to the obtaining of God's favour, and are prescribed by God to that end: it follows from thence, first, that the observance of these things is the highest obligation that lies upon mankind, and that our utmost care, application, and diligence, ought to be exercised in the search and performance of them; because there is nothing in this world that is of any consideration in comparison with eternity. Secondly, that seeing one man does not violate the right of another, by his erroneous opinions, and undue manner of worship, nor is his perdition any prejudice to another man's affairs; therefore the care of each man's salvation belongs only to himself. But I would not have this understood, as if I meant hereby to condemn all charitable admonitions, and affectionate endeavours to reduce men from errors; which are indeed the greatest duty of a Christian. Any one may employ as many exhortations and arguments as he pleases, towards the promoting of another man's salvation. But all force and compulsion are to be forborn. Nothing is to be done imperiously. Nobody is obliged in that manner to yield obedience unto the admonitions or injunctions of another, farther than he himself is persuaded. Every man, in that, has the supreme and absolute authority of judging for himself; and the reason is, because nobody else is concerned in it, nor can receive any prejudice from his conduct therein.

But besides their souls, which are immortal, men have also their temporal lives here upon earth; the state whereof being frail and fleeting, and the duration uncertain, they have need of several outward conveniences to the support thereof, which are to be procured or preserved by pains and industry; for those things that are necessary to the comfortable support of our lives, are not the spontaneous products of nature, nor do offer themselves fit and prepared for our use. This part, therefore, draws on another care, and necessarily gives another employment. But the pravity of mankind being such, that they had rather injuriously prey upon the fruits of other men's labours than take pains to provide for themselves; the necessity of preserving men in the possession of what honest industry has already acquired, and also of preserving their liberty and strength, whereby they may acquire what they farther want, obliges men to enter into society with one another; that by mutual assistance and joint force, they may secure unto each other their properties, in the things that contribute to the comforts and happiness of this life; leaving in the meanwhile to every man the care of his own eternal happiness, the attainment whereof can neither be facilitated by another man's industry, nor can the loss of it turn to another man's prejudice, nor the hope of it be forced from him by any external violence. But forasmuch as men thus entering into societies, grounded upon their mutual compacts of assistance, for the defence of their temporal goods, may nevertheless be deprived of them, either by the rapine and fraud of their fellow-citizens, or by the hostile violence of foreigners; the remedy of this evil consists in arms, riches, and multitudes of citizens; the remedy of others in laws; and the care of all things relating both to the one and the other is committed by the society to the civil magistrate. This is the original, this is the use, and these are the bounds of the legislative, which is the supreme power in every commonwealth. I mean, that provision may be made for the security of each man's private possessions; for the peace, riches, and public commodities of the whole people, and, as much as possible, for the increase of their inward strength against foreign invasions.

These things being thus explained, it is easy to understand to what end the legislative power ought to be directed, and by what measures regulated, and that is the temporal good and outward prosperity of the society, which is the sole reason of men's entering into society, and the only thing they seek and aim at in it; and it is also evident what liberty remains to men in reference to their eternal salvation, and that is, that every one should do what he in his conscience is persuaded to be acceptable to the Almighty, on whose good pleasure and acceptance depends his eternal happiness; for obedience is due in the first place to God, and afterwards to the laws.

But some may ask, 'What if the magistrate should enjoin any thing by his authority, that appears unlawful to the conscience of a private person?' I answer, that if government be faithfully administered, and the counsels of the magistrate be indeed directed to the public good, this will seldom happen. But if perhaps it do so fall out, I say, that such a private person is to abstain from the actions that he judges unlawful; and he is to undergo the punishment, which is not unlawful for him to bear; for the private judgment of any person concerning a law enacted in political matters, for the public good, does not take away the obligation of that law, nor deserve a dispensation. But if the law indeed be concerning things that lie not within the verge of the magistrate's authority; as, for example, that the people, or any party amongst them, should be compelled to embrace a strange religion, and join in the worship and ceremonies of another church; men are not in these cases obliged by that law, against their consciences; for the political society is instituted for no other end, but only to secure every man's possession of the things of this life. The care of each man's soul, and of the things of heaven, which neither does belong to the commonwealth, nor can be subjected to it, is left entirely to every man's self. Thus the safeguard of men's lives, and of the things that belong unto this life, is the business of the commonwealth; and the preserving of those things unto their owners is the duty of the magistrate; and therefore the magistrate cannot take away these worldly things from this man, or party, and give them to that; nor change property amongst fellow subjects, no not even by a law, for a cause that has no relation to the end of civil government; I mean for their religion; which, whether it be true or false, does no prejudice to the worldly concerns of their fellow subjects, which are the things that only belong unto the care of the commonwealth.

'But what if the magistrate believe such a law as this to be for the public good?' I answer: as the private judgment of any particular person, if erroneous, does not exempt him from the obligation of law, so the private judgment, as I may call it, of the magistrate, does not give him any new right of imposing laws upon his subjects, which neither was in the constitution of the government granted him, nor ever was in the power of the people to grant; and least of all, if he make it his business to enrich and advance his followers and fellow-sectaries with the spoils of others. But what if the magistrate believe that he has a right to make such laws, and that they are for the public good; and his subjects believe the contrary? Who shall be judge between them? I answer, God alone; for there is no judge upon earth between the supreme magistrate and the people. God, I say, is the only judge in this case, who will retribute unto every one at the last day according to his deserts; that is, according to his sincerity and uprightness in endeavouring to promote piety, and the public weal and peace of mankind. But what shall be done in the mean while? I answer: the principal and chief care of every one ought to be of his own soul first, and, in the next place, of the public peace: though yet there are few will think it is peace there, where they see all laid waste. There are two sorts of contests amongst men; the one managed by law, the other by force: and they are of that nature, that where the one ends, the other always begins. But it is not my business to inquire into the power of the magistrate in the different constitutions of nations. I only know what usually happens where controversies arise, without a judge to determine them. You will say then the magistrate being the stronger will have his will, and carry his point. Without doubt. But the question is not here concerning the doubtfulness of the event, but the rule of right.

But to come to particulars. I say, first, No opinions contrary to human society, or to those moral rules which are necessary to the preservation of civil society, are to be tolerated by the magistrate. But of those indeed examples in any church are rare. For no sect can easily arrive to such a degree of madness, as that it should think fit to teach, for doctrines of religion, such things as manifestly undermine the foundations of society, and are therefore condemned by the judgment of all mankind: because their own interest, peace, reputation, every thing would be thereby endangered.

Another more secret evil, but more dangerous to the commonwealth, is when men arrogate to themselves, and to those of their own sect, some peculiar prerogative covered over with a specious show of deceitful words, but in effect opposite to the civil rights of the community. For example: we cannot find any sect that teaches expressly and openly, that men are not obliged to keep their promise; that princes may be dethroned by those that differ from them in religion; or that the dominion of all things belongs only to themselves. For these things, proposed thus nakedly and plainly, would soon draw on them the eye and hand of the magistrate, and awaken all the care of the commonwealth to a watchfulness against the spreading of so dangerous an evil. But nevertheless, we find those that say the same things in other words. What else do they mean, who teach that 'faith is not to be kept with heretics'? Their meaning, forsooth, is, that the privilege of breaking faith belongs unto themselves: for they declare all that are not of their communion to be heretics, or at least may declare them so whensoever they think fit. What can be the meaning of their asserting that 'kings excommunicated forfeit their crowns and kingdoms'? It is evident that they thereby arrogate unto themselves the power of deposing kings: because they challenge the power of excommunication as the peculiar right of their hierarchy. 'That dominion is founded in grace', is also an assertion by which those that maintain it do plainly lay claim to the possession of all things. For they are not so wanting to themselves as not to believe, or at least as not to profess, themselves to be the truly pious and faithful. These therefore, and the like, who attribute unto the faithful, religious, and orthodox, that is, in plain terms, unto themselves, any peculiar privilege or power above other mortals, in civil concernments; or who, upon pretence of religion, do challenge any manner of authority over such as are not associated with them in their ecclesiastical communion; I say these have no right to be tolerated by the magistrate; as neither those that will not own and teach the duty of tolerating all men in matters of mere religion. For what do all these and the like doctrines signify, but that they may, and are ready upon any occasion to seize the government, and possess themselves of the estates and fortunes of their fellow-subjects; and that they only ask leave to be tolerated by the magistrates so long, until they find themselves strong enough to effect it.

Again: That church can have no right to be tolerated by the magistrate, which is constituted upon such a bottom, that all those who enter into it, do thereby, *ipso facto*, deliver themselves up to the protection and service of another prince. For by this means the magistrate would give way to the settling of a foreign jurisdiction in his own country, and suffer his own people to be listed, as it were, for soldiers against his own government. Nor does the frivolous and fallacious distinction between the court and the church afford any remedy to this inconvenience; especially when both the one and the other are equally subject to the absolute authority of the same person; who has not only power to persuade the members of his church to whatsoever he lists, either as purely religious, or as in order thereunto; but can also enjoin it them on pain of eternal fire. It is ridiculous for any one to profess himself to be a Mahometan only in religion, but in every thing else a faithful subject to a Christian magistrate, whilst at the same time he acknowledges himself bound to yield blind obedience to the mufti of Constantinople; who himself is entirely obedient to the Ottoman emperor, and frames the famed oracles of that religion according to his pleasure. But this Mahometan, living amongst Christians, would yet more apparently renounce their government, if he acknowledged the same person to be head of his church, who is the supreme magistrate in the state.

Lastly, Those are not at all to be tolerated who deny the being of God. Promises, covenants, and oaths, which are the bonds of human society, can have no hold upon an atheist. The taking away of God, though but even in thought, dissolves all. Besides also, those that by their atheism undermine and destroy all religion, can have no pretence of religion whereupon to challenge the privilege of a toleration. As for other practical opinions, though not absolutely free from all error, yet if they do not tend to establish domination over others, or civil impunity to the church in which they are taught, there can be no reason why they should not be tolerated.

It remains that I say something concerning those assemblies, which being vulgarly called, and perhaps having sometimes been conventicles, and nurseries of factions and seditions, are thought to afford the strongest matter of objection against this doctrine of toleration. But this has not happened by any thing peculiar unto the genius of such assemblies, but by the unhappy circumstances of an oppressed or ill-settled liberty. These accusations would soon cease, if the law of toleration were once so settled, that all churches were obliged to lay down toleration as the foundation of their own liberty; and teach that liberty of conscience is every man's natural right, equally belonging to dissenters as to themselves; and that nobody ought to be compelled in matters of religion either by law or force. The establishment of this one thing would take away all ground of complaints and tumults upon account of conscience. And these causes of discontents and animosities being once removed, there would remain nothing in these assemblies that were not more peaceable, and less apt to produce disturbance of state, than in any other meetings whatsoever. But let us examine particularly the heads of these accusations.

You will say, that 'assemblies and meetings endanger the public peace, and threaten the commonwealth'. I answer: if this be so, why are there daily such numerous meetings in markets, and courts of judicature? Why are crowds upon the Exchange, and a concourse of people in cities suffered? You will reply, these are civil assemblies; but those we object against are ecclesiastical. I answer; it is a likely thing indeed, that such assemblies as are altogether remote from civil affairs should be most apt to embroil them. O, but civil assemblies are composed of men that differ from one another in matters of religion; but these ecclesiastical meetings are of persons that are all of one opinion. As if an agreement in matters of religion were in effect a conspiracy against the commonwealth: or as if men would not be so much the more warmly unanimous in religion, the less liberty they had of assembling. But it will be urged still, that civil assemblies are open, and free for any one to enter into; whereas religious conventicles are more private, and thereby give opportunity to clandestine machinations. I answer, that this is not strictly true; for many civil assemblies are not open to every one. And if some religious meetings be private, who are they, I beseech you, that are to be blamed for it? those that desire, or those that forbid their being public? Again: you will say, that religious Communion does exceedingly unite men's minds and affections to one another, and is therefore the more dangerous. But if this be so, why is not the magistrate afraid of his own church; and why does he not forbid their assemblies, as things dangerous to his government? You will say, because he himself is a part, and even the head of them. As if he were not also a part of the commonwealth, and the head of the whole people.

Let us therefore deal plainly. The magistrate is afraid of other churches, but not of his own; because he is kind and favourable to the one, but severe and cruel to the other. These he treats like children, and indulges them even to wantonness. Those he uses as slaves; and how blamelessly soever they demean themselves, recompenses them no otherwise than by galleys, prisons, confiscations, and death. These he cherishes and defends: those he continually scourges and oppresses. Let him turn the tables: or let those dissenters enjoy but the same privileges in civils as his other subjects, and he will quickly find that these religious meetings will be no longer dangerous. For if men enter into seditious conspiracies, it is not religion inspires them to it in their meetings, but their sufferings and oppressions that make them willing to ease themselves. Just and moderate governments are every where quiet, every where safe. But oppression raises ferments, and makes men struggle to cast off an uneasy and tyrannical yoke. I know that seditions are very frequently raised upon pretence of religion. But it is as true, that, for religion, subjects are frequently ill treated, and live miserably. Believe me, the stirs that are made proceed not from any peculiar temper of this or that church or religious society; but from the common disposition of all mankind, who, when they groan under any heavy burthen, endeavour naturally to shake off the yoke that galls their necks. Suppose this business of religion were let alone, and that there were some other distinction made between men and men, upon account of their different complexions, shapes, and features, or that those who have black hair, for example, or gray eyes, should not enjoy the same privileges as other citizens; that they should not be permitted either to buy or sell, or live by their callings; that parents should not have the government and education of their own children; that they should either be excluded from the benefit of the laws, or meet with partial judges: can it be doubted but these persons, thus distinguished from others by the colour of their hair and eyes, and united together by one common persecution, would be as dangerous to the magistrate, as any others that had associated themselves merely upon the account of religion? Some enter into company for trade and profit: others, for want of business, have their clubs for claret. Neighbourhood joins some, and religion others. But there is one thing only which gathers people into seditious commotions, and that is oppression.

You will say; what, will you have people to meet at divine service against the magistrate's will? I answer; why, I pray, against his will? Is it not both lawful and necessary that they should meet? Against his will, do you say? That is what I complain of. That is the very root of all the mischief. Why are assemblies less sufferable in a church than in a theatre or market? Those that meet there are not either more vicious, or more turbulent, than those that meet elsewhere. The business in that is, that they are ill used, and therefore they are not to be suffered. Take away the partiality that is used towards them in matters of common right; change the laws, take away the penalties unto which they are subjected, and all things will immediately become safe and peaceable: nay, those that are averse to the religion of the magistrate, will think themselves so much the more bound to maintain the peace of the commonwealth, as their condition is better in that place than elsewhere; and all the several separate congregations, like so many guardians of the public peace, will watch one another, that nothing may be innovated or changed in the form of the government: because they can hope for nothing better than what they already enjoy; that is, an equal condition with their fellow-subjects, under a just and moderate government. Now if that church, which agrees in religion with the prince, be esteemed the chief support of any civil government, and that for no other reason, as has already been shown, than because the prince is kind, and the laws are favourable to it; how much greater will be the security of a government, where all good subjects, of whatsoever they be, without any distinction upon account of religion, enjoying the same favour of the prince, and the same benefit of the laws, shall become the common support and guard of it; and where none will have any occasion to fear the severity of the laws, but those that do injuries to their neighbours, and offend against the civil peace!

That we may draw towards a conclusion. 'The sum of all we drive at is, that every man enjoy the same rights that are granted to others.' Is it permitted to worship God in the Roman manner? Let it be permitted to do it in the Geneva form also. Is it permitted to speak Latin in the market-place? Let those that have a mind to it, be permitted to do it also in the church. Is it lawful for any man in his own house to kneel, stand, sit, or use any other posture; and clothe himself in white or black, in short or in long garments? Let it not be made unlawful to eat bread, drink wine, or wash with water in the church. In a word: whatsoever things are left free by law in the common occasions of life, let them remain free unto every church in divine worship. Let no man's life, or body, or house, or estate, suffer any manner of prejudice upon these accounts. Can you allow of the presbyterian discipline? Why should not the episcopal also have what they like? Ecclesiastical authority, whether it be administered by the hands of a single person, or many, is every where the same; and neither has any jurisdiction in things civil, nor any manner of power of compulsion, nor any thing at all to do with riches and revenues.

Ecclesiastical assemblies and sermons, are justified by daily experience, and public allowance. These are allowed to people of some one persuasion: why not to all? If any thing pass in a religious meeting seditiously, and contrary to the public peace, it is to be punished in the same manner, and no otherwise, than as if it had happened in a fair or market. These meetings ought not to be sanctuaries of factious and flagitious fellows: nor ought it to be less lawful for men to meet in churches than in halls: nor are one part of the subjects to be esteemed more blameable for their meeting together than others. Every one is to be accountable for his own actions; and no man is to be laid under a suspicion, or odium, for the fault of another. Those that are seditious, murderers, thieves, robbers, adulterers, slanderers, &c. of whatsoever church, whether national or not, ought to be punished and suppressed. But those whose doctrine is peaceable, and whose manners are pure and blameless, ought to be upon equal terms with their fellow-subjects. Thus if solemn assemblies, observations of festivals, public worship, be permitted to any one sort of professors; all these things ought to be permitted to the presbyterians, independents, anabaptists, Arminians, quakers, and others, with the same liberty. Nay, if we may openly speak the truth, and as becomes one man to another, neither pagan, nor Mahometan, nor Jew, ought to be excluded from the civil rights of the commonwealth, because of his religion. The Gospel commands no such thing. The church, 'which judgeth not those that are without', 1 Cor. v. 11, wants it not. And the commonwealth, which embraces indifferently all men that are honest, peaceable, and industrious, requires it not. Shall we suffer a pagan to deal and trade with us, and shall we not suffer him to pray unto and worship God? If we allow the Jews to have private houses and dwellings amongst us, why should we not allow them to have synagogues? Is their doctrine more false, their worship more abominable, or is the civil peace more endangered, by their meeting in public, than in their private houses? But if these things may be granted to Jews and pagans, surely the condition of any Christians ought not to be worse than theirs, in a Christian commonwealth.

You will say, perhaps, yes, it ought to be: because they are more inclinable to factions, tumults, and civil wars. I answer: is this the fault of the Christian religion? If it be so, truly the Christian religion is the worst of all religions, and ought neither to be embraced by any particular person, nor tolerated by any commonwealth. For if this be the genius, this the nature of the Christian religion, to be turbulent and destructive of the civil peace, that church itself which the magistrate indulges will not always be innocent. But far be it from us to say any such thing of that religion, which carries the greatest opposition to covetousness, ambition, discord, contention, and all manner of inordinate desires; and is the most modest and peaceable religion that ever was. We must therefore seek another cause of those evils that are charged upon religion. And if we consider right, we shall find it to consist wholly in the subject that I am treating of. It is not the diversity of opinions, which cannot be avoided; but the refusal of toleration to those that are of different opinions, which might have been granted, that has produced all the bustles and wars, that have been in the Christian world, upon account of religion. The heads and leaders of the church, moved by avarice and insatiable desire of dominion, making use of the immoderate ambition of magistrates, and the credulous superstition of the giddy multitude, have incensed and animated them against those that dissent from themselves, by preaching unto them, contrary to the laws of the Gospel, and to the precepts of charity, that schismatics and heretics are to be outed of their possessions, and destroyed. And thus have they mixed together, and confounded two things, that are in themselves most different, the church and the commonwealth. Now as it is very difficult for men patiently to suffer themselves to be stripped of the goods, which they have got by their honest industry; and contrary to all the laws of equity, both human and divine, to be delivered up for a prey to other men's violence and rapine; especially when they are otherwise altogether blameless; and that the occasion for which they are thus treated does not at all belong to the jurisdiction of the magistrate, but entirely to the conscience of every particular man, for the conduct of which he is accountable to God only; what else can be expected, but that these men, growing weary of the evils under which they labour, should in the end think it lawful for them to resist force with force, and to defend their natural rights, which are not forfeitable upon account of religion, with arms as well as they can? That this has been hitherto the ordinary course of things, is abundantly evident in history: and that it will continue to be so hereafter, is but too apparent in reason. It cannot indeed be otherwise, so long as the principle of persecution for religion shall prevail, as it has done hitherto, with magistrate and people; and so long as those that ought to be the preachers of peace and concord, shall continue, with all their art and strength, to excite men to arms, and sound the trumpet of war. But that magistrates should thus suffer these incendiaries, and disturbers of the public peace, might justly be wondered at, if it did not appear that they have been invited by them unto a participation of the spoil, and have therefore thought fit to make use of their covetousness and pride, as means whereby to increase their own power. For who does not see that these good men are indeed more ministers of the government than ministers of the Gospel; and that by flattering the ambition, and favouring the dominion of princes and men in authority, they endeavour with all their might to promote that tyranny in the commonwealth, which otherwise they should not be able to establish in the church? This is the unhappy agreement that we see between the church and the state. Whereas if each of them would contain itself within its own bounds, the one attending to the worldly welfare of the commonwealth, the other to the salvation of souls, it is impossible that any discord should ever have happened between them. 'Sed pudet haec opprobria', &c. God Almighty grant, I beseech him, that the Gospel of peace may at length be preached, and that civil magistrates, growing more careful to conform their own consciences to the law of God, and less solicitous about the binding of other men's consciences by human laws, may, like fathers of their country, direct all their counsels and endeavours to promote universally the civil welfare of all their children; except only of such as are arrogant, ungovernable, and injurious to their brethren; and that all ecclesiastical men, who boast themselves to be the successors of the apostles, walking peaceably and modestly in the apostles' steps, without intermeddling with state affairs, may apply themselves wholly to promote the salvation of souls. Farewell.

Perhaps it may not be amiss to add a few things concerning heresy and schism. A Turk is not, nor can be either heretic or schismatic to a Christian; and if any man fall off from the Christian faith to Maho-metism, he does not thereby become a heretic, or a schismatic, but an apostate and an infidel. This nobody doubts of. And by this it appears that men of different religions cannot be heretics or schis-matics to one another.

We are to inquire, therefore, what men are of the same religion: concerning which, it is manifest that those who have one and the same rule of faith and worship are of the same religion, and those who have not the same rule of faith and worship are of different religions. For since all things that belong unto that religion are contained in that rule, it follows necessarily, that those who agree in one rule are of one and the same religion; and vice versa. Thus Turks and Christians are of different religions; because these take the Holy Scriptures to be the rule of their religion, and those the Koran. And for the same reason, there may be different religions also, even amongst Christians. The papists and the Lutherans, though both of them profess faith in Christ, and are therefore called Christians, yet are not both of the same religion: because these acknowledge nothing but the Holy Scriptures to be the rule and foundation of their religion; those take in also traditions and decrees of popes, and of all these together make the rule of their religion. And thus the Christians of St. John, as they are called, and the Christians of Geneva, are of different religions; because these also take only the Scriptures, and those, I know not what traditions, for the rule of their religion.

This being settled, it follows, First, That heresy is a separation made in ecclesiastical communion between men of the same religion, for some opinions no way contained in the rule itself. And secondly, That amongst those who acknowledge nothing but the Holy Scriptures to be their rule of faith, heresy is a separation made in their Christian communion, for opinions not contained in the express words of Scripture.

Now this separation may be made in a twofold manner:

First, When the greater part, or, by the magistrate's patronage, the stronger part, of the church separates itself from others, by excluding them out of her communion, because they will not profess their belief of certain opinions which are not to be found in the express words of Scripture. For it is not the paucity of those that are separated, nor the authority of the magistrate, that can make any man guilty of heresy; but he only is an heretic who divides the church into parts, introduces names and marks of distinction, and voluntarily makes a separation because of such opinions.

Secondly, When any one separates himself from the communion of a church, because that church does not publicly profess some certain opinions which the Holy Scriptures do not expressly teach.

Both these are 'heretics, because they err in fundamentals, and they err obstinately against knowledge'. For when they have determined the Holy Scriptures to be the only foundation of faith, they nevertheless lay down certain propositions as fundamental, which are not in the Scripture; and because others will not acknowledge these additional opinions of theirs, nor build upon them as they were necessary and fundamental, they therefore make a separation in the church, either by withdrawing themselves from the others, or expelling the others from them. Nor does it signify any thing for them to say that their confessions and symbols are agreeable to Scripture, and to the analogy of faith: for if they be conceived in the express words of Scripture, there can be no question about them; because those are acknowledged by all Christians to be of divine inspiration, and therefore fundamental. But if they say that the articles which

54

they require to be professed are consequences deduced from the Scripture, it is undoubtedly well done of them to believe and profess such things as seem unto them so agreeable to the rule of faith: but it would be very ill done to obtrude those things upon others, unto whom they do not seem to be the indubitable doctrines of the Scripture. And to make a separation for such things as these, which neither are nor can be fundamental, is to become heretics. For I do not think there is any man arrived to that degree of madness, as that he dare give out his consequences and interpretations of Scripture as divine inspirations, and compare the articles of faith, that he has framed according to his own fancy, with the authority of the Scripture. I know there are some propositions so evidently agreeable to Scripture, that nobody can deny them to be drawn from thence: but about those therefore there can be no difference. This only I say, that however clearly we may think this or the other doctrine to be deduced from Scripture, we ought not therefore to impose it upon others as a necessary article of faith, because we believe it to be agreeable to the rule of faith; unless we would be content also that other doctrines should be imposed upon us in the same manner; and that we should be compelled to receive and profess all the different and contradictory opinions of Lutherans, Calvinists, remonstrants, anabaptists, and other sects, which the contrivers of symbols, systems, and confessions, are accustomed to deliver unto their followers as genuine and necessary deductions from the Holy Scripture. I cannot but wonder at the extravagant arrogance of those men who think that they themselves can explain things necessary to salvation more clearly than the Holy Ghost, the eternal and infinite wisdom of God.

Thus much concerning heresy; which word in common use is applied only to the doctrinal part of religion. Let us now consider schism, which is a crime near akin to it: for both those words seem unto me to signify an 'ill-grounded separation in ecclesiastical communion, made about things not necessary'. But since use, which is the supreme law in matter of language, has determined that heresy relates to errors in faith, and schism to those in worship or discipline, we must consider them under that distinction.

Schism then, for the same reasons that have already been alleged, is nothing else but a separation made in the communion of the church, upon account of something in divine worship, or ecclesiastical discipline, that is not any necessary part of it. Now nothing in worship or discipline can be necessary to Christian communion, but what Christ our legislator, or the apostles, by inspiration of the Holy Spirit, has commanded in express words.

In a word: he that denies not any thing that the Holy Scriptures teach in express words, nor makes a separation upon occasion of any thing that is not manifestly contained in the sacred text; however he may be nicknamed by any sect of Christians, and declared by some, or all of them, to be utterly void of true Christianity; yet in deed and in truth this man cannot be either a heretic or schismatic.

These things might have been explained more largely, and more advantageously; but it is enough to have hinted at them, thus briefly, to a person of your parts.   .

THE DEVELOPMENT OF LOCKE'S BELIEF IN TOLERATION

J. W. Gough

Locke's famous *Letter Concerning Toleration* was not published till 1689, not long before the *Two Treatises of Government* and the *Essay Concerning Human Understanding*, but the question of toleration had been occupying his mind for many years before this. In the *Treatises*, in which he incorporated the doctrines which had been advocated for a generation and more by a whole school of political writers, he summed up the Whig support for constitutionalism and opposition to arbitrary government. So also his belief in toleration, which was based on the same general principles as his political theory, was the fruit of long reading and reflection on a question of burning topical interest. In England, the intolerance of the Laudian church, and later of the Presbyterians in the Long Parliament, had led the Protestant sectaries to urge the necessity for religious liberty. Across the Atlantic the intolerant Calvinism of Massachusetts had aroused a similar controversy, which can be paralleled by the struggle for recognition by the Arminians in Holland and the Huguenots in France. With many of the sectaries the plea for toleration had been the outcome of their circumstances: they found themselves in the position of a persecuted minority, and had they been numerous enough to impose their beliefs on others some of them might have been as intolerant as their persecutors. But there were others whose belief in religious liberty was more profound than this. Such was Oliver Cromwell himself, under whose protectorate some measure of toleration, for the Protestant sects if not for Roman Catholics or Anglicans, had actually been secured for a time. Such also was Dr John Owen, the Independent divine who was Dean of Christ Church while Locke was an undergraduate there.

After all, if toleration in the end was necessitated in practice by the multiplicity and variety of the sects, religious liberty was logically

57

the outcome of the Protestant belief that each individual (with God's assistance) could interpret scripture for himself. To the rational spirit, which became more widespread as the seventeenth century advanced, an intolerant dogmatism seemed out of place, and began to give way before the latitudinarian idea that essential Christianity could be reduced to a few fundamental beliefs, compared with which all other matters, whether of doctrine or ritual, were relatively unimportant. Alongside this there appeared the idea of 'natural religion', which subsequently reached its fullest development among the Deists, but which had much earlier roots. Just as natural law, which was God's will for human conduct, could be discerned by the faculty of reason, so, it was thought, the principles of religion, with which morality was closely connected, were founded in nature and could be discerned, independently of revelation or of ecclesiastical authority, by natural reason. Those who thought thus would be inclined to regard many of the subjects in dispute between the different churches as inessential trivialities. To many minds, also, the rationalism of the age meant a more purely secular outlook, which was sceptical of ecclesiastical dogma, and more inclined to be influenced by practical than by theological considerations. Dissent was strong among the mercantile classes, and they were not slow to argue that English traders suffered in comparison with the Dutch whose prosperity they ascribed to the religious liberty allowed in Holland. Writers like Shaftesbury, Temple, Petty and others stressed these arguments, and it can hardly be doubted that this appeal to material interest contributed powerfully to reinforce the more purely intellectual grounds in favour of toleration.[1]

Locke, who was the son of Puritan parents, whose education both at Westminster and at Oxford had been in a Puritan atmosphere, and who subsequently became closely associated with the sceptical and tolerant Shaftesbury, was in fundamental sympathy with this rationalist point of view.[2] In politics the attitude he adopted, in common with the Whigs, was one of resistance to the dogmatic authoritarianism professed by the Tories with the support of the established church. Instead of their conception of church and state as so integrally linked together in one divinely organized society that membership of the one essentially involved membership of the other, he regarded the state as a voluntary union of individuals for the specific and limited purposes of settling disputes, preserving order and protecting life and property. Corresponding with this was his view of a church as, similarly, a voluntary union of individuals for specific purposes, namely, 'the public worship of God in such manner as they believe will be acceptable to the Deity for the salvation of their souls'.[3] This being so, each society will have its own laws and conditions of membership, but neither has any right to interfere in the affairs of the other for purposes which are purely the other's concern. Thus it is the state's business to keep the peace, but it is none of the state's business to impose civil penalties in order to enforce obedience to the laws of the church. The proper method of enforcing such obedience is the hope of rewards and fear of punishments in the other world, except that, as the church has to maintain its existence in this world, it may expel members who do not accept its principles or obey its regulations. Here we see the essential points round which Locke's advocacy of toleration always centred.

That his concern with this subject dated back to 1660 has been known since Lord King reprinted part of the preface to a then unpublished treatise of that date, entitled *Question: Whether the Civil Magistrate may lawfully impose and determine the use of indifferent things in reference to Religious Worship.*[4] Investigation of the Lovelace Collection of Locke's papers has revealed a good deal more than Lord King disclosed about this treatise, and has also shown that Locke's attitude to toleration was already defined in 1659. This appears from a letter to one S.H., thanking him for a book he had sent on toleration, which Locke declares that he has read with great pleasure and admiration. He hopes there will be a second and enlarged edition, and to this end he gives advice on how to make the book more effective polemically, suggesting that the author could improve it by tracing the history of toleration down to recent times and dealing with conditions in Holland, France and Poland. Locke's doubt was whether S.H. was wise in advocating a general toleration for all, including Roman Catholics, and he gave reasons for thinking such wide indulgence dangerous.[5] Dr W. von Leyden who calendared the Lovelace papers in the Bodleian Library, identified S.H. with Henry Stubbe (it was apparently Locke's habit, when denoting someone by his initials, to reverse their order), who was a friend of Hobbes and had been a contemporary of Locke's at Westminster and Christ Church. The book in question, published in 1659, must have been Stubbe's *An Essay in Defence of the Good Old Cause; or a Discourse concerning the Rise and Extent of the Power of the Civil Magistrate in Reference to Spiritual Affairs ...*, in the course of which the writer claimed to vindicate Sir Henry Vane from the 'false aspersions of

Mr Baxter'. Locke never ceased to think it unsafe to extend toleration to Roman Catholics (whom in this respect he bracketed with atheists), because Roman Catholics not only taught that faith need not be kept with heretics, but owed allegiance to a foreign potentate who pretended that kings forfeited their crowns if he excommunicated them.

For Locke the essential question was thus a political one. It was not a question of freedom of conscience, or of intellectual freedom, in the abstract. It was a question of the extent of the power of the civil magistrate in religious affairs. In civil affairs, as we have seen,[6] Locke held that civil magistrates and governments had absolute power, but in religious affairs they could interfere only in so far as such interference was necessary for civil purposes, such as the preservation of peace, and did not go beyond matters 'indifferent'. This was the line he took in the treatise he composed in 1660, in reply to a pamphlet published anonymously in that year with the title, *The Great Question concerning Things Indifferent in Religious Worship Briefly Stated*. Dr von Leyden has shown that the author of this was another old Westminster, Edward Bagshaw (the younger), who, like Locke, also became a student of Christ Church. Bagshaw championed the extreme sectarian view that the civil magistrate could never interfere in any religious matters; but Locke, while agreeing that the magistrate had no power to touch things necessary for the worship of God, and determined and revealed by God as such, argued that indifferent things are subject to the magistrate's interference, since the way they are determined is not necessary for the maintenance of religion, but may affect questions of peace and order. The Lovelace Collection contains a copy of Bagshaw's pamphlet; and each of Locke's arguments in the treatise, which consists of thirty-six quarto sheets, is introduced by a quotation from Bagshaw, to which it is a reply.[7] Locke discussed his controversy with Bagshaw with other Oxford friends, as appears from letters to him from Samuel Tilly and Gabriel Towerson of All Souls, while a couple of pages at the end of the treatise contain a draft of a letter from him, dated Pensford,[8] 11 December 1660, and signed 'John Locke', which Dr von Leyden thinks was probably addressed to Towerson, who seems to have instigated him to write the treatise. It looks as if Locke intended to publish it, possibly anonymously like Bagshaw's pamphlet itself, but he never did so, and with characteristic caution he subsequently crossed out the draft letter and tried (not quite successfully) to make both his signature and the word 'Pensford' illegible. The letter to

Towerson summarizes the contents of the treatise, and contains a number of sentences which also occur at the end of the Preface to the reader. The passages printed by Lord King consist only of some excerpts from this preface, which is written in Locke's hand on six sides of a sheet of paper, originally folded and now bound separately from the treatise itself.[9]

From this it seems clear that, in his disgust at the fanatical excesses of the Interregnum, Locke not only at first welcomed the Restoration, but was prepared to attribute a greater authority to the government than he thought proper in later years. After declaring that 'there is no one can have a greater respect and veneration for authority than I', he remarks that from earliest childhood he has found himself 'in a storm, which has lasted almost hitherto', so that he 'cannot but entertain the approaches of a calm with the greatest joy and satisfaction', and he feels bound, therefore, 'both in duty and gratitude to endeavour the continuance of such a blessing by disposing men's minds to obedience to that government which has brought with it the quiet settlement which even our giddy folly had put beyond the reach not only of our contrivance but hopes'. His wish is that men will not 'hazard again the substantial blessings of peace and settlement in an over zealous contention about things which they themselves confess to be little, and at most are but indifferent'. Experience, he continues, has taught him that 'a general freedom is but a general bondage', and 'were the part of freedom contended for by our author [sc. Bagshaw] generally indulged in England, it would prove only a liberty for contention, censure and persecution'. He is no believer, therefore, in 'a liberty to be Christians so as not to be subjects. All the freedom I can wish my country or myself, is to enjoy the protection of those laws which the prudence and providence of our ancestors established, and the happy return of His Majesty has restored'. In the political theory of his maturity Locke upheld the traditional English constitution based on a limited monarchy and fundamental law, but in this preface he gave expression to markedly less 'liberal' views.

Locke opens the treatise itself by laying down certain propositions, which are of considerable interest, as showing that at this early date he had already formulated some of the basic principles of his political theory, and they are therefore worth quoting:

In order to the clearer debating this question, besides
the granting my author's two suppositions, viz: (i) That a

Christian may be a magistrate, (ii) that there are some things indifferent, it will not be amiss to premiss some few things about these matters of indifferency, viz:

1.   That were there no law there would be no moral good or evil, but man would be left to a most entire liberty in all his actions, and could meet with nothing which would not be purely indifferent, and consequently, that which doth not lie under the obligation of any law is still indifferent.

2.   That nobody hath a natural original power and disposure of this liberty of man but only God himself, from whose authority all laws do fundamentally derive their obligation, as being either immediately enjoined by him, or framed by some authority from him.

3.   That wherever God hath made known his will, either by the discovery of reason, usually called the law of nature, or the revelations of his word, there nothing is left man but submission and obedience, and all things within the compass of this law are necessarily and indispensably good or evil.

4.   That all things not comprehended in that law are perfectly indifferent, and as to them man is naturally free, but yet so much master of his own liberty that he may by compact convey it over to another, and invest him with a power over his actions, there being no law of God forbidding a man to dispose of his liberty and obey another. But on the other side, there being a law of God enforcing fidelity and truth in all lawful contracts, it obliges him after such resignation and agreement to submit.

Locke's fifth proposition emphasizes the necessity, if life in society is to be possible, for 'every particular man' to 'part with this right to his liberty'[10] and entrust the government with supreme power.

Indifferency and the powers of the magistrate were being debated at length in numerous publications about this time, and at Christ Church, which in the course of the year 1660 was presided over by no less than four deans of varying outlook and policy in these matters, such indifferent things as the wearing of surplices were in utter disorder.[11] It was against this background that Locke rejected Bagshaw's plea for religious liberty. Bagshaw rested his claim for complete freedom, in everything not expressly commanded or forbidden in scripture, on faith and revelation, but Locke argued that natural law and reason made it evident that only limited toleration was consistent with life in society. He agreed that right and wrong were determined by the law of nature or the will of God, but indifferent things must be subject to the civil magistrate, since he was responsible for the maintenance of public order.

Locke's attitude in 1660 thus appears to be definitely conservative, but at the same time he maintained that his doctrine did not involve any damaging loss of liberty. 'Besides the submission I have for authority', he wrote, 'I have no less a love of liberty, without which a man shall find himself less happy than a beast, slavery being a condition that robs us of all the benefits of life, and embitters the greatest blessings'.[12] Locke also argued that

> if the supreme authority be conferred on the magistrate by the consent of the people, ... then it is evident that they have resigned up their liberty of action into his disposure, and so all his commands are but their own votes, and his edicts their own injunctions made by proxies which by mutual contract they are bound to obey.[13]

This and other passages are worth attention for the indication they give of what Locke meant by consent. It seems remarkable, to say the least, that he should recognize the impotence of the individual's vote in face of an adverse majority, and at the same time conclude the preface to this treatise by remarking that 'it would be a strange thing if anyone amongst us should question the obligation of those laws which are not ratified nor imposed on him but *by his own consent* in Parliament'. It seems probable that he thought of this consent as embodied in the contract by which, it was supposed, every man surrendered his own individual liberty of action at the origin of the state; and in a previous study we have already noticed the un-convincing arguments by which he sought to show that the same consent could be ascribed to later generations.[14] The best explanation I can offer of Locke's apparent satisfaction with this is that the notion of consent in parliament had become such a commonplace of the constitution that when he was not paying special attention to what representation really involved (and sometimes even when he was) he was apt to give it the same everyday uncritical acceptance as the rest of his fellow countrymen seem to have done, then as well as since.

Besides the treatise in reply to Bagshaw, Locke also composed a short Latin treatise on the same subject, entitled *An Magistratus Civilis possit res adiaphoras in divini cultus ritus asciscere, eosque populo imponere? Aff.*[15] This differs in form and substance from the English treatise.[16] It makes no mention of Bagshaw's pamphlet, but after some definitions of 'magistrate', 'religious worship' and 'indifferent things', with discussions about the nature of law and the duty of civil obedience, deals more generally, and in a more scholastic manner, with the question of the rights of magistrates. Locke purported to preserve liberty of conscience, but he defined it in a very narrow way, arguing that if the magistrate gave orders concerning things indifferent, a man must obey them, but as he need not inwardly assent, his judgement remained free. We may doubt the value of a liberty to think without the liberty to act on one's thoughts, and in later life Locke ceased to argue in this style and came to hold that in religion there were no indifferent things; but he continued to maintain that the civil magistrate could always demand full obedience when this was necessary for peace and security. In view of Locke's numerous quotations from Hooker in the *Second Treatise of Government*, it is interesting to observe that in both the English and the Latin treatises on the civil magistrate he cites Hooker in support of his view.[17] In the English treatise Hooker's name is coupled with that of Dr Sanderson, while the first draft of the Latin treatise refers to the Bishop of Lincoln, and Dr von Leyden concluded that the Latin treatise was written not before the autumn of 1660, for Robert Sanderson, who had been Regius Professor of Divinity at Oxford, was consecrated Bishop of Lincoln on 28 October in that year. Locke cancelled the reference to the bishop in his final draft of the Latin treatise, although in fact his argument owed more to Sanderson than to Hooker.[18]

In his *Life of John Locke* (1876) Fox Bourne quoted[19] some extracts from a work, consisting of forty-six pages of manuscript, said to be in Locke's hand, and preserved among the Shaftesbury papers in the Public Record Office, entitled *Reflections upon the Roman Commonwealth*. This is not dated, but Fox Bourne thought it belonged to the year 1660, and might have been written before the treatise on the civil magistrate which we have just dealt with. It shows considerable knowledge of Roman history and historians, and political convictions from which Locke 'never greatly swerved'. The constitution is, perhaps, chiefly remarkable for the liberality of the religious institutions, which, begun by Romulus and completed by Numa, are commended for their simplicity and wisdom. Some of the phraseology of this essay, together with its advocacy of 'comprehension', and the belief that the essentials of religion could be reduced to one or two simple articles, without 'clogging it with creeds and catechisms and endless niceties about the essences, properties and attributes of God', certainly seem to have a Lockean sound. On the other hand, these views were common to the Whigs and latitudinarians in general, and the power the magistrate is here allowed to exercise in religious matters differs from what Locke elsewhere attributes to the civil authorities. Locke's favourite distinction was between things morally good or bad, which a man is obliged to do or to abstain from, and things 'indifferent', and it is in the latter that the magistrate might (in certain circumstances) intervene; but here the suggestion is that the lawgiver may 'venture to enjoin' belief in 'the common principles of religion' which 'all mankind agree in'. Internal evidence therefore makes it doubtful whether Locke was really the author of this essay at all. It has been attributed to the third Lord Shaftesbury, but it has been shown to be in fact the first part of Walter Moyle's *Essay upon the Roman Government.*[20]

It is clear from entries in Locke's commonplace book, dated 1661,[21] that he gave a good deal of attention to questions about the nature of the church, and the power of the government in religious matters, and that he soon advanced from the position he had taken up in the treatise against Bagshaw. Under the heading *Sacerdos* he noted that 'though the magistrate have a power of commanding or forbidding things indifferent which have a relation to religion, yet this can only be within that Church whereof he himself is a member'. He may 'forbid such things as may tend to the disturbance of the peace of the commonwealth', whether people think them civil or religious; but he may not 'order and direct even matters indifferent in the circumstances of a worship, or within a Church whereof he is not professor or member'. Rites and ceremonies are 'a thing different and independent wholly from every man's concern in the civil society, which hath nothing to do with a man's affairs in the other world. . . . The magistrate hath here no more right to intermeddle than any private man'. This rather hesitant and illogical compromise was already an advance on 1660; but in 1689 Locke confines the magistrate's power to purely civil affairs; it 'extends not to the establishing of any articles of faith, or forms of worship, by the force of his laws', and the fact that a magistrate is a member of a particular church gives him no more power, as a magistrate, to interfere in its religious affairs than in the religious affairs of any other church.

Another entry, headed *Ecclesia*, develops Locke's position a little further. He finds support in Hooker for the notion that the church is a supernatural but voluntary society: voluntary, because, like other societies, the 'original of it' is 'an inclination unto sociable life and a consent to the bond of association which is the law and order they are associated in'; supernatural, because 'part of the bond of their association is a law revealed concerning what worship God would have done unto him, which natural reason could not have discovered'. From these premisses Locke draws four conclusions: (1) the secular power 'which is purely natural' cannot compel anyone to belong to any one of the many existing churches, (2) nobody can 'impose any ceremonies unless positively and clearly by revelation injoined', (3) only the revealed part of the bond of association is an unalterable law; the other, being human, 'depends wholly on consent, and so is alterable, and a man is held by such laws, or to such a particular society, no longer than himself doth consent', (4) churches do not (as Hooker seems to imply) originate from our inclination to a sociable life, for this can be fully satisfied in other societies, but 'from the obligation man, by the light of reason, finds himself under, to own and worship God publicly in the world'.[22]

In these brief notes we can see already formed Locke's basic ideas on the voluntary character of societies, and of the church as one of them; and of the relationship in this connection between God's will and man's natural reason. The theoretical structure of his political philosophy, of which his theory of toleration was a corollary, is already here in outline. It was confirmed and substantiated by further reading and reflection, and required only to be more fully worked out in the light of experience of practical affairs. This practical experience Locke gained meanwhile through his association with Shaftesbury, but it was not till after the publication of some of Filmer's works in 1679 that he determined to write at full length on the principles of government. In the intervening years, however, though he published nothing, his papers show that questions about the churches and toleration occupied a large part of his thoughts.

To this period belong *The Fundamental Constitutions for the Government of Carolina*, of which the original draft, in Locke's handwriting, dated 21 June 1669, is among the Shaftesbury papers in the Public Record Office. Charles II granted a charter for this colony to eight Lords Proprietors, among whom Ashley (later Lord Shaftesbury) was prominent and Locke, who was in effect Ashley's confidential secretary, was closely concerned in the drafting of this scheme; and the text, as subsequently adopted by the Lords Proprietors, after being published in a volume entitled *A Collection of Several Pieces of*

Mr. John Locke (1720), was included in later collected editions of Locke's *Works*. It seems to be generally agreed, however, that though Locke drafted this, the scheme itself was not his.[23] To students of his thought it is perhaps mainly of interest on account of the extremely liberal religious clauses it contains. In effect, colonists were to profess a belief in God, consent to worship him, and make no secret of their belief: with these provisos, any seven persons could establish a church of their own, and worship God in whatever manner they thought fit, so long as they did not interfere with a like freedom for others, or speak seditiously about the government. There was also a clause (which we are told 'was not drawn up by Mr Locke, but inserted by the chief of some of the proprietors, against his judgment, as Mr Locke himself informed one of his friends')[24] providing that when the colony was sufficiently developed Anglican churches should be established and these only should be subsidized by the government.

Shaftesbury himself believed in religious liberty, and even if Locke did no more than draft this constitution, the comprehensiveness of its religious arrangements and their freedom from any rigid tests are entirely in accord with his views. Fox Bourne suggested that 'whether Locke originated those generous arrangements or not, he was certainly responsible for the wording of them, in which the generosity was clearly expressed'. This is confirmed by some letters to Locke preserved in the Lovelace Collection, notably three letters on Carolina from Sir Peter Colleton, the second of which (undated, but endorsed '1673') refers to 'that excellent form of government in the composure of which you had so great a hand',[25] and a letter from Nicholas Toinard, dated 16 September 1679, in which the writer says he has heard that Locke has been revising the article on religion in the constitutions of Carolina.[26]

Two years before the Carolina scheme, Locke had completed the draft of what Fox Bourne called 'by far the most important of Locke's early writings'.[27] We have already noticed entries in his commonplace book on the subject of the church and religious worship. In 1667 he assembled his conclusions on this subject in an orderly form, under the heading *An Essay Concerning Toleration*. It appears from the last sentence that he contemplated writing more on the same subject, but he does not seem to have done so. The essay dates from the beginning of his acquaintance with Ashley, and it is possible that Ashley encouraged him to write it. Locke evidently took a great deal of trouble over the composition of this essay, for four variant versions of it are in existence, the last of which, a copy in the handwriting of an amanuensis, contains a number of alterations, cancellations and additional passages in Locke's own hand.[28] The version printed in Fox Bourne's *Life of John Locke*[29] was taken from a draft, in Locke's handwriting, among the Shaftesbury papers. The other two versions are both in America, one in the Huntington Library in California, the other in Locke's commonplace book in Mr Houghton's private collection. Lord King[30] printed the end of this, with the concluding sentence 'sic cogitavit J. Locke' and the date (1667), with which Locke not infrequently ended the memoranda he made of his philosophical reflections.

In this essay Locke makes clear at the outset that his theory of toleration is the logical consequence of his theory of the nature of society and government.

> If men could live peaceably and quietly together, without uniting under certain laws, and entering[31] into a common-wealth, there would be no need at all of magistrates or politics, which were only made to preserve men in this world from the fraud and violence of one another.

Whether the government be in the hands of a monarch *jure divino*, or of magistrates deriving their authority 'from the grant and consent of the people', the functions of a ruler are strictly limited to 'securing the civil peace and property of his subjects'. In reference to toleration, he continues, 'the opinions and actions of men ... divide themselves into three sorts'. First, 'all purely speculative opinions and divine worship', such as 'the belief of the Trinity, purgatory, transubstantiation, antipodes.[32] Christ's personal reign on earth, &c.', and 'the place, time, and manner of worshipping my God'. With these society and government have no concern. Second, 'all practical opinions and actions in matters of indifferency', which 'in their own nature are neither good nor bad but yet concern society and men's conversations with one another'. Third, there are 'moral virtues and vices', which 'concern society and are also good or bad in their own nature'.

Only the first of these have 'an absolute and universal right to toleration'. In the second category Locke includes

> all practical principles or opinions, by which men think themselves obliged to regulate their actions with one another; as that men may breed their children, or dispose of their estates, as

they please; that men may work or rest when they think fit; that polygamy and divorce are lawful or unlawful; that flesh or fish is to be eaten or abstained from at certain seasons, and so on. These opinions, and the actions following from them, with all other things indifferent, have a title also to toleration; but yet only so far as they do not tend to the disturbance of the state, or do not cause greater inconveniences than advantages to the community.

The magistrate, therefore, 'may prohibit the publishing of any of these opinions when in themselves[33] they tend to the disturbance of the government', and may command or forbid any actions resulting from these opinions in so far as they affect 'the peace, safety and security of his people'. But he must be careful to make no laws and impose no restraints beyond what are so necessitated; nor should he force any man to renounce an opinion or assent to the contrary, because such a compulsion 'cannot alter men's minds; it can only force them to be hypocrites'. A similar principle applies to the third category. 'However strange it may seem', Locke declares, 'the lawmaker hath nothing to do with moral virtues and vices ... any otherwise than barely as they are subservient to the good and preservation of mankind under government.' As a result, Locke thinks that while the magistrate 'ought not to command the practice of any vice', he is not bound to punish all vices, but may tolerate some, 'for, I would know, what government in the world doth not?' Locke briefly discusses the problem of men who find the restrictions imposed by the magistrate conflict with the 'sincere persuasions of their own consciences'. He thinks such men should do what their consciences require of them, in so far as they can do so without violence, 'but withal are bound at the same time quietly to submit to the penalty the law inflicts on such disobedience. . . . And certainly he is a hypocrite, and only pretends conscience', Locke declares, 'who will not, by obeying his conscience and submitting also to the law, purchase heaven for himself and peace for his country, though at the rate of his estate, liberty, or life itself'. We are apt to scoff nowadays at this doctrine of 'passive obedience', and it may indeed seem supine if applied indiscriminately, as it sometimes was by seventeenth-century high churchmen. But not everyone is heroic enough to resist actively, and even passive obedience may require considerable courage; and if the magistrate's interference is restricted by conditions such as Locke lays down, recalcitrants have no valid grounds for complaint.

Having dealt with toleration as a question of the magistrate's duty, Locke proceeds to discuss 'what he ought to do in prudence', with special reference to the papists and the 'fanatics' – 'an opprobrious name' for Protestant dissenters, which he thinks should be 'laid aside and forgotten'. For the kind of reasons we have already noticed, he would exclude papists from toleration: besides, 'they think themselves bound to deny it to others'. As for the dissenters, if they cannot be persuaded to part with their opinions, it is useless to try and force them to do so by persecuting them. We may 'persuade them to lay by their animosities, and become friends to the state, though they are not sons of the church'.

In the earlier drafts of his essay Locke expressed doubts whether it would be prudent for the government to tolerate all dissenting sects, especially if they 'herd themselves into companies with distinction from the public', and seem to the magistrate 'visibly to threaten the peace of the state'. The Quakers, in particular, 'were they numerous enough to become dangerous to the state, would deserve the magistrate's care and watchfulness to suppress them', largely, it seems, because of their refusal to take off their hats. Locke even went on to suggest that if 'any fashion of clothes distinct from that of the magistrate and those that adhere to him should spread itself and become the badge of a very considerable part of the people', this might give the government reasonable cause to forbid it.

In the final version of the essay, however, Locke deleted these passages and substituted a markedly more permissive one. He now rejected the idea that political security necessitated such uniformity, lest when people form sects they 'may occasion disorder, conspiracies and seditions ... and endanger the government'. Instead he declared that if this were so 'all discontented and active men must be removed, and whispering must be less tolerated than preaching, as much more likely to carry on and foment a conspiracy'. If the formation of separate unions or corporations is not to be allowed, 'all charters of towns, especially great ones, are presently to be taken away'; but union in religion, he now felt sure, was no more a threat to the government than union in the privileges of a corporation.

Locke also inserted a passage which significantly modified his earlier doctrine about indifferency.

'Twill be said [he wrote] that if a toleration shall be allowed as due to all the parts of religious worship, it will shut out the magistrate's power from making laws about those things over which it is acknowledged on all hands that he has a power, viz. things indifferent, as many things made use of in religious worship are, viz. wearing a white or a black garment, kneeling or not kneeling, &c. To which I answer that in religious worship nothing is indifferent, for it being the using of those habits, gestures, &c., and no other, which I think acceptable to God in my worshipping of him, however they may be in their own nature perfectly indifferent, yet when I am worshipping my God in a way I think he has prescribed and will approve of, I cannot alter, omit or add any circumstances in that which I think the true way of worship.

Thus while Locke continued to maintain the principle that the magistrate had a right to exercise control over indifferent things, in effect he excluded the whole concept of indifferency from the sphere of religion.

Though differing in form and arrangement, this essay anticipated the main arguments and conclusions of the *Epistola de Tolerantia* of 1689, and was based on the fundamental thesis which Locke adhered to consistently all through his life. In the preface to his translation William Popple declared that 'absolute liberty, just and true liberty, equal and impartial liberty, is the thing that we stand in need of'. This, however, was going too far, for Locke never believed in 'absolute liberty'. Besides excluding papists and atheists, he always gave the magistrate a right to interfere in religious matters, where peace and public order necessitated it. As he grew older, however, he undoubtedly came to lay less emphasis on the justification for interference, and more on the need for freedom of thought and worship. His biographer praises him because he 'went far beyond the most liberal of the independents' in pleading for 'the utmost freedom of opinion in religious matters ... to all outside the limits of the national church',[34] restraining them only if their social or political views ran contrary to the true interests of the community, and also 'went far beyond the most liberal of the latitudinarian churchmen' in his plea for comprehension, 'so broadening the area of doctrine and so simplifying the methods of ritual appointed for the national church as to leave to most reasonable persons very little excuse indeed for refusing to belong to it'.[35]

Not everyone, however, not even the firmest believers in religious liberty and freedom of thought, would endorse the admiration implied in this account of Locke's theory. In the first place, now as much as then, there is the difficulty of accepting his notion that the essentials of religious faith could be reduced to a few broad tenets which were a kind of lowest common factor between all the Christian churches.[36] Then again, his conception of the church as a voluntary society (irrespective of any arguments which can be used in favour of the voluntary principle in the modern state) is as false historically as his theory, with which it is connected, that the origin of all societies, the state included, is in the consent of contracting individuals. His view on the nature of the church, and of the place of authority (whether clerical or secular) in religious matters, suffers too, as does his whole political and social theory, from his exaggerated belief in the capacity of the human intellect to make a rational choice in a field where historical traditions and habits, and only too often ignorant prejudices, are the dominant factors.[37]

Locke regarded himself as a churchman, but his churchmanship was of a very loose and unorthodox kind, in some respects exceeding even the limits of latitudinarianism; and though he never sympathized with sectarian extremism, his conception of the church, and of its relation to the state, was typical of nonconformity. Though not a separatist himself, he championed the right of separatists to form their own independent churches, and this was the root of his belief in toleration.[38] Even his intolerance of atheism was a consequence of the same belief in the right of free individuals to form voluntary societies by consent; for the atheist, in disbelieving in God, disbelieves in the author of the law of nature. Such disbelief undermines the obligation to keep promises and contracts, which is what holds society together. Atheism, therefore, is potentially anarchy.[39]

Locke's sympathy with the nonconformists, which indeed he shared with the Whig party generally, is exhibited clearly in an unpublished treatise against Edward Stillingfleet, then Dean of St Paul's, with whom, as Bishop of Worcester, Locke was later to be engaged in a lengthy theological controversy. Lord King printed some extracts from this treatise, under the title *A Defence of Nonconformity*, explaining that Locke wrote it in answer to a sermon of Stillingfleet's against the nonconformists (1680) and to Stillingfleet's rejoinder (1683) to Presbyterian and Independent replies to his sermon.[40] This explanation is not entirely correct, for Stillingfleet's rejoinder, entitled *The Unreasonableness of Separation*, was in fact published in 1681.[41] The treatise is in the Lovelace Collection, and consists of a large bundle of some 160 folio sheets. Lord King's extracts were taken from only a few sheets towards the end, and he overlooked the important fact, to which Dr von Leyden drew attention, that while the manuscript is partly in Locke's hand, and partly in that of his amanuensis Brownover, it is mainly in the hand of James Tyrrell. It was probably written at Tyrrell's house at Oakley between 1681 and 1683.

Few modern readers would wish to read more than Lord King printed of these detailed arguments in justification of the right of dissenters from the established church to form independent churches. Their general trend is in accordance with the views that Locke had already expressed, and was to repeat in his published works. The fact that Tyrrell had the largest share in this treatise, however, is of interest, in view of their common concern about this time to reply to Filmer's *Patriarcha*. The Lovelace Collection also contains a number of letters from Tyrrell to Locke on various subjects, including the law of nature, in which they shared an interest.[42]

We thus come to the best known of Locke's writings on toleration. The original of it he wrote in Latin, under the title, *Epistola de Tolerantia*, while he was in exile in Holland, and addressed to his Remonstrant theologian friend Philip van Limborch. Limborch had it published, under a pseudonym, in Holland, and it was quickly translated into English by a Unitarian friend of Locke's, William Popple, who had it published, anonymously, under the title *A Letter Concerning Toleration*. There is no need here to summarize this famous work again, particularly as it largely reproduces, albeit in a different form, the conclusions Locke had arrived at years before, and had more than once committed to writing. Nor is it necessary to add more to what his biographers have already told us about the reception it met with, and the later *Letters* he wrote in defence of the views he had expressed.[43]

His support of toleration was not the only flank he exposed to attack from Tory and Anglican quarters, where some of his philosophical and theological opinions were branded as heretical, and it seems clear that though he was not, as he was accused of being, a Socinian, his theology was in fact what would now be called Unitarian.[44] The conclusion of this study, however, is no place to embark on a discussion of the theological controversies in which Locke was so much occupied in his later years. Historically, the battle for toleration was already almost won when the *Letter* was published, for it was impossible that the old intolerant uniformity should be maintained after the revolution. Locke was disappointed at the time that the bill for comprehension was rejected, just as its predecessor had been at the Restoration, and the measure of indulgence actually accorded to dissenters by the so-called Toleration Act was much less complete than he would have wished. But in spite of a brief setback at the end of Anne's reign, the principle of toleration was now firmly established, and became more widely accepted as the eighteenth century ran its course. To this result the reading of Locke's published work contributed its share, even though he had said nothing new. The importance of Locke's *Letter* in the history of toleration, like the importance of his *Two Treatises of Government* in the history of civil liberty, lies not in its novelty or originality, nor in any remarkable or radical liberality. His works were persuasive in their age because of their orderliness and reasonableness and philosophical temper; and these qualities they owed in no small measure to being based on lifelong convictions reinforced by years of study and reflection.

NOTES

1   See A. A. Seaton, *The Theory of Toleration under the Later Stuarts* (Cambridge 1911), cc. 2 and 3.

2   According to Burnet (*Own Time*, ii c.1, edited by Airy, i, 172), Shaftesbury was 'a Deist at best'. Though brought up in Puritan surroundings, Locke was never a Puritan himself. He supported the rights of dissenters, but his real affinity was with the liberal school of divines to which Cudworth and Tillotson, Patrick and Isaac Barrow belonged (cf. H. R. Fox Bourne, *The Life of John Locke*, 2 vols (London 1876), vol. i, p. 310).

3   R. Klibansky (ed.), John Locke, *Epistola de Tolerantia: A Letter on Toleration*, translated by J. W. Gough (Oxford 1968), p. 71. See above p. 20. See also Locke's paper, dated 1673–4, 'On the difference between civil and ecclesiastical power', endorsed 'Excommunication', among the Lovelace papers, and printed in Lord King, *Life of John Locke* (Bohn's edn), p. 300. In this he works out in parallel columns the comparison between 'Civil Society or the State' and 'Religious Society or the Church', an arrangement which emphasizes his fundamental concept of both church and state as associations of individuals. Actually he describes churches as more voluntary than states, for while men 'are combined into civil societies in various forms, as force, chance, agreement or other accidents have happened to constrain them', and governments once established can command their subjects' continued obedience, 'church membership is perfectly voluntary, and may end whenever anyone pleases without any prejudice to himself' (ibid., p. 304).

4   King, op cit., p. 7.

5   Draft of the letter in Bodl. MS. Locke c.27, f.I.

6 J. W. Gough, 'The separation of powers and sovereignty', in his *John Locke's Political Philosophy: Eight Studies* (Oxford 1973), p. 119.

7 Bodl. MS. Locke e. 7. It is possible, as Lord King suggested, that Locke refrained from publication when the scheme of comprehension with the Presbyterians broke down, and it became clear that the post-Restoration parliament was determined to impose a policy of Anglican uniformity. Locke, who disliked public controversy, may well have felt that in these circumstances there would be no point in publishing his treatise. Cf. P. Abrams (ed.), John Locke, *Two Tracts on Government* (Cambridge 1967), pp. 12–15.

8 Locke's home in north Somerset, where he was staying with his parents at this time. See Abrams, op cit., p. 11.

9 Bodl. MS. Locke c. 28, ff. 1–2. The full texts of Locke's writings on this occasion, with an Introduction discussing in detail the circumstances that led to his composing them, have been published by Abrams, op cit.

10 Locke first of all wrote 'native right' and 'primitive liberty', but crossed out the adjectives.

11 Abrams, op cit., pp. 30ff.

12 Preface to the reader, printed in Abrams, op cit., p. 120.

13 Abrams, op cit., p. 126.

14 J. W. Gough, 'Government by consent', in his *John Locke's Political Philosophy: Eight Studies* (Oxford 1973).

15 This consists of eighteen manuscript pages in Locke's handwriting (Bodl. MS. Locke c. 28, ff. 3–20). Another draft of it, in Locke's handwriting, will be found in the notebook entitled *Lemmata* (Bodl. MS. Locke e. 6), which also contains drafts of six of his Latin essays on the law of nature. The similarity to them in the form of the title will be observed.

16 Latin text and an English translation in Abrams, op cit., pp. 185ff., 210ff.

17 In the English treatise he is 'the learned and reverend Mr. Hooker', in the Latin 'doctissimus Hooker'. The epithet 'judicious' which appeared on the title page of a series of extracts from Hooker published in 1675, was, according to the *OED*, first applied to him in 1626, in Thomas Jackson's commentary on the Creed.

18 His reasons for so doing are discussed by Abrams, op cit., pp. 70ff.

19 Fox Bourne, op cit., vol. i, pp. 147ff.

20 W. Moyle, *Works* (1726), vol. i, p. 3. See H. F. Russell Smith, *Harrington and his Oceana* (Cambridge 1914), pp. 139, 143, 217–18.

21 Dr Abrams (op cit., p. 9) doubts the existence of this book, but there undoubtedly exists a book, with the date of Locke's birth and the words 'Adversaria 1661' at the beginning, as described by Lord King (op cit., p. 282). It is in America, in the private collection of Mr Arthur Houghton, Jr, and a microfilm (MS. Film 77) is available for English readers in the Bodleian Library. One difficulty is that its present contents only partially correspond with the contents as described by King. Abrams says that the passages King quoted 'come from two separate notebooks' and are all plainly dated by Locke as entries made after 1680.

King was not an impeccably accurate transcriber, but it seems to me at least doubtful that he should have been so careless as to have said that he was copying from one notebook what in fact he was copying from two. A possible explanation is that what was in King's time one book may have since been split up, and in the process pages may have been displaced. This is only a conjecture, but it would account for the curious fact that the entry marked *Sacerdos*, which King quoted as one continuous passage, is now in two discontinuous sections, with one of the versions of the 1667 *Essay Concerning Toleration* between them. No doubt, while Locke started his commonplace book in 1661, some of the entries in it were made years later, and Abrams may well be right in his contention that there is nothing in Locke's papers before 1667 that shows support for religious toleration.

22 King, op cit., pp. 286ff., 295.
23 Locke's *Works* also contain a paper entitled *A Letter from a Person of Quality to his Friend in the Country*, which arose out of the proceedings in the Lords over a bill imposing the so-called Bishops' Test (1675). Shaftesbury seems to have got Locke to write out an account of his opposition to this bill. This was privately printed, but it was ordered to be burned by the common hangman, and Locke denied the authorship of it. See King, op cit., p. 39; Fox Bourne, op cit., vol. i, pp. 238ff., 336; H. O. Christophersen, *A Bibliographical Introduction to the Study of John Locke* (Oslo 1930), p. 9.
24 Fox Bourne, op cit., vol. i, p. 240.
25 Bodl. MS. Locke, c. 6, f. 213.
26 Bodl. MS. Locke, c. 20. The Constitutions are also referred to in a letter to Locke from H. Justel (MS. Locke c. 12).
27 Fox Bourne, op cit., vol. i, p. 165.
28 This final version is in Bodl. MS. Locke c. 28, ff. 21–32.
29 Fox Bourne, op cit., vol. i, pp. 174–94.
30 King, op cit., p. 156.
31 'entering' in the final version in the Lovelace Collection. The copy printed by Fox Bourne read 'growing'. Locke's alteration is a significant indication of his voluntarist theory of the nature of the state.
32 It must be remembered that in the seventeenth century the possibility of antipodes was a theoretical and controversial question. It is worth noticing that in the final version Locke added a passage making it clear that the existence of God was not to be regarded as a speculative opinion, 'it being the foundation of all morality', without which men would be like wild beasts, 'incapable of all society'.
33 'in themselves' inserted in the final version in the Lovelace Collection.
34 This is an exaggeration, for Locke would not have approved of the more extreme demands of some of the sectaries. He would have thought them anarchical, which indeed they were.
35 Fox Bourne, op cit., vol. i, p. 167.
36 In his *Second Vindication of the Reasonableness of Christianity* (1697) he reduced the creed to 'the believing of Jesus of Nazareth to be the Messiah', but he added that this involves 'receiving him for our Lord and King, promised and sent from God, and so lays upon all his subjects

an absolute and indispensable necessity of assenting to all that they can attain of the knowledge of what he taught, and of a sincere obedience to all that he commands' (Fox Bourne, op cit., vol. ii, p. 409).

37 Cf. Seaton, op cit., pp. 263–8.

38 On this aspect of Locke's theory cf. F. Lezius, *Der Toleranzbegriff Lockes und Pufendorfs* (Leipzig 1900). He points out that Pufendorf simply wanted freedom for the individual to interpret matters of faith for himself, but Locke pleaded for liberty to join in nonconformist sects.

39 His intolerance of Roman Catholics, perhaps only to be expected of a Protestant and a Whig in seventeenth-century England, was scarcely more than the result of prejudice, but this, too, he could justify rationally, on the ground that Roman Catholics are potentially disloyal subjects of a Protestant government.

40 Bodl. MS. Locke c. 34; King, op cit., p. 346.

41 His original sermon against the nonconformists was published under the title, *The Mischief of Separation*. It was answered by Dr Owen of Christ Church, Richard Baxter, and a number of others. See Fox Bourne, op cit., vol. i, p. 456.

42 In 1692 Tyrrell published an English abridgement of Richard Cumberland's Latin work on the law of nature.

43 See Klibansky (ed.), op cit., containing, besides introduction and notes, the Latin text with a new English translation.

44 See H. McLachlan, *The Religious Opinions of Milton, Locke and Newton* (Manchester 1941), pp. 69–114.

JOHN LOCKE AND THE CASE FOR TOLERATION

Maurice Cranston

Toleration is a disagreeable subject. This is because the question of toleration arises only in connection with disagreeable things: heresy, subversion, prostitution, drug-abuse, pornography, abortion and cruelty to animals. It can hardly be edifying for the mind to dwell on such subjects. But if there were not things we disapproved of, the concept of 'toleration' need not be introduced at all. It would be enough to talk about 'liberty' or 'freedom'. When we speak of people's liberty or freedom, no criticism is implied of the use to which they put their freedom. Indeed the words 'liberty' and 'freedom' have such an exalted emotive content that some writers would have their use restricted to the rightful exercise of choice: 'Only the good man', said Milton, 'can be free.' That may or may not be so; but we can say that only the undesirable or at any rate, the undesired, is a candidate for toleration.

T. S. Eliot once said, 'The Christian does not want to be tolerated.' He did not mean, as some readers supposed, that the Christian wanted martyrdom. He simply meant that the Christian did not wish to be 'put up with', to be 'endured' – which is what being tolerated means: the Christian desired something better – respect, humour, esteem; to be positively welcomed and wanted as a member of society.

D'Alembert says the same thing about actors in the *Encyclopedia*. He says they should not be tolerated: they should be treated as the equals of everyone else.

In a recent book which emerged from studies organized at York by the Morrell Trust, Mr Peter Nicholson argues that 'toleration is not a second-best, a necessary evil, a putting-up with what we have to for the sake of peace and quiet, but a positive good, a virtue distinctive of the best people and the best societies'.[1]

I am not so sure about this; I am inclined to think that toleration is a second-best, but a second-best to be cherished in an imperfect world. What is more, since toleration comes on to the agenda only in connection with undesirable things, it demands of its champions considerable skills of advocacy.

One striking feature about the Morrell Trust book is that while the chapters written on the more abstract level tend, with Mr Nicholson, to exalt toleration as a virtue, other chapters, dealing with its application in practical policy, seem to call for a diminished range of toleration, less toleration of fascist speech, for example, is recommended by one author, and less toleration of pornography is recommended by another.

This is by no means uncommon in the literature of the subject: we find philosophers pleading for a general toleration, and then, in a list of what should be denied toleration, including things that the unreflective reader might have been quite content to tolerate. One is reminded of those insurance policies which offer in large type cover against all eventualities, and then attach in small print a schedule excluding several of the risks for which one is most likely to claim indemnity.

To some extent this charge can, I think, be brought against the leading champion of toleration in the history of British philosophy, John Locke. But I hope to show that it is not a ruinous criticism.

Locke worked out the main lines of his theory of toleration in the year 1667, at the age of 35, when he had left his place as an Oxford don to live in London as a household physician and domestic philosopher to the Whig leader, the first Earl of Shaftesbury. Shaftesbury in parliament was an advocate of religious toleration, and indeed this was one of the things that recommended him to Charles II, who also believed in toleration and who promoted Shaftesbury partly because he considered him an ally against the majority in parliament who wanted to impose the Anglican religion on everyone. However, it soon emerged that the two men had different conceptions of what religious toleration should mean in practice. The king wanted toleration primarily for the benefit of Roman Catholics. Shaftesbury wanted it exclusively for Protestant dissenters. Behind this was a difference over secular policy: Shaftesbury was anti-French, and regarded the Roman Catholics as tools of French aggrandizement; Charles II was pro-French, and without being in the least pious, preferred Catholic to Protestant devotions. Friendship soon turned to hostility between Shaftesbury and the king; and in this situation,

Shaftesbury invited Locke to draw up a theoretical argument in support of religious toleration as he understood it.

Locke had not always been of Shaftesbury's mind. His earliest writings on the subject are directed against toleration. In his Oxford days, in 1661, he had written a pamphlet asserting that 'by appointment of the great sovereign of heaven and earth we are born subjects to the will and pleasure of another' – our earthly sovereign, who 'must necessarily have an absolute and arbitrary power over all indifferent actions of his people' including the forms and content of religious worship.

Locke never published this early pamphlet, and he had doubtless come to repudiate such views before he met Shaftesbury. We have evidence of Locke's opinions in the form of a series of memoranda he prepared for Shaftesbury[2] in 1667. It sets out in skeleton form some of the arguments for toleration that he was to expound in writings for publication in the 1680s and afterwards, but it is given a certain emphasis, imposed by the demands of Shaftesbury's campaign.

In his early memoranda Locke divides men's actions and opinions into three kinds. The first concerns speculative opinions and methods of divine worship. These, he says, are no concern of the civil magistrate, or as we should say, of the state. The second are opinions and actions which, however good or bad in themselves, impinge on other people. This category – which resembles Mill's class of 'other-regarding actions' – Locke suggests may come within the province of the law. He illustrates the type with examples: 'belief in divorce and polygamy, and belief in freedom to breed children and dispose of estates'.[3]

'These opinions and the actions following from them', he writes, 'have a title to toleration, but only so far as they do not tend to the disturbance of the state or do not cause greater inconvenience than advantage to the community.'[4]

Locke went on to say that the magistrate ought not to force a man to renounce opinions of this kind (because force cannot alter a man's inner belief) but might prohibit the *publication* of such opinions, if such an interdiction was deemed 'necessary for the peace, safety or security of the people'. And, of course, the magistrate was even more clearly entitled to prohibit any actions which might be injurious to the public good.

Locke's third class of actions were those which were inherently good or bad, namely virtues or vices. Here he insisted that magistrates had 'nothing to do with the good of men's souls'.[5] It was not

the magistrate's duty 'to punish every vice'. His only duty was to
keep the peace.

How were these principles to be applied to the situation of
England in 1667? Locke argued that all Protestant dissenters should
be tolerated because their beliefs and methods of worship, however
erroneous in the eyes of the bishops or the Anglican majority in
parliament, were in no way inimical to the tranquillity of the realm.
Besides, if the dissenters were not tolerated, they were likely to
continue to emigrate to other countries and deprive England of their
wealth and talents.

The same considerations, however, Locke refused to apply to the
Roman Catholics. Their opinions, he claimed, were 'destructive of
all governments except the Pope's'. Roman Catholics should not be
allowed to congregate or to publish because they constituted a threat
to the peace, safety and security of the kingdom.[6]

Here we enter a very controversial area, and a dangerous one. In
fact, I think it might not be at all wise to draw attention to Locke's
writings on toleration in Northern Ireland today, in view of the
extent of religious intolerance in that province; since the more
bigoted Protestant sectarians might well be encouraged by Locke's
argument to claim a rational justification for their prejudices.

But we have to remember that Locke was writing for a different
time and in a different context. The great churches of the world
today have moved away from their old mutual intolerance towards
the ecumenical ideal, but in the sixteenth century and the seventeenth century confessional divisions were powerful agents of
national discord. In England in the reign of Charles II disputes
around the question of tolerating Roman Catholicism, and
especially the question of whether Charles's Roman Catholic
brother James should be allowed to accede to the throne, were
carrying the kingdom once more to the brink of civil war. It was a
situation which led to both Shaftesbury and Locke withdrawing into
exile in Holland. And it was in exile in Holland that Locke produced
his most famous and eloquent contribution to the subject: his Latin
Epistola de Tolerantia, written in November 1685, but not published
until 1689.

Another thing that we must remember is that Locke was writing
for a world where religious faith was intense and virtually universal.
He was not asking people to extend freedom to something which
most of them considered a very great wrong, heresy. Moreover,
unlike John Stuart Mill, and indeed unlike Voltaire, writing his

Traité sur la tolerance in 1762, Locke himself was a man with deep religious sentiments of his own. So it would not have been enough, or at all appropriate for him, to invoke in this connection the general argument for a natural right to liberty such as he sets forth in his *Second Treatise of Government*. He had to present to Christian readers a Christian case for religious toleration.

One might have expected the *révocation* of the Edict of Nantes to make him more impassioned on the subject of Catholics. I think it is not generally remembered today how cruel and barbarous was the repression of the Huguenots in France in 1685. Protestants who refused to convert, under orders of Louis XIV, were beaten, pillaged, dragooned, their children were taken from them; men were sent to the galleys or driven into exile.

Locke wrote his *Epistola de Tolerantia* immediately after the *révocation* and clearly he has these events in mind when he writes:

> Let us deal plainly. The magistrate is afraid of other churches, but not of his own because he is kind and favourable to the one, but severe and cruel to the other. These he treats like children, and indulges them even into wantonness. Those he uses as slaves.

Even so, Locke does not use the *révocation* as a reason to attack Catholics. The really aggressive attacks on 'Papists' which occur in the memoranda Locke wrote for Shaftesbury are not repeated in his calm writings on toleration. He still proposed to exclude Catholics from toleration, but he argues in conspicuously less impassioned terms, and indeed, only indirectly against them.

Locke does not refer to France by name: everybody knew what was happening there, and we can hardly doubt that those events did much to undermine the allegiance of the English people to James II, and smoothed the way for the Revolution of 1688. Locke is no longer the polemical writer he was in his earlier memoranda, working in the service of a politician. He is a philosopher. He does not dwell on the horrors of the Huguenots' suffering. He simply suggests all the time that the alternative to toleration is persecution, and that persecution, in turn, can be understood to mean the kind of things that were done in France after the *révocation* of the Edict of Nantes.

The central theme of Locke's *Epistola de Tolerantia* is the radical distinction, as he sees it, between the church and the state. The state, or commonwealth, he describes as a 'society of men constituted only for the procuring, preserving and advancing their own civil interests'. Civil interests, he goes on to explain, are 'life, liberty, health and indolency of body, and the possession of outward things, such as money, lands, houses, furniture and the like'.[7]

The civil magistrate, as head of the state, has the duty 'by the impartial execution of equal laws' to secure the 'just possession of these things belonging to *this* life'. In order to secure the enforcement of the law, the magistrate is 'armed with the force and strength of all his subjects'.[8] Now Locke insists that 'the whole jurisdiction of the magistrate reaches only to these matters'.[9] Spiritual matters, the care of souls, have nothing to do with him 'because his power consists only in outward force', while 'true and saving religion consists in the inward persuasion of the mind'.[10] The care of souls is the function of the church. The church Locke defines as a 'voluntary society of men, joining themselves together of their own accord in order to the public worshipping of God and . . . the salvation of their souls'.[11]

The church then is voluntary in a sense in which the state is not voluntary. Locke does not enlarge on this point in this work but we know from his other writings that he regards the state as having originated in a social contract made by our ancestors, which imposes obligations on us even though it is not a contract we have actually made ourselves. The church is different. 'Nobody is born a member of any Church',[12] he asserts. 'But everyone joins himself voluntarily to that society in which he has found that profession and worship which is truly acceptable to God.'

Many Christians, of course, would disagree with this description of the church: but it is a crucial feature of Locke's theory.

The functions of the church, according to Locke, are:

1   The organization of public worship.
2   The 'regulation of men's lives according to the rules of virtue and piety'.[13]

In this business of regulating lives, the church 'may not employ force on any occasion whatever'.[14] Force is the monopoly of the magistrate. The laws of the church must be imposed by other means, by 'exhortations, admonitions and advice',[15] the ultimate sanction being excommunication. No other sanction is permissible. Even excommunication does not deprive a man of his civil rights: for civil rights are not the business of religion.

Correspondingly, religion is not the business of the state. Assuredly, most magistrates do try to enforce religions. But they cannot succeed, Locke says, for while force can make a man go through the outward movements of ritual observance, it cannot compel a man's mind or save a man's soul;[16] it can only produce a hypocrite if it makes a man pretend to conform by observance only. Force can never produce that 'faith and inward sincerity' which alone can 'procure acceptance with God'.[17]

The state and the church have neither any right to interfere in the business of the other, because, as Locke writes, 'the Church itself is a thing absolutely separate and distinct from the Commonwealth. The boundaries on both sides are fixed and immovable. He jumbles heaven and earth together, things most remote and opposite who mixes these two societies'.[18]

It follows from this, that the magistrate ought to tolerate all religious societies, or churches, that men choose to form among themselves. For the business of these religious societies 'is nothing but what is lawful for every man in particular to take care of – I mean the salvation of their souls: nor is there any difference between the national Church, and other separated congregations'.[19] Indeed, Locke adds, this toleration must extend beyond dissenting Christians to all societies which acknowledge God. 'Neither pagan nor Mohametan nor Jew ought to be excluded from the civil rights of the commonwealth, because of his religion. The gospel commands no such thing.'[20]

What are the limits of toleration? – Are they the same limits to which Locke drew attention, twenty years earlier, in his memoranda for Shaftesbury? In the *Epistola de Tolerantia*, Roman Catholics are not, by name, excluded from toleration. Indeed Locke seems to be pleading this time for Catholics to be treated like any other sect. He writes: 'If a Roman Catholic believes that to be really the body of Christ which another man calls bread, he does no injury thereby to his neighbour',[21] or again, 'Is it permitted to speak Latin in the market place? Let those that have a mind to it, be permitted also to do it in Church.'[22] The whole tone of the *Epistola* is very different from that of the early memoranda he wrote for Shaftesbury. On the other hand, Locke sets out limits to toleration which are precisely those invoked in those memoranda and to be invoked again later to refuse toleration to Roman Catholics. He enumerates four classes of religious societies which he authorizes the magistrate to proscribe: first, there are churches which proclaim 'opinions contrary to human society, or to those moral rules which are necessary to the preservation of civil society'.[23] Second, there are churches 'which arrogate to themselves, or to those of their own sect, some prerogative opposite to the civil right of the community'.[24] Third, there are churches 'constituted on such a bottom, that all those who enter into it, do thereby *ipso facto* deliver themselves up to the protection and service of another prince'.[25] Without referring directly to Catholics, Locke set these two last categories down so as to be able to justify withholding toleration from Catholics.

The fourth and last category of persons denied toleration by Locke are not those assembled in churches, but individuals, namely atheists. This may seem quaint in our world, but Locke was very much a man of his time in thinking that people who did not believe in God could not be bound by oaths; and for Locke, a contractualist through and through, there could be no secure society among men without valid oaths and pledges. In seventeenth-century England, torn as it was by civil wars and revolutions, oath-taking was a conspicuous feature of national life. Fortunately, perhaps, not many people at that time admitted to being atheists, so few would feel injured by Locke's unwillingness to tolerate atheists.

One of several curious facts about Locke's *Epistola de Tolerantia* is that he refused to admit being the author of it, even to the friend in Holland to whom it was supposed to be addressed – the initials on the title page, it afterwards emerged, were a coded form[26] of Locke's name and that of the Dutch friend who shared his interest in the theory of toleration, Philip van Limborch, Professor of Theology at the Remonstrant seminary in Amsterdam. As for the English translation, undertaken by Locke's friend William Popple and published by Locke's publisher and friend Awnsham Churchill in London at the end of the year 1689, Locke always claimed that that translation had been made 'without my privity'.[27]

Now although Locke was far from truthful about matters he wished to conceal (and he was an unusually secretive man) I think he did not see Popple's preface or introductory note to the translation, for Popple says things that are simply at variance with Locke's point of view.

There is one especially striking phrase in Popple's preface: 'Absolute liberty, just and true liberty, equal and impartial liberty, is the thing we stand in need of.' This was Popple's demand. It was not Locke's. Locke wanted toleration, not 'absolute liberty'. Locke was an Anglican. Popple was a radical nonconformist. In fact Popple's approach to religious toleration offers an interesting contrast to that of Locke. He is also an interesting man. He was born in Hull in 1638, a nephew of Andrew Marvell; he prospered as a merchant, and found time both to translate books about religion and philosophy and to write several of his own, notably in 1687 one called *A Rational Catechism*. Popple was not a Quaker, but he had a Quakerish outlook and was a friend of William Penn.

William Penn was by no means hostile to Catholics, and was indeed a personal friend of James II. He had been persecuted for his religious beliefs, but persecuted by Anglicans, not Catholics. It was Anglicans who expelled him from Oxford, who imprisoned him in the Tower of London for publishing an unlicensed pamphlet, and the Catholic James II who released him – together with 1,200 other Quakers who had been jailed by the Anglicans. Quakers were persecuted in the Calvinist American colonies, but tolerated in Lord Baltimore's Catholic colony of Maryland. Penn had no reason to be suspicious of Catholics; and neither had Popple, who had done well as a merchant in the Catholic city of Bordeaux.

William Popple seems to have been too independent a dissenter even to join the Quakers: his *Rational Catechism* accepts revelation, but gives far more prominence to reason, and he was an ardent champion of what is properly called freedom of conscience as distinct from religious toleration.

How does his position differ from Locke's position? Up to a point, what is said in Popple's writings is not substantially different from the argument set forth in Locke's Latin letter. Locke, at that time, was the lonely man in exile, as much an outsider as Popple, and one cannot fail to notice that in these pages Locke draws no distinction between churches and sects, between one voluntary religious society and another.

However, by the year 1689, when Popple published his translation of Locke's Latin letter, Locke was no longer a lonely man in exile. At the beginning of that year, he had returned to England in the company of the princess who was to become Queen Mary II, and was promptly put into that position of which so many philosophers have dreamed – that of confidential adviser to a potent monarch. Plato at Syracuse, Bacon at the court of James I, Voltaire with Frederick II, Diderot with Catherine the Great – Locke might have had even more influence than these if his health had been robust enough for him to accept the invitations pressed on him by William III.

In the event, he remained in the background, informally advising several leading politicians; but he was extremely conscious of participating in a great undertaking – the reconstruction of England which the Revolution had made possible: and that included the reconstruction of the Church of England.

Soon after his arrival he sent news – again in Latin – to Philip van Limborch about debates in parliament about the future of religious institutions in the kingdom.

> Toleration [he wrote] is now discussed under two forms 'comprehension' and 'indulgence'. By the first, it is proposed to enlarge the bounds of the church, so that by the abolition of some ceremonies, many people may be made to conform. By the other is designed the toleration of those who are either unwilling or unable to unite with the Church of England, even on the proposed conditions. [28]

Locke himself, it is clear, was much in favour of the policy of 'comprehension'. His own Christianity was of the minimal kind; he did not think it required of the believer assent to any dogmas in excess of the propositions that Christ is the Messiah and that the soul is immortal. On the other hand, he shared with the 'judicious Hooker', as he called him, the ideal conception of the Church of England as a society to which all Englishmen would belong, an institution, so to speak, of cultural cohesion, holding the community together in shared bonds of fellowship and common habits of worship.

Not, of course, that Locke wanted too much worship. Time should not be spent in prayer that could be more profitably employed in work. Too much ritual, like too many dogmas, bred dissension. The plainer the church, the simpler the creed, the less anyone could object to, or find reasons for not joining. The policy of 'comprehension' would solve the problem of religious dissent by removing from the national church anything that could provoke dissent. Philip van Limborch, in his reply to Locke, expressed the view that 'truly Christian toleration' was 'well represented under the two heads of comprehension and indulgence'.

> God grant [he added] that by embracing all who by the rule of the gospel are not shut out from heaven, England may give us the spectacle of a truly Catholic and Christian Church. . . . If, however, comprehension should prove too narrow, the wider indulgence might offer a way of providing for the security of

all, if those whom their conscience, whether wrongly or rightly informed, does not permit to join themselves to the Great Church were allowed to meet together without fear of punishment.[29]

That letter was written early in April 1689. In his reply Locke wrote

As to the establishment of toleration in our country, I do not altogether despair, though it is proceeding very slowly – The Scots are as keen in their aversion to episcopal governance as we are in holding to it, and they have put this first in their list of grievances. All right-minded persons who favour sane and moderate counsels, hope for some relaxation in the attitude of extremists on either side.[30]

In the end, the two kingdoms had to have each its own national church, and William III had to be head of the Anglican Church in England and of the Presbyterian Church in Scotland. Locke, whose whole outlook was that of an Englishman and not that of a Britisher, had no reason to deplore this separation. The Church of England satisfied his desire for a national church. He had always wanted such a church, although he makes only a passing reference to it in his *Epistola de Tolerantia*.

Even so, as Limborch remarked in one of his letters to the author, Locke's *Epistola de Tolerantia* was really a plea for what had come to be called *indulgence*; and Limborch suggested it should be published together with another pamphlet on *Peace in the Church* by Samuel Strimesius, since that was a plea for what had come to be called *comprehension*. Locke could not disagree. He wanted both *comprehension* and *indulgence*, and in the situation of post-revolutionary England, he had come to give comprehension priority over indulgence.

Popple wanted neither. And he says so in his preface to his translation of Locke's Latin letter.

We have need of more generous remedies than have yet been made use of in our distemper. It is neither Declarations of Indulgence nor Acts of Comprehension, such as have yet been practised or projected among us that can do the work, the first will but palliate, that second increase our Evil.[31]

He then goes on to say that 'absolute liberty' is the thing we stand in need of.

Popple's position is clear: he does not want one dominant national church, with minor denominations on the side, tolerated as dissenting sects. In short, he does not want what Locke wants. He wants equal liberty for all. He was disappointed by the Toleration Act which William and Mary signed on 24 May 1689. Locke was pleased, as we know from the letter he wrote in June to Limborch.

> No doubt you will have heard before this that Toleration has now at last been established by law in our country . . . . I hope that with these beginnings the foundations have been laid of that liberty and peace in which the church of Christ is one day to be established. None is entirely debarred from his own form of worship or made liable to penalties, except the Romans, provided only that he is willing to take the oath of allegiance and to renounce transubstantiation and certain dogmas of the Roman Church.[32]

Locke had reason to be well-satisfied with the kind of Church of England which emerged from the Revolution settlement. It was led by bishops who shared, for the most part, his latitudinarian approach, if few were altogether as unitarian or Socinian as he was. It was a church signally lacking in fanaticism or enthusiasm; broad, tranquil and tolerant. The very architecture of the churches that were built in early eighteenth-century England bear witness to this spirit – they could almost be libraries with spires on top, temples of good sense, good taste and good behaviour, bearing witness to what Locke called 'the reasonableness of Christianity'. Of course, in time there was a reaction – Wesleyan, Evangelical, Tractarian, Revivalist movements demanding a more intense religion, but for the great part of the eighteenth century the Church of England remained peacefully and calmly Lockean.

Locke's interest in the problem of toleration was not confined to religious toleration. He wrote about, and influenced policy in areas which are relevant to the wider problem of toleration. One of these he put under the heading of 'naturalization'.

This was to do with the acceptance into England, and to English civil society of Huguenot refugees from French persecution. The arguments he offered were economic ones. The refugees, he pointed out, would bring assets to England: their industrial and commercial skills, and their manpower. Even those who had nothing to offer but their labour would be useful. Locke believed that a large population was better than a small one. Just as it was bad for the national economy when natives such as the Puritans left the country, so it was good for the economy if foreigners such as the Huguenots settled in the country. Even the least skilled should be welcomed, since their presence would tend to bring down the cost of labour.

In our trade-union-minded days, of course, this last argument would not receive a sympathetic hearing. The English workers could hardly be expected to want to see their wages reduced: but Locke's belief was that the cost of living would go down with the cost of labour, so that English workers would not in the long run be worse off. In any case Locke knew well enough that he was defending an unpopular cause. In putting forward economic arguments for the naturalization of Huguenots he did not think he needed to counter an economic argument, but rather to use economic arguments against xenophobia, against an emotional and unreflective unwillingness to have French people settle among us. That is why we have to see his thought on naturalization as part of his theory of toleration. He does not expect the English public to embrace the French settlers as brothers. He simply asks them to put up with them.

Present-day discussions of toleration often turn on questions which Locke considered in rather different contexts. For example, the Morrell Trust book on *Aspects of Toleration* has quite a lot to say about censorship, obscenity, blasphemy, sedition. Now, Locke was squarely against censorship as it existed in his time. When the Act for the Regulation of Printing, which had been passed under Charles II in 1662, came up for renewal in 1692, Locke argued against renewal, but in doing so he did not appeal to the natural right to liberty. He simply argued that the monopoly conferred on the Stationers Company made books unnecessarily expensive and often hard to obtain.

When the act lapsed, censorship lapsed with it, that is censorship in the sense of pre-publication licensing or import licensing of books. The freedom of the press was established, although, of course, the publication of obscenity, blasphemy, libel and sedition could be prosecuted under other acts; and the censorship in stage plays prior to performances remained in force.

I cannot imagine that Locke would have considered the interdictions placed on blasphemy, obscenity and so forth as a limitation of freedom, because Locke did not understand freedom in the Hobbesian sense as the silence of the law; but rather as the exercise of natural rights under the law. Law, provided it was a just law, served in Locke's eyes to perfect freedom and not to limit it.

Now, I think Locke was always clear in his own mind as to what should and what should not be tolerated: but what is not so clear is who has the duty of suppressing what is not to be tolerated. For all the absolute separation of church and state in his theory, it is not clear what kind of evils are to be dealt with by the church alone and what are to be punished by the state.

Moreover, the emphasis changes in his successive writings on toleration. In the early memorandum he seems to be saying that the state should leave the enforcement of morality to the church. He says it is not the duty of the magistrate to 'punish every vice', or busy himself with matters that have no bearing on the security and tranquillity of civil society.[33]

In the *Epistola de Tolerantia*, written in 1685, Locke seems to be saying that it is *everybody's* duty to uphold morality. For he writes – without drawing any distinction between the magistrates, the church and laity:

> Whoever, therefore, is sincerely solicitous about the kingdom of God, and thinks it his duty to endeavour the enlargement of it amongst men, ought to apply himself with no less care and industry to the rooting out of [these] immoralities than to extirpation of sects.

The immoralities Locke names are 'adultery, fornication, uncleanness, lasciviousness, idolatry and such things . . . concerning which the Apostle has expressly declared that they who do them shall not inherit the kingdom of God'.[34]

In his *Second Letter for Toleration*, written in English in 1691, Locke writes:

> I will boldly say that if magistrates will severely and impartially set themselves against vice, in whomsoever it is found, and leave men to their own consciences in their articles of faith and worship, true religion will spread wider and be more fruitful in the lives of its professors.[35]

In the *Third Letter for Toleration*, written in 1692, Locke says: 'As for the toleration of corrupt manners and the debaucheries in life, neither our author nor I do plead for it, but say it is properly the magistrate's business, by punishments to restrain and suppress them.'[36]

Whether there is a change of view here, or merely a change of emphasis, it is clear that Locke, in his most mature writings on toleration, assigned to the civil magistrate a specific duty to enforce morality. On the other hand, it is equally clear that he still expected the church to play the major role in upholding morality by its distinctive method of 'exhortation, admonition and excommunication'.

The more effective the church in the performance of this task, the less need will there be for intervention by the state. And since Locke lived at a time when most men respected the authority of their church or sect, he did not feel it necessary to spell out the circumstances in which the civil magistrate would have to act to enforce morality. In saying that a magistrate has a duty to enforce morality, he was not giving assent to the views of his extreme Puritan contemporaries that the magistrate should enforce such things as the observance of the Sabbath. The Gospel, he noted, required a Christian to observe the Sabbath, therefore the Christian would freely observe the Sabbath because he would wish to obey the injunctions of the Apostles. Any failure to observe the Sabbath was to be a matter for the church to correct by its own appropriate means and not for the magistrate to regulate by force.

I have tried in this lecture to put forward two suggestions. First, that Locke's theory of toleration can best be understood in relation to the circumstances which prompted him to write as he did: and to draw attention to the extent to which his perspective changed as he moved from being an Oxford don to being the adviser to an opposition politician, and then from being in solitary exile to being an adviser to government undertaking the radical restructuring of the kingdom. But I have also tried to suggest that Locke was writing as a philosopher, with an argument of universal relevance, as much relevance to the problems of toleration in the England of today as of 300 years ago.

The enduring relevance of his argument on 'naturalization' needs no underlining on my part. Everyone knows today that Hitler's repression of the Jews was far more extreme than the worst that was done by Louis XIV against the Huguenots. What is less well remembered is the unwillingness of democratic governments to offer refuge to victims of that persecution. Since I myself was engaged in refugee work in the months of the 'phoney-war', I have vivid memories of the obstacles that the British authorities put in the way of admitting, let alone naturalizing, any non-Aryan alien. Thousands were denied a visa, and perished.

The economic science of the time seems to have held that Great Britain was overpopulated, and that further emancipation would increase unemployment, especially in the bourgeois professions, where the trade unions were strongest and most unyielding. In the event, I think it is true to say that the non-Aryan refugees who did manage to scale the walls of this fortress proved the truth of Locke's argument: they added greatly to the wealth, scientific, industrial and cultural, of this country, and its defence capacity.

The Huguenots were victims of religious intolerance in Catholic France; the Jews were for generations victims of religious intolerance in Christian Europe. It has been suggested by some historians that religious intolerance in Europe declined because religious faith declined. The propagation of scepticism by the Enlightenment is thought to have done more to end persecution than the promotion of Christian tolerance by Christian writers such as Locke. This interpretation of events would be more convincing if intolerance had really continued to decline as religious faith declined. In fact, what took place was an increase of intolerance motivated by forces other than religious fanaticism. Persecution of the Jews, for example, came to be renewed on racial instead of religious grounds. Ideology – and not only totalitarian ideology – has proved in the present century just as powerful a motor of intolerance as religion ever was.

Locke, I think, was always well aware of the strength of prejudice, and that even in addressing fellow Christians, it was not enough to appeal for Christian charity; he had to show that it was in man's interest to adopt a policy of toleration, or to show that the refusal of toleration was unreasonable. To a great extent we can perhaps say that Locke's battle for religious toleration has been won – not in the Islamic world, to be sure, and not in Ireland; but among Christians generally.

But what of toleration in spheres other than the specifically religious? Here, I am bound to think he would accuse us of too much toleration in some areas, and too little toleration in others, of having no coherent principles of toleration.

There are, however, certain problems in conceiving how Locke's own principles might be applied to twentieth-century society. Neither the national church, nor the independent churches or sects, have the authority over men's minds and behaviour that they had in the seventeenth century. What, in such circumstances, can exercise the duty of protecting morality that Locke assigns to the church or churches? It seems to me clear from what he says about 'us all' having a duty in this matter, that he would expect 'society itself' to undertake it.

Now to use the expression 'society itself' is to think of John Stuart Mill, and of Mill's famous protest in his essay *On Liberty* that society itself had become a tyrant – practising collectively over the individuals who compose it 'a social tyranny more formidable than many kinds of political oppression . . . enslaving the soul itself'.

Of course, Locke did not live in Victorian England; but even so, I cannot imagine him having much sympathy with John Stuart Mill in this matter. From Locke's point of view, to take away the authority of first the church, then of the society itself, would leave the state as the only source of authority, and that really would be a formula for enslavement.

On the other hand, people are mistaken who think of Locke as a champion of the 'minimal state' or the 'night-watchman state'. We must not conclude on the strength of some of his utterances that he thought the function of the state was limited to the protection of lives, liberties and properties of individuals. He also thought it included the promotion of the public good, and these last purposes occupied more and more of his attention in the years that followed the Revolution of 1688.

He certainly did not shrink from proposing the enlargement of state activity in the realm of economic organization. Locke was a mercantilist in economics; he was very far from being a *laissez-faire* liberal like Adam Smith or Hayek. One thing we can confidently say that he would not understand if he were to return to this kingdom today is how we can tolerate over 3 million unemployed people on the dole. He was unwilling to tolerate even a few thousand idle people on relief in his time.

If he could apply the techniques he advocated, he would simply take them off welfare and put them to work in jobs in the national interest, at lower wages if need be than those already in the trades. If the trade unions objected, Locke would surely suppress the unions as combinations acting against the national interest.

Locke wanted to see reasonableness introduced into the ordering of civil society; and I think he would consider that we fall far short of that modest ideal today, in what we tolerate, and what we do not. For example, we tolerate prostitution, but we suppress the means by which prostitution may be conducted discreetly, namely the *maisons closes*, and tolerate means by which it is conducted offensively; we have discovered that smoking tobacco in cigarettes is as harmful as smoking cannabis, yet we allow the one activity to be practised publicly and widely advertised, and make the other subject to criminal prosecution; we regale the public, in our wonderful mass media, with glamorous imaginary scenes of crime and violence, and yet we protest if it spreads over into real life; we have adopted a good many of John Stuart Mill's permissive ideas about private behaviour, but have made it harder than it was in Mill's time for any political opinion to be allowed a public hearing (including, as we all know, university campuses). We claim to be able to distinguish between soft pornography (which may be sold in any newsagent in the land) and hard pornography (which may not even be exhibited in private clubs), but we refuse to distinguish between soft and hard drugs in our efforts – our remarkably unsuccessful efforts – to suppress narcotics. And on what principles do we decide whether to tolerate, or to penalize, cruelty to animals? At an English court recently, a man who beat a hedgehog to death was acquitted of a charge of cruelty because a hedgehog is a wild animal, and English laws offer protection from cruelty only to the tame, as if domesticated animals feel pain and wild animals do not.

There seems to be something incorrigibly illogical about our attitudes in all these fields. And this, I am afraid, represents an actual challenge to Locke's whole philosophy. For Locke is famous for having worked from a far more pleasing conception of human nature than that of Hobbes or the Calvinists of his time. He depicted human beings as essentially reasonable so that in the end reason was bound to prevail over passion. The experience of his age seemed to prove it. Locke's foreign admirers who visited England soon after his death – people such as Montesquieu and Voltaire – were impressed by everything they saw – the freedom, the toleration, the good sense; they found us uniquely 'a nation of philosophers'. Even if the whole human race was not reasonable, at least the English were.

We do not hear such compliments today. And perhaps we do not deserve them.

NOTES

1   John Horton and Susan Mendus (eds), *Aspects of Toleration* (London 1985), p. 166.
2   The copy Locke gave to Shaftesbury is preserved at the Public Record

Office (Shaftesbury Papers 30/24/47/I). Three other drafts are known to exist (Maurice Cranston, *John Locke: A Biography* (Oxford 1957), p. 111). It is possible that this memorandum has to be read as an exercise in 'speech writing' done by Locke for Shaftesbury's use: and parts may even have been dictated by Shaftesbury.

3   Cranston, op cit., p. 112.
4   ibid.
5   ibid.
6   ibid. Locke writes with unaccustomed passion in these pages against the 'Papists' as he calls them. 'Papists are not to enjoy the benefit of toleration because, where they have power, they think themselves bound to deny it to others' (cited in Fox Bourne, *The Life of John Locke*, 2 vols (London 1876), vol. i, p. 187). 'It being impossible, either by indulgence or severity to make papists, whilst papists, friends to your government.... I think they ought not to enjoy the benefit of toleration' (ibid., p. 188).

> Add to this that papacy, having been brought in upon the ignorant and zealous world by the art and industry of their clergy and kept up by the same artifice, backed by power and force, is the most likely of any religion to decay where the secular power handles them severely.   (ibid., pp. 188–9)

7   See above, p. 17.
8   ibid.
9   ibid.
10 ibid., p. 18.
11 ibid., p. 20.
12 ibid.
13 ibid., p. 14.
14 ibid., p. 22.
15 ibid.
16 ibid., p. 18.
17 ibid., p. 32.
18 ibid., p. 26.
19 ibid., p. 33.
20 ibid., p. 51.
21 ibid., p. 41.
22 ibid., p. 50.
23 ibid., p. 45.
24 ibid.
25 ibid., p. 46.
26 Cranston, op cit., p. 320.
27 ibid., p. 321.
28 ibid., p. 314.
29 E. S. de Beer (ed.), *The Correspondence of John Locke*, 8 vols (Oxford 1974), vol. iii, pp. 587–8.
30 ibid., p. 597.
31 See above, p. 12.
32 de Beer, op cit., p. 633.

33 He goes on to declare, 'Yet, give me leave to say, however strange it may seem, that the law-maker hath nothing to do with moral virtues and vices ... any otherwise than barely as they are subservient to the good and preservation of mankind under government' (Fox Bourne, op cit., vol. i, p. 181).

34 This kind of language does not appear in the memoranda Locke wrote for Shaftesbury. Nor should we expect to find it. Shaftesbury was eager to have ammunition to use against Popery; but given his way of life, he would not have appreciated attacks on sexual immorality.

35 *The Works of John Locke, Esq.*, 4 vols (London 1727), vol. ii, p. 261.

36 ibid., p. 414.

LOCKE: TOLERATION AND THE RATIONALITY OF PERSECUTION

Jeremy Waldron

I

This is a paper about John Locke's argument for toleration, or, more accurately, it is a paper about the main line of argument which appears in Locke's work *A Letter on Toleration.*[1] It is *not* intended – as so many papers on Locke's political philosophy are these days – as an historical analysis of his position. I am not going to say very much at all about the development (in some ways the quite remarkable development) of Locke's views on the subject, or about the contemporary debate on religious toleration in which Locke, first as an academic then as a political agitator, was involved, or about the historical circumstances of the *Letter*'s composition.[2] Rather, I want to consider the Lockean case as a political argument – that is, as a practical intellectual resource that can be abstracted from the antiquity of its context and deployed in the modern debate about liberal theories of justice and political morality.[3] To put it bluntly, I want to consider whether Locke's case is worth anything as an argument which might dissuade someone here and now from actions of intolerance and persecution.[4]

There is a further somewhat more abstract reason for examining the Lockean argument. In its content and structure the Lockean case is quite different from the more familiar and more commonly cited arguments of John Stuart Mill.[5] Even if, as I shall claim, it turns out to be an inadequate and unconvincing argument, one that in the last resort radically underestimates the complexity of the problem it addresses, still its distinctive structure and content tell us a lot about the possibilities and limits of liberal argumentation in this area. Those insights and the contrast with the more familiar arguments of

Mill may well contribute considerably to our understanding of modern liberal theories of toleration and the 'neutral' state.[6]

II

I have said that I am going to concentrate on the main line of argument in the *Letter on Toleration*. But perhaps it is worth saying a word or two about one subordinate line of argument that I will largely overlook in the rest of my discussion.

At the beginning of the *Letter*, Locke takes some pains to emphasize the peculiarly Christian character of toleration. 'The toleration of those that differ from others in matters of religion', he maintains, is not only consistent with and 'agreeable to' the gospel of Jesus Christ (p. 65, p. 16) but actually required by Christian teaching. Persecution, he points out, with the denial of love and charity which it involves, is repugnant to the Christian faith (pp. 59–65, pp. 14–17).

Historically, there is no doubting the importance of this aspect of Locke's case. As an *ad hominem* argument addressed to the Christian authorities, it is of course devastating for it exposes an evident and embarrassing inconsistency between the content of their theory and their practice in propagating it. It is significant that much of the immediate reaction to the publication of the *Letter* concerned this part of the Lockean case and that many of the issues taken up in Locke's boring and inordinately repetitive *Second*, *Third*, and (mercifully) uncompleted *Fourth Letter on Toleration* had to do with the argument from Christian premises.[7]

But, however effective and historically important this line of argument might have been, it is uninteresting from a philosophical point of view. We are interested in the question of whether the state *as such* is under a duty of toleration and we want an argument addressed to state officials in their capacity as wielders of the means of coercion, repression and persecution. An argument which addresses them instead in their capacity as members of a Christian congregation is insufficiently general to be philosophically interesting because it leaves us wondering what if anything we would have to say to someone who proposed persecution in the name of a more militant and less squeamish faith. Certainly, it would be an untidy and unsatisfactory state of affairs if we had to construct a fresh line of argument for toleration to match each different orthodoxy that was under consideration.

Locke, I think, recognizes this, and the bulk of the *Letter* is devoted to considerations which proceed on a more general front and which purport to show the *irrationality* of intolerance and not just its uncongeniality to a particular religious point of view. It is this argument – the argument by which Locke attempts to show that religious persecution is irrational – that I want to examine in my paper.

III

An argument for toleration is an argument which gives a reason for not interfering with a person's beliefs or practices even when we have reason to hold that those beliefs or practices are mistaken, heretical or depraved. (Questions of toleration do not arise in relation to beliefs or practices which are regarded as good or true.)[8]

I take it that this is *not* achieved simply by announcing that the enforcement of correct religious belief or practice is not the *function* of the state, or by saying, in the famous terms of the Wolfenden Report, that matters of religion, like personal morality and immorality, are 'not the law's business'.[9] That sort of talk just begs the question. At most it gives us the *conclusion* we want to reach but it does not help us to discharge the obligation to argue for that conclusion. But Locke, I am afraid, is often interpreted as having said little more than this. For example, in the entry under 'Toleration' in his recent *Dictionary of Political Thought*, Roger Scruton gives us the following account of Locke's argument:

> it is not within the competence of the state to discern the truth of religious doctrines, nor is it the function of the state to save men's souls; rather the state exists to protect men's rights and may use force to that end alone. *Hence*, there ought to be toleration in matters of religion.[10]

When this sort of functionalist talk is in the air, we do well to remember Max Weber's observation that it is impossible to define the state in terms of its functions and that historically 'there is scarcely any task that some political association has not taken in hand'.[11] Among all the tasks that states have undertaken, the question of which fall into the class of the *proper* functions of government is an important one; but it has to be a matter of argument, not of essentialist definition.

Since the state cannot be defined in terms of its functions, the best way of defining it, Weber suggested, was in terms of its characteristic *means*: the means, such as the organized monopoly of legitimate force in a given territory, which are deployed to carry out whatever ends a state may happen to undertake.[12] Now if we can give such a *modal* definition of the state – if we can define it in terms of its distinctive and characteristic means, then we may have the basis for an argument about its proper ends or functions along the following lines.

A state by definition is an organization which uses means of type M. But means of type M are ill-fitted for producing ends of type E. They never produce E-type effects (but perhaps at best mockeries or travesties of them). Therefore it is irrational to use M-type means in order to produce (genuine) E-type effects – and irrational in one of the most straightforward and least contestable instrumental senses. Therefore, given the type of means that it uses, it is irrational for the state to pursue E-type ends. Therefore – and in this sense – the pursuit of E-type ends cannot be one of the proper functions of government.

That, it seems to me, is the form of an interesting and evidently acceptable line of argument. It is an argument from available means to possible ends – from a modal definition to a (negative) functionalist conclusion. And, in a very compressed form, it captures the structure of the main line of argument in the *Letter on Toleration* that I want to examine.

Locke, like Weber, defines the state in terms of the characteristic means at its disposal. In the *Second Treatise*, he tells us: 'Political power ... I take to be a right of making laws with penalties of death.'[13] Similarly, in the *Letter on Toleration* he distinguishes the means available to the magistrate from those available to the ordinary man of good will in civil society: 'Every man is entitled to admonish, exhort, and convince another of error, and lead him by reasoning to accept his own opinions. But it is the magistrate's province to give orders by decree and compel with the sword' (p. 69, p. 19).

Looking at the matter in more detail, Locke characterizes the power of the magistrate at three levels. Sometimes it is described symbolically in terms of the paraphernalia of force and terror: 'fire and the sword' (p. 61, p. 15; p. 63, p. 16; p. 89, p. 28; p. 115, p. 38; etc.), 'rods and axes' (p. 89, p. 28) and 'force and blood' (p. 113, p. 37). Sometimes it is described (along Weberian lines) in terms of the way in which force is organized in a political community: 'the magistrate is armed with force, namely with all the strength of his subjects' (p. 67, p. 17).[14] And sometimes it is characterized in legalistic terms – 'impartially enacted laws' (p. 67, p. 17), 'laying down laws' (p. 91, p. 28) and 'legal censure' (p. 115, p. 39) – and in punishments such as the deprivation of property (p. 61, p. 15; p. 69, p. 18; etc.), imprisonment (p. 69, p. 18), mutilation and torture (p. 61, p. 15; p. 69, p. 18) and execution (p. 61, p. 15). But the emphasis is everywhere on *force*: that is, on the coercive nature of penalties – 'if no penalties are attached to them, the force of laws vanishes' (p. 69, p. 19) and, somewhat less importantly, on the possibility of direct physical compulsion. The fact that governments and their officials work by coercive force while other organizations do not is the fundamental premise of Locke's argument and the basis of his distinction between church and state.[15]

It is true that Locke says a number of things which might lead a careless reader to believe that he wants to define government in functional terms. For example, early in the *Letter on Toleration*, he says in an apparently definitional tone: 'The commonwealth seems to me to be a society of men constituted only for preserving and advancing their civil goods' (p. 66, p. 17), where civil goods are defined as 'life, liberty, bodily health, . . . and the possession of outward things', etc. (p. 67, p. 17). But he makes it absolutely clear in the *Letter* that he regards this as something to be established, as a task to be fulfilled (p. 65, p. 17). He takes it as the conclusion, not a premise, of his argument:

> that the whole jurisdiction of the magistrate is concerned only with those civil goods, and that all the right and dominion of the civil power is bounded and confined solely to the care and advancement of these goods; and that it neither can nor ought in any way to be extended to the salvation of souls, the following considerations seem to me to prove.
>
> (p. 67, pp. 17–18)

And then he gives the arguments that I shall examine in a moment. Elsewhere in the *Letter* the functional theory of government is described explicitly as a *conclusion* (p. 71, p. 19) and as something which in the course of his argument he has *proved* (p. 91, p. 28). Those like Scruton and also J. D. Mabbott (in his summary of Locke's arguments) who represent it as a premise are therefore doing Locke a grave disservice.[16]

Having defined government in terms of its means, Locke then argues that those means – laws, threats, the sword – are not capable of producing genuine religious belief in the minds of the citizens who are subjected to them. Sincere and genuine (as opposed to feigned or counterfeited) belief cannot be produced by these means; so it is irrational for the authorities to use them for that purpose. Thus, from a rational point of view, the state, defined in the way Locke wants to define it, cannot have among its functions that of promoting genuine religion. And since, on Locke's definition, toleration is nothing but the absence of force deployed for religious ends,[17] it follows that the state is rationally required to be tolerant.

That is a preliminary summary of a sophisticated argument. It gives us an idea of the lie of the land; and it has the great heuristic merit of indicating by inequitable exaggeration the extent of the argument's defects and limitations. Let me now discuss it in a little more detail.

IV

The crux of the argument – the step which dominates it and on which everything else depends – is the claim that religious belief cannot be secured by the coercive means characteristic of state action. This is the essence of Locke's challenge to the rationality of religious persecution: that what the persecutors purport to be up to is something that, in the nature of the case, they cannot hope to achieve.

To make this case, he needs to show that this is true *in principle*. It is not enough to show that coercion is *inefficient* as a means of religious discipline or that it is less efficient than the citizens' means of argument and persuasion. For that would leave open the possibility of using coercion as a last resort, and it would also make the case for toleration vulnerable to a reassessment of the relative values of the various effects of coercive action. Locke needs to show impossibility here. He must show that there is a gap between political means and religious ends which cannot in principle be bridged.

On Locke's account, that causal gap between political coercion and religious belief is framed, as it were, by two important propositions: (1) that coercion works by operating on a person's will, that is, by pressurizing his decision-making with the threat of penalties; and (2) that belief and understanding are not subject to the human will, and that one cannot acquire a belief simply by intending or deciding to believe. If I do not believe in the truth of the Resurrection, for example, there is nothing I can do, no act of will that I can perform, to *make* myself believe it. (There is no way of holding my mouth or concentrating which is going to get me into the state of having this belief.) Of course, I may change my mind about the Resurrection, and people often do. But there is a sense in which even if that happens it is not my doing: it happens rather as a result of the work of what Locke calls 'light and evidence' on the understanding and not as the upshot of *my* conscious decision-making.

The effect of these two claims then – that coercion works through the will and that belief is not subject to the will – if they are true, is to render religious belief or unbelief effectively immune from coercive manipulation. Laws, Locke says, are of no force without penalties (p. 69, p. 18), and the whole point of penalties is to bring pressure to bear on people's decision-making by altering the pay-offs for various courses of action, so that willing one particular course of action (the act required or prohibited by law) becomes more or less attractive to the agent than it would otherwise be. But this sort of pressurizing is crazy in cases of actions which men are incapable of performing no matter how attractive the pay-off or unattractive the consequences. Sincerely believing a proposition that one takes to be false (like jumping 20 feet into the air) is an action in this category. As Locke puts it: 'what is gained in enjoining by law what a man cannot do, however much he may wish to do it? To believe this or that to be true is not within the scope of our will' (p. 121, p. 41). The imposition of belief, then, by civil law has been shown to be an absurdity. Intolerance and persecution, at least for religious reasons, have been shown to be irrational.

This is the sort of conclusion that every moral philosopher dreams of when he starts out making an argument. To justify his belief that a certain practice is wrong, he does not want to have to appeal in a Humean fashion to contingent desires and attitudes: he can never be certain that his audience shares them, and even if they do this sort of argument often appears to establish nothing more than the undesirability of the practice. Rather he wants to be able to show (if he can) that the wrong practice is also an irrational practice – that it involves in itself the sort of inconsistency or rational absurdity which every philosopher wants to avoid in his life as well as in his arguments.[18] Everyone in his audience – or at least everyone in his philosophical audience – accepts standards of rationality; they are part of the tools of the trade, even for one who is, in other respects, the most rabid of moral sceptics. So the possibility of appealing to those standards to establish substantive moral conclusions has been one of the recurring dreams of western moral philosophers, at least since Kant. (It finds its latest manifestation in the work of Alan Gewirth.)[19] And here, in the *Letter on Toleration*, we find John Locke engaged in an early attempt to do the same sort of thing.

V

This is the crux of Locke's argument for toleration. Before going on to indicate some of the difficulties in the argument, I want to make two or three general observations.

The first point to notice is that this argument for toleration does not rest on any religious doubt, religious scepticism or epistemic misgivings in relation either to the orthodox position Locke is considering or to the beliefs and practices that are being tolerated. It is sometimes said that toleration is the child of doubt, and that there is a philosophical as well as a historical connection between the rise of secular liberalism and the decline of religious certainty. Similarly, it is often said that there is a philosophical as well as a historical connection between liberal doctrine and doubts about the objectivity of ethics.[20] I have to confess that these conceptual connections escape me; and that the view that moral non-cognitivism generates a principle of ethical *laissez-faire* seems to me simply incoherent.[21] Be that as it may, Locke (like most of the great thinkers in the early liberal tradition) has little truck with arguments of this sort. He is adamant that there is a God, that His existence can be established very readily,[22] that this God requires certain things of us in the way of ethical practice, belief and worship, and 'that man is obliged above all else to observe these things, and he must exercise his utmost care, application and diligence in seeking out and performing them' (pp. 123–5, pp. 42–3). We should, however, note that although Locke believed that there is 'only one way to heaven', he did suggest at one point that the case for toleration might be even stronger if there were more than one right answer to questions about religious practice: 'if there were several ways, not even a single pretext for compulsion could be found' (p. 91, p. 29). But this is a mistake. The truth of something like religious pluralism (analogous to the moral pluralism that Joseph Raz discusses)[23] would still leave open the question of what to do about those heretics who, faced with a whole array of different routes to salvation, *still* persist in choosing a deviant and mistaken path. Just as faced with a variety of goods, men may still choose evil, so faced with a variety of true religions men may still choose error and blasphemy.

Certainly, Locke was confidently of the opinion that most of the groups and sects he proposed to tolerate (such as Jews who disbelieved the New Testament and heathens who denied most of the old as well) had got these matters objectively and evidently wrong. He was prepared to 'readily grant that these opinions are false and absurd' (p. 123, p. 41). His argument, then, did not depend on any misgivings about contemporary orthodoxy (though in fact he did not support contemporary Anglicanism in all the details of its faith and liturgy); nor was it based on any suspicion, however slight, that at the last trump the sects that he proposed to tolerate might turn out to have been right all along. His position was rather that a false belief, even if it is objectively and demonstrably false, cannot be changed by a mere act of will on the part of its believer, and that it is therefore irrational to threaten penalties against the believer no matter how convinced we are of the falsity of his beliefs. Locke's view, then, is not like the main theme in J. S. Mill's essay *On Liberty* that persecution is irrational because it tends to suppress doctrines which may turn out to have been worth preserving (for one reason or another).[24] It is more like Mill's subordinate argument that the state of mind produced by coercive indoctrination is so far from genuine belief as to call in question the rationality of one who is trying to inculcate it.[25]

There is one line of argument present in the *Letter* which may make us think that Locke was taking a sceptical position on religious matters. Locke was very concerned by the fact that if a magistrate or a ruler were to require certain religious beliefs or practices of us, there would be no guarantee that the religion he favoured would be correct.

> Princes are born superior in power, but in nature equal to other mortals. Neither the right nor the art of ruling carries with it the certain knowledge of other things, and least of all true religion. For if it were so, how does it come about that the lords of the earth differ so vastly in religious matters?
>
> (p. 95, p. 30)

But at most this is scepticism about the religious discernment of princes, not scepticism about religious matters as such. Locke maintains that 'a private man's study' is every bit as capable of revealing religious truth to him as the edicts of a magistrate (p. 93, p. 29). He insists that each man is *individually* responsible for finding 'the narrow way and the strait gate that leads to heaven' (p. 71, p. 19) and that God will excuse no man for a failure to discharge this responsibility on grounds of duress or obedience to orders. If the magistrate makes a mistake and I obey him, then *I* bear the responsibility and the cost I face may be everlasting perdition: 'What security can be given for the kingdom of heaven?' (p. 95, p. 30). Locke adds one further point, which, in his view, 'absolutely determines this controversy' (p. 99, p. 32) by distinguishing religious from other forms of paternalism:

> even if the magistrate's opinion in religion is sound . . . yet, if I am not thoroughly convinced of it in my own mind, it will not bring me salvation. . . . I may grow rich by an art that I dislike, I may be cured of a disease by remedies I distrust; but I cannot be saved by a religion I distrust, or by worship I dislike. It is useless for an unbeliever to assume the outward appearance of morality; to please God he needs faith and inward sincerity. However likely and generally approved a medicine may be, it is administered in vain if the stomach rejects it as soon as it is taken, and it is wrong to force a remedy on an unwilling patient when his particular constitution will turn it to poison.
>
> (pp. 99–101, p. 32)

One may be forced to be free, to be healthy or to be rich, but 'a man cannot be forced to be saved' (p. 101, p. 32). Religious truth must be left to individual conscience and individual discernment alone. So there are here certainly individualistic doubts about the abilities of princes; but none of these points is consistent with any more far-reaching doubts about truth or knowledge in matters of religion.

There is one further line of argument, connected with this, which does have a slightly stronger sceptical content. This is the worry at the back of Locke's mind that an argument for the imposition of Christian beliefs and practices by a Christian magistrate would seem to yield, by universalization, an argument for the imposition of pagan beliefs and practices by a pagan magistrate:

> For you must remember that the civil power is the same everywhere, and the religion of every prince is orthodox to himself. If, therefore, such a power be granted to the civil magistrate in religious matters, as that at Geneva, for example,

he may extirpate by force and blood the religion which there is regarded as false or idolatrous; by the same right another magistrate, in some neighbouring country may oppress the orthodox religion, and in the Indies the Christian.[26]

(p. 113, p. 37)

Notice that this is a good argument only against the following rather silly principle: (P1) that the magistrate may enforce *his own* religion or whatever religion *he thinks* is correct. It is not a good argument against the somewhat more sensible position (P2) that a magistrate may enforce the religion, whatever it may be, which is *in fact* objectively correct. It may, of course, be difficult to tell, and perhaps impossible to secure social agreement about, whether the view that the magistrate believes is correct is in fact the correct view. (P2 is what Gerald Dworkin has called a 'non-neutral' principle, and the social implementation of non-neutral principles is always problematic.)[27] But opposition to intolerance based on awareness of these difficulties is not opposition to intolerance as such, but only opposition to particular cases of it. Like the argument discussed in section II above, this is not an argument for toleration in general. Suppose, however, that the notion of objective truth in religious matters were a chimera. Would we then be able to make any distinction between P1 and P2? It may be thought that the answer is 'no' and therefore (working backwards) that Locke, who saw no difference between them, must have been sceptical about the objectivity of religious belief. And one does get a sense, especially in the *Third Letter Concerning Toleration*, that Locke may be inclined to move in this direction.[28] Be that as it may, we should note that a rigorous sceptic could still draw a distinction between P1 and P2. If there were no objective truth, P1 could be implemented as before (perhaps on Hobbesian grounds of public order);[29] but P2 would not now licence the enforcement of any religious belief at all.

VI

The second general point I want to make concerns the way in which the case for toleration fits into the general structure of Locke's political philosophy.

I am not sure whether we ought to attach any significance to the fact that the subject of religious toleration is not mentioned at all in the *Two Treatises of Government*. There may be an historical explanation: if we take the *Letter on Toleration* to have been drafted after

1685[30] and we accept something like Peter Laslett's dating of the composition of the *Two Treatises*,[31] then we can say that Locke may well not have formulated his final tolerationist position sufficiently clearly at the time the *Treatises* were drafted to include reference to it there. Even so, it is surprising. Religious toleration was one of Locke's abiding preoccupations and one of the most contested political issues of the age. It is odd that he should make no reference to it in a treatise concerned with the functions and limits of government.

Indeed, the occasional references to religion in the *Second Treatise* indicate, if anything, that the legitimate Lockean state need not be a secular one at all. In the chapters on resistance and revolution, Locke suggests that a people may be entitled to rise up against their prince if he has by his actions or negligence endangered 'their estates, liberties, lives . . . and perhaps their religion too'.[32] He implies throughout that the failure of the later Stuarts to prosecute and enforce the laws against Catholicism amounted to subversion of the constitution.[33] (This, however, is complicated by the fact that even in the *Letter on Toleration* Locke indicated that he was disposed to exclude Catholics, as he excluded atheists, from the scope of the toleration that he was arguing for (pp. 131–5, pp. 45–7). We cannot go into the grounds for this here; but it had to do mainly with his suspicion that members of both classes would make bad citizens.) The indications in the *Second Treatise* seem to be that a legitimate state may have an established and constitutionally sanctioned religion and an established pattern of religious discrimination; and that it would be permissible for Lockean individuals to agree on such arrangements when they moved out of the state of nature.

However, I am inclined to regard these indications as superficial: arguably they have more to do with the political events of the 1670s than with Locke's deepest convictions in political philosophy. I want to see now whether it is possible to accommodate the argument for toleration within the framework of the political theory of the *Second Treatise*.

The view in the *Second Treatise* is that a state has no greater power than that delegated to it by its citizens. Specifically, what the magistrate has at his disposal is the executive power which everyone previously had in the State of Nature to prosecute and punish transgressions of natural law.[34] This power is resigned into the hands of the community and entrusted to the magistrate on entry to civil society. No doubt the magistrate will organize that power efficiently, making it much more effective than the sum of the dispersed powers of the same individuals in the State of Nature.[35] (That, after all, is the whole point of the shift to civil society.) But the substance of the power is exactly the same as the individuals' natural right to punish.

The question about toleration, then, is a question not just about the limits of *state* force but about the limits of the use of force by any agency or any individual at all. (It is significant that in Locke's discussion of excommunication (p. 79, p. 23), he insists that, while it is permissible for a church (like any private club) to expel a recalcitrant member, nevertheless 'care must be taken that the sentence of excommunication carry with it no insulting words or rough treatment, whereby the ejected person may be injured in any way, in body and estate'.) So since the doctrine applies to individual force, let us consider its application to individuals in the State of Nature who have retained their natural right to punish: do they have a right to punish heretics and persecute religious deviance? If they do, there seems no reason why that power should not be vested in the community as a whole when civil society is set up. Let us assume for the sake of argument (what Locke certainly believed, as we saw in section V above) that the heresy whose toleration is in question really *is* heresy and that the deviant religious sect really *is* acting in defiance of God's commands so far as their beliefs and practices are concerned. If a heretic is defying God's law (and remember that the law of nature, for Locke, derives all its normative force from the fact that it is God's law), do the rest of us have a natural right to punish him? On Locke's view the natural right to punish has two purposes – reparation for wrongful injury done, and *restraint* in the sense of coercive deterrence.[36] Clearly, reparation is out of the question in the religious case. Locke takes the Protestant view that a heretic does no injury to anyone but himself and God (pp. 123–5, pp. 42–3) – and, of course, it is not for us to collect compensation on behalf of the Almighty. That leaves the function of restraint. But if the argument of the *Letter* goes through, then restraint is also out of the question, since coercive deterrence can have no effect on the formation or maintenance of heretical beliefs. The right to punish may not be exercised in these cases, then, because it would serve no useful purpose, and punishment when it serves no useful purpose is wrong on the Lockean account.[37] So, since individuals have no right to punish heretics, governments cannot acquire any such right either, for 'nobody can transfer to another more power than he has himself'.[38] It follows that it is wrong to set up any sort of confessional state or established church when we move out of the State of Nature, if this is going to involve the use of political power for religious purposes.

This argument would not work were Locke to countenance any sort of retributive justification for punishment. For we might then be justified in using force and inflicting pain and loss on heretics simply in order to punish them for their (undoubted) sins without any further purpose of deterrence, reform or reparation in mind. Force used in this way could not be conceived as a means to any end apart from the immediate infliction of suffering; its employment, therefore, could not be criticized as irrational in the sense of being incapable of attaining the ends at which it was aimed. In a recent book, W. von Leyden has argued that Locke's theory of punishment *is* (partly) retributive.[39] If he is correct, then there is an enormous gap in the argument for toleration. But the passages cited by von Leyden do not support his view. It is true that Locke says that punishment should be such as to make the criminal 'repent' of his crime.[40] But since repentance involves, among other things, forming the belief that one's criminal conduct was wrong, the same argument can be used to establish that force is inapposite to this end as Locke used to establish that it was inapposite to more direct coercion and deterrence. Von Leyden notes that Locke makes occasional use of the language of retribution and desert: but when 'retribute' is used early in the *Second Treatise* Locke immediately links it in a definitional way to reparation and restraint;[41] moreover he uses desert only in the sense of proportionality[42] and he is adamant elsewhere in the *Treatise* that proportionality of punishment is strictly determined by the damage that has been suffered and thus by the reparation that is to be recouped.[43]

VII

The third general point I want to make about Locke's argument concerns its structure and the sort of toleration it entails.

Locke's position is a *negative* one: toleration, as he says in his *Second Letter* on the subject, is nothing but the absence or 'removing' of force in matters of religion.[44] The argument is about the irrationality of coercive persecution and it entails nothing more than that that sort of activity ought not to be undertaken. Nothing is entailed about the positive value of religious or moral diversity. Unlike Mill, Locke does not see anything to be gained from the existence of a plurality of views, or anything that might be lost in monolithic unanimity, in these matters. There is nothing in his argument to justify a policy of fostering religious pluralism or of providing people with a meaningful array of choices.

Even more important, we need to see that Locke's negative argument is directed not against coercion *as such*, but only against *coercion undertaken for certain reasons* and with certain ends in mind. The argument concerns the rationality of the would-be persecutor and his purposes; it is concerned about what happens to his rationality when he selects means evidently unfitted to his ends. Coercion, as we know, is in Locke's view unfitted to religious ends. But if it is being used for other ends to which it is not so unfitted (such as Hobbesian ends of public order), then there can be no objection on the basis of this argument, even if *incidentally* some church or religious sect is harmed. The religious liberty for which Locke argues is defined *not* by the actions permitted on the part of the person whose liberty is in question, but by the motivations it prohibits on the part of the person who is in a position to threaten the liberty. It is what Joseph Raz has called elsewhere 'a principle of restraint'.[45] Thus it is not a right to freedom of worship as such, but rather, and at most, a right not to have one's worship interfered with for religious ends.

This point is emphasized quite nicely by an example that Locke uses towards the end of the *Letter on Toleration*. In the course of considering various practices that heathen sects may engage in, Locke takes up the case of animal sacrifice. He begins by saying that if people want to get together and sacrifice a calf, 'I deny that that should be forbidden by law' (p. 109, p. 36). The owner of the calf is perfectly entitled to slaughter the animal at home and burn any bit of it he pleases. The magistrate cannot object when the slaughter takes on a religious character – for the element that makes it a religious *sacrifice* (and therefore an affront to God in the eyes of decent Anglicans) is precisely the internal aspect of belief which political power can never reach. *However*, Locke goes on, suppose the magistrate wants to prohibit the killing and burning of animals for non-religious reasons:

> if the state of affairs were such that the interest of the commonwealth required all slaughter of beasts to be forborne for a while, in order to increase the stock of cattle destroyed by some murrain; who does not see that in such a case the magistrate may forbid all his subjects to kill any calves for any use

whatever? But in this case the law is made not about a religious but a political matter, and it is not the sacrifice but the slaughter of a calf that is prohibited.

(p. 111, p. 37)

But, of course, the *effect* of the economic ban on animal slaughter may be exactly the same as a ban that was religiously inspired. Perhaps in both cases the religious sect in question will wither and die out as its congregation, deprived of their favourite ceremony, drift off to other faiths. But what matters for Locke's purposes is not coercion as such or its effects, but the reasons that motivate it. If the reasons are religious, the coercion is irrational. But if the reasons are economic or political, then the argument for toleration gets no grip whatsoever despite the fact that the coercion may discriminate unequally in its consequences against a particular group. There may, of course, be other arguments against this sort of inequity, but they are not based on a Lockean principle of toleration.

I have emphasized this point because it seems to be relevant to some of the modern formulations of the liberal position on religion, personal morality and conceptions of the good life. Recently, philosophers like Ronald Dworkin and Bruce Ackerman have formulated that position in terms of a requirement of neutrality: the state and its officials are required to be *neutral* as between the various moral conceptions of the good life that various citizens may hold.[46] But the question arises: what does neutrality involve? Is it just a requirement of impartiality or is it some stronger constraint of equal treatment? Does it involve, as Alan Montefiore has claimed, an effort to help and hinder the contending parties in equal degree?[47] And if it does require such evenhandedness, is it in practical terms *possible* for a government to be neutral in that sense?

In Locke's account of toleration, we have the basis for a conception of neutrality which is very narrow indeed and quite light in the burden that it places on the liberal state. The government and its officials are required to be neutral only in the *reasons* for which they take political actions. They must not act *in order to* promote particular religious objectives. Beyond that no wider neutrality is required. They need pay no attention to the evenness of the impact of their actions on those with whom they are dealing.

Compare now the conceptions of neutrality generated by some of the other familiar lines of liberal argument. If we wanted to use John Stuart Mill's argument about the dialectical value of religious, philosophical and ethical diversity, then our conception of neutrality would be somewhat more strenuous. For if a sect, such as the animal sacrifice cult, dies out as a result of government action, that is a loss to religious and cultural diversity, and therefore a loss to the enterprise of seeking the truth, no matter what the reason for the action was. *Mill's* liberal government, then, unlike Locke's, must take care to see that diversity is not threatened even incidentally by its actions; and if it is threatened, it must weigh up carefully the value of the loss against the other ends it hopes to achieve by the coercion.[48] Similarly, if our argument for liberal neutrality has to do with the respect that a government owes to the autonomous moral and religious development of its citizens, then again a more strenuous requirement than Locke's will be generated. The government will be obliged not merely to refrain from religiously or morally inspired persecution, but to avoid any action which, in its effects, may **frustrate or undermine individuals' choices and their self-constitution in these areas.**

An important point emerges from all this. The idea of liberal neutrality, like that of toleration, is an abstract concept in political theory of which various conceptions are possible.[49] These conceptions differ considerably in the practical requirements they generate and the burdens they impose on governments. Which conception we opt for is not a matter of preference – it is not a matter of which we find most congenial to our political 'intuitions'. Rather it is a matter of the *line of argument* that we want to put forward. Locke's argument yields one conception of liberal neutrality, Mill's another, and so on. It follows, therefore, that an enterprise like that of Bruce Ackerman, in his recent book *Social Justice in the Liberal State*, is completely misguided. Ackerman puts forward a principle of liberal neutrality which he claims can be defended by any one of at least four distinct lines of argument. (Both Mill's argument and something like Locke's feature on his menu.)[50] He professes indifference as to which line of justification is adopted, claiming that the liberal ought to be as tolerant about that issue as he is about conceptions of the good life.[51] But if I am right, this promiscuity about justification may have disastrous consequences. The different lines of argument do not converge on a single destination: each argument yields a distinct conception which in turn generates distinct and practically quite different principles of political morality and social justice. So the liberal cannot afford to be indifferent or offhand about the justificatory task. The line of justification that is taken *matters* for the articulation of the position he wants to adopt.

VIII

Let us return now, finally, to the details of the Lockean argument. The nub of the case, you will recall, was his claim that there is an unbridgeable causal gap between coercive means and religious ends – the gap which, as I put it, is framed by these two propositions that 'Coercion works on the will' and 'Belief cannot be affected by the will.' So long as these two frames remain in place, the irrationality of using coercive means for religious ends is evident.

We have already seen one reason for questioning the first of these propositions. Coercion, or more generally force, may be applied to a person not in order to put pressure on his will but simply in order to punish him, retributively, for the wrong he has done. But it is with the second of the two propositions that I am now chiefly concerned.

The second proposition is not argued for by Locke at any length in the *Letter on Toleration*. All Locke says is that 'light is needed to change men's opinions, and light can by no means accrue from corporeal suffering' (pp. 69–71, p. 19). One looks naturally to the *Essay Concerning Human Understanding* for further elaboration, for the claim is primarily epistemological in character. We find there very little in the way of argument either. Locke does touch on the point in Book IV of the *Essay*,[52] but what he says is not entirely congenial to the argument put forward in the *Letter*.

The basic position that Locke defends in this part of the *Essay* is that 'our knowledge is *neither wholly necessary, nor wholly voluntary*'. He explains two senses in which knowledge is not voluntary. First, 'men that have senses cannot choose but have some *ideas* by them', and what a man sees (for example) 'he cannot see otherwise than he does':

> It depends not on his will to see that *black* which appears *yellow*, nor to persuade himself that what actually *scalds* him feels *cold*; the earth will not appear painted with flowers, nor the fields covered in verdure, whenever he has a mind to it: in the cold winter, he cannot help seeing it cold and hoary. . . .

Second, once ideas have been received, the processes of the understanding go to work on them more or less automatically. Once men have received ideas from their senses, 'if they have memory, they cannot but retain some of them; and if they have any distinguishing faculty, cannot but perceive the agreement or disagreement of some of them with one another'. And if men have in their minds names for these ideas, then propositions expressing the agreement or disagreement which their understanding has discerned will necessarily be accepted as true.[53]

None of this is subject to the will so none of it can be coerced. Thus far the toleration argument is supported. What, then, according to the *Essay* is voluntary in the formation of beliefs? Locke answers: 'all that is *voluntary* in our knowledge is the *employing* or witholding any of our faculties from this or that sort of object, and a more or less accurate survey of them'.[54]

Though a man with his eyes open cannot help but see, he can decide which objects to look at, which books to read and more generally which arguments to listen to, which people to take notice of and so on. In this sense, if not his beliefs then at least the sources of his beliefs are partly under his control.

All this is familiar and evidently true. But it opens up a first and fatal crack in the framework of Locke's argument for toleration. Suppose there are books and catechisms, gospels and treatises, capable of instructing men in the path of the true religion, if only they will read them. Then although the law cannot compel men coercively to believe this or that because it cannot compel the processes of the understanding, it can at least lead them to water and compel them to turn their attention in the direction of this material. A man may be compelled to learn a catechism on pain of death or to read the gospels every day to avoid discrimination. The effect of such threats and such discrimination may be to increase the number of people who eventually end up believing the orthodox faith. Since coercion may therefore be applied to religious ends by this indirect means, it can no longer be condemned as in all circumstances irrational.

The case is even stronger when we put it the other way round. Suppose the religious authorities know that there are certain books that would be sufficient, if read, to shake the faith of an otherwise orthodox population. Then, although again people's beliefs cannot be controlled directly by coercive means, those who wield political power can put it to work indirectly to reinforce belief by banning everyone on pain of death from reading or obtaining copies of these heretical tomes. Such means may well be efficacious even though they are intolerant and oppressive; and Locke, who is concerned only with the rationality of persecution, provides no argument against them.

Once we catch the drift of this criticism, we begin to see how the rest of Locke's case falls apart. His case depended on the Protestant importance he attached to sincere belief: 'All the life and power of true religion consists in the inward and full persuasion of the mind; and faith is not faith without believing'. So long as our attention is focused on the state of belief itself and *its* immunity from interference, Locke's argument is safe. But now we are starting to look at the epistemic apparatus that surrounds and supports belief – the apparatus of selection, attention, concentration and so on – which, although it does not generate belief directly, nevertheless plays a sufficient role in its genesis to provide a point of leverage. Even if belief is not under the control of one's will, the surrounding apparatus may be; and that will be the obvious point for a rational persecutor to apply his pressure.

Perhaps the following sort of response may be made on Locke's behalf.[55] What matters for the purposes of true religion is genuine belief. But belief to be genuine must be based on the free and autonomous activity of the mind, choosing and selecting its own materials and its own evidence, uncoerced and undetermined by outside factors. Belief-like states generated in the mind of an individual on the basis of a coerced input of ideas are not genuine in this sense; they are more like the states of mind of an individual who has been brainwashed or subjected incessantly to propaganda. Such an individual may look like a believer from the outside – and he may even feel like a believer from the inside (he is not merely mouthing formulas to evade punishment) – but nevertheless, in virtue of the history of their causation, his beliefs do not count as genuine.[56] Since it is genuine belief that the religious authorities are interested in securing, it will therefore be irrational for them to resort even to the sort of indirect coercion I have been describing.

I have two worries about this line of argument. First, it is difficult to see why the 'free' input of ideas should *matter* so much in determining what counts as genuine belief. We have said already that it is not a phenomenological matter of whether beliefs generated in this way *feel* more genuine than beliefs generated on the basis of coercively determined input. So is the point rather that belief-like states which are not 'genuine' in this sense cannot perform some or all of the *functions* we expect beliefs to perform? Are they functionally deficient in some way? Are they, for example, like brainwashed 'beliefs', peculiarly resistant to logical pressure and to requirements of consistency? That, I suppose, is a possibility. But I find it hard to imagine what sort of epistemology or philosophy of mind could possibly connect the *external* conditions under which sensory input was acquired with the functional efficacy of the beliefs generated on the basis of that input. If I am forced at the point of a bayonet to look at the colour of snow, is my consequent belief that snow is white likely to function differently from the corresponding belief of someone who did not need to be forced to take notice of this fact?

Second, this approach appears to place such great demands on the notion of *genuine belief* as to lead us to doubt the genuineness of everything we normally count as a belief in ordinary life. In *most* cases (not just a few), the selection of sensory input for our understanding is a matter of upbringing, influence, accident or constraint; freedom (in any sense that might plausibly be important) and autonomy seem to play only minor roles. But if this yields the conclusion that most religious belief is not 'genuine' anyway, then we have offered the persecutors an easily defensible position: they can now say that their intention is not to inculcate 'genuine' belief (since that is impossible for most people anyway), but simply to generate in would-be heretics beliefs which are the same in content and status as those of the ordinary members of orthodox congregations. Against this proposal, it would seem, Locke has nothing to say.

We may attack the question of the relation between belief and *practice* in the constitution of religious faith in a similar sort of way. Locke is relying on the view that practice – outward conformity to certain forms of worship – by itself without genuine belief is nothing but empty hypocrisy which is likely to further imperil rather than promote the salvation of the souls of those forced into it. But this is to ignore the possibility that practice may stand in some sort of generative and supportive relation to belief – that it too may be part of the apparatus which surrounds, nurtures and sustains the sort of intellectual conviction of which true religion, in Locke's opinion, is composed. So here we have another point of leverage for the theocrat. A law requiring attendance at Matins every morning may, despite its inefficacy in the immediate coercion of belief, nevertheless be the best and most rational indirect way of avoiding a decline in genuine religious faith.

Some of these points were raised by Jonas Proast in a critique of Locke's *Letter*, to which the latter responded in his *Second* and subsequent *Letters Concerning Toleration*.[57] Proast had conceded

Locke's point that beliefs could not be imposed or modified directly by coercive means, but he insisted that force applied 'indirectly and at a distance' might be of some service in concentrating the minds of recalcitrants and getting religious deviants to reflect on the content of the orthodox faith.[58] Force may be unable to inculcate truth directly, but it may remove the main obstacles to the reception of the truth, namely, 'negligence' and 'prejudice'.[59]

Despite the enormous amount of ink that he devoted to his response, Locke failed to provide any adequate answer to this point. He said that it would be difficult to distinguish sincere and reflective dissenters from those whose religious dissent was negligent, slothful or based on removable prejudice; and he insisted that it would certainly be wrong to use force indiscriminately on all dissenters when its proper object could only be a certain subset of them. This is undoubtedly correct. But now the case in principle against the use of force in religious matters has collapsed into a purely pragmatic argument: force *may* be serviceable, only it is likely to be difficult to tell *in which cases* it will be serviceable. In place of the knock-down argument against the use of political means for religious ends, we have now an argument to the effect that political means must not be used indiscriminately and without great care for religious ends. Because the in-principle argument has collapsed, the sharp functional distinction between church and state that Locke was arguing for goes with it. We can no longer say that the magistrate's power is *rationally inappropriate* in the service of true religion. Everything now depends on how sure the magistrate is that the deviants he is dealing with have prejudiced and negligent minds. It is impossible, therefore, to agree with J. D. Mabbott that Locke provides a 'complete and effective' response to Proast's critique.[60] On the contrary, the response he provides completely and effectively demolishes the substance of his position.

IX

I do not see any other way of reconstructing Locke's argument to meet the criticisms that I have outlined. Religious faith, and more generally moral commitment, are complex phenomena. Yet Locke has relied, for his indictment of the rationality of persecution, on a radical and distorted simplification of that complexity. A charge of irrationality based on that sort of simplification is likely to be returned with interest!

It is possible that the gist of Locke's position is correct. Perhaps at a very deep level, there *is* something irrational about intolerance and persecution; perhaps ultimately reason and liberal commitment do converge in this respect. But, on the face of it, it seems unlikely that this convergence is going to take place at the level of *instrumental* rationality. Censors, inquisitors and persecutors have usually known exactly what they were doing, and have had a fair and calculating idea of what they could hope to achieve. If our only charge against their enterprise was hopeless and instrumentally irrational from the start, then we perhaps betray only our ignorance of their methods and objectives, and the irrelevance of our liberalism to their concerns. If by their persistence they indicate that they *do* have a viable enterprise in mind, then there comes a point when the charge of instrumental irrationality must be dropped (on pain of misunderstanding), and a more direct challenge to their actions taken up.

At this point, what one misses above all in Locke's argument is a sense that there is anything *morally* wrong with intolerance, or a sense of any deep concern for the *victims* of persecution or the moral insult that is involved in the attempt to manipulate their faith. What gives Locke's argument its peculiar structure and narrowness is that it is, in the end, an argument about agency rather than an argument about consequences. It appeals to and is concerned with the interests of the persecutors and with the danger that, in undertaking intolerant action, they may exhibit a less than perfect rationality. Addressed as it is to the persecutors in *their* interests, the argument has nothing to do with the interests of the victims of persecution as such; rather those interests are addressed and protected only incidentally as a result of what is, in the last resort, prudential advice offered to those who are disposed to oppress them.

We have already seen that an argument based on a concern for the moral interests of the potential victims of intolerance would differ considerably from Locke's argument. Not being an argument about rational agency, it would not merely be a principle of restraint on reasons, but would generate more strenuous and consequentially more sensitive requirements for political morality. Perhaps this is why Locke avoided that line. But one cannot help feeling too that part of the explanation lies in the fatal attraction of ethical rationalism: that if only we can show that intolerance is irrational we may be excused from the messy business of indicating the reasons why it is *wrong*.[61]

NOTES

1 First page references in the text are to John Locke, *Epistola de Tolerantia: A Letter on Toleration*, edited by R. Klibansky and translated by J. W. Gough (Oxford 1968), second references are to page numbers in this edition.

2 For the development of Locke's views on toleration, see M. Cranston, *John Locke: A Biography* (London 1957), pp. 44ff., 59–67, 111–13, 125–33, 314–21, 331ff. See also J. D. Mabbott, *John Locke* (London 1973), pp. 171–5; and J. W. Gough, 'Introduction' to the Klibansky and Gough edition of the *Letter*, op cit., pp. 1ff. For detailed accounts of the historical circumstances of the *Letter*'s composition, see R. Klibansky, 'Preface' to the Klibansky and Gough edition, op cit.; and M. Montuori, 'Introduction' to John Locke, *A Letter Concerning Toleration*, edited by M. Montuori (The Hague 1963).

3 It is of course controversial whether Locke's political arguments can be abstracted and deployed in this way. For the suggestion that there may be dangers here, see Q. Skinner, 'Meaning and understanding in the history of ideas', *History and Theory*, 8 (1969); and J. Dunn, *The Political Thought of John Locke: An Historical Account of the 'Two Treatises of Government'* (Cambridge 1969), chs 1 and 19. For a less pessimistic view, see D. Boucher, 'New histories of political thought for old', *Political Studies*, 31 (1983).

4 I use 'persecute' in its dictionary sense of 'to harass, afflict, hunt down, put to death, esp. for religious . . . opinions' (*Chambers Twentieth Century Dictionary*, edited by A. M. MacDonald (London 1977), p. 994) as a general term to cover all acts at variance with toleration. Jonathan Harrison pointed out to me that the word also has emotive and evaluative connotations. Clearly it would be wrong to *rely* on these for the purposes of argument: I do not intend to and I hope I have not done so.

5 J. S. Mill, *On Liberty* (1859), edited by C. V. Shields (Indianapolis and New York 1956).

6 For modern theories of this kind, see especially J. Rawls, *A Theory of Justice* (Oxford 1971), pp. 201–34, 325–32; R. M. Dworkin, 'Liberalism', in S. Hampshire (ed.), *Public and Private Morality* (Cambridge 1978); and B. Ackerman, *Social Justice in the Liberal State* (New Haven and London 1980).

7 For the reception of the *Letter*, see Cranston, op cit., pp. 331ff. For the *Second, Third*, and *Fourth Letters Concerning Toleration*, see *The Works of John Locke*, 11th edn (London 1812), vol. VI, pp. 59–274.

8 For a contrary view see Joseph Raz, 'Autonomy, toleration and the harm principle', in S. Mendus (ed.), *Justifying Toleration* (Cambridge 1985), pp. 137–55.

9 *Report of the Committee on Homosexual Offences and Prostitution* 1957, Cmd. 247, para. 62.

10 R. Scruton, *A Dictionary of Political Thought* (London 1982), p. 464 (the emphasis is mine).

11 M. Weber, 'Politics as a vocation' (1918) in H. Gerth and C. Wright Mills (eds), *From Max Weber: Essays in Sociology* (London 1970), p. 77;

see also M. Weber, *Economy and Society*, 3 vols, edited by G. Roth and C. Wittich (Berkeley, Los Angeles and London 1978), vol. I, p. 55.

12 Weber, 'Politics as a vocation', op cit., p. 78; Weber, *Economy and Society*, op cit., vol. I, pp. 55–6.

13 John Locke, *Two Treatises of Government* (1689), edited by P. Laslett (Cambridge 1960), II, section 3.

14 See also ibid., II, section 86, and – for the organization of force – II, section 137.

15 This incidentally undermines John Dunn's view that force and violence are presented in Locke's works as the ways of beasts and the solvents of society and civilization (Dunn, op cit., p. 165). A more accurate view is that Locke's account of force is profoundly ambiguous: rightful force is the essence of politics, while force without right is the epitome of bestiality.

16 For Scruton's account, see note 10 above and the text thereto; see also Mabbott, op cit., p. 176 (first premise of Mabbott's argument ii).

17 Locke defines it explicitly in these terms in the *Second Letter,* in *Works,* op cit., vol. VI, p. 62.

18 For some interesting questions about this assumption, see Robert Nozick, *Philosophical Explanations* (Cambridge, Mass. 1981), pp. 405–9.

19 Alan Gewirth, *Reason and Morality* (Chicago and London 1978), see especially pp. 22ff.

20 See, for example, R. M. Unger, *Knowledge and Politics* (New York and London 1976), p. 76: 'From the start, liberal political thought has been in revolt against the concept of objective value.' (Historically, of course, such a claim is utterly groundless.)

21 See the excellent argument by G. Harrison, 'Relativism and tolerance', in P. Laslett and J. Fishkin (eds), *Philosophy, Politics and Society*, 5th series (Oxford 1979), p. 273.

22 See John Locke, *An Essay Concerning Human Understanding* (1690), edited by J. Yolton (London 1961), book IV, chs III (section 21) and X.

23 See Raz, op cit., note 8.

24 Mill, op cit., ch. II.

25 ibid., pp. 43, 49–50.

26 I am grateful to David Edwards and Tom Baldwin for impressing on me the need to treat this as a separate and important line of argument for toleration.

27 G. Dworkin, 'Non-neutral principles', in Norman Daniels (ed.), *Reading Rawls: Critical Studies of 'A Theory of Justice'* (Oxford 1975), p. 124.

28 cf. Locke, *Third Letter*, in *Works*, op cit., vol. VI, pp. 143ff.

29 For Hobbes's views on toleration, see T. Hobbes, *Leviathan* (1651), edited by C. B. Macpherson (Harmondsworth 1968), chs 18 and 31.

30 See Klibansky, 'Preface' to the Klibansky and Gough edition of the *Letter*, op cit., pp. ixff.; also Montuori's 'Introduction' to his edition, op cit., pp. xv–xxii.

31 P. Laslett, 'Introduction' to his edition of Locke, *Two Treatises*, op cit., part III.

32 Locke, *Two Treatises*, op cit., II, section 209.

33 ibid., II, sections 210, 214, 225.

34 ibid., II, sections 8–12, 86, 126.
35 ibid., II, section 137.
36 ibid., II, sections 7–12.
37 For the doctrine that punishment should be waived when it does not serve these aims, see ibid., II, section 159.
38 ibid., II, section 135.
39 W. von Leyden, *Hobbes and Locke: The Politics of Freedom and Obligation* (London 1982), pp. 115ff.
40 See Locke, *Two Treatises*, op cit., II, section 8 (lines 21–3).
41 ibid., II, section 8 (lines 5ff.).
42 ibid., II, section 87 (lines 8–10).
43 ibid., II, section 184.
44 See note 17 above.
45 J. Raz, 'Liberalism, autonomy and the politics of neutral concern', in P. French, T. Uehling and H. Wettstein (eds), *Midwest Studies in Philosophy VII: Social and Political Philosophy* (Minneapolis 1982), pp. 90–1; see also C. L. Ten, *Mill on Liberty* (Oxford 1980), p. 40.
46 See note 6 above; R. M. Dworkin, op cit., p. 127; Ackerman, op cit., p. 11.
47 A. Montefiore, *Neutrality and Impartiality: The University and Political Commitment* (Cambridge 1975), p. 5. For a useful discussion, see Raz, 'Liberalism', op cit.
48 See, for example, Mill, op cit., pp. 53–4, 58, 63–4.
49 For the distinction between concept and conceptions, see Rawls, op cit., pp. 9–10, and R. M. Dworkin, *Taking Rights Seriously*, revised edn (London 1978), pp. 134–6, 226. This idea is indirectly linked to the views of Gallie on conceptual disagreement: see W. B. Gallie, 'Essentially contested concepts', *Proceedings of the Aristotelian Society*, 56 (1955–6), 167. For discussions of this idea, see William Connolly, *The Terms of Political Discourse*, 2nd edn (Oxford 1983), chs 1 and 5–6; and J. N. Gray, 'Political power, social theory and essential contestibility', in D. Miller and L. Siedentop (eds), *The Nature of Political Theory* (Oxford 1983).
50 Ackerman, op cit., pp. 11–12.
51 ibid., p. 359.
52 Locke, *Essay*, op cit., book IV, ch. XIII.
53 ibid., sections 1–2.
54 ibid., section 2.
55 I am grateful to Joseph Raz for suggesting this line of argument to me. He is not responsible for any inadequacies in its formulation here.
56 For an interesting discussion, see D. Dennett, 'Mechanism and responsibility', in Ted Honderich (ed.), *Essays on Freedom of Action* (London 1973).
57 J. Proast, *The Argument of the Letter Concerning Toleration Briefly Considered and Answered* (Oxford 1690). See 'Introduction' to the Klibansky and Gough edition of the *Letter*, op cit., p. 32ff.; also Mabbott, op cit., pp. 180–2.
58 Proast is quoted in these terms by Locke in the *Second Letter*, in *Works*, op cit., vol. VI, p. 69.

59 ibid., p. 74.
60 Mabbott, op cit., p. 182.
61 This paper was first presented at the Morrell Conference on Toleration organized in the Politics Department of the University of York in September 1983. I am grateful to Tom Baldwin, David Edwards, Judy Evans, Peter Jones, Onora O'Neill, Albert Weale and especially Joseph Raz for their comments, questions and criticisms.

JOHN LOCKE: AUTHORITY, CONSCIENCE AND RELIGIOUS TOLERATION[1]

P. J. Kelly

In 1700 John Locke added a further chapter, 'Of Enthusiasm', to the fourth edition of his *An Essay Concerning Human Understanding*.[2] In the course of this chapter he wrote:

> Upon this occasion I shall take the liberty to consider a third Ground of Assent, which with some Men has the same Authority, as is as confidently relied on as either Faith or Reason, I mean Enthusiasm. Which laying by Reason would set up Revelation without it. Whereby in effect it takes away both Reason and Revelation, and substitutes in the room of it, the ungrounded Fancies of a Man's own Brain, and assumes them for a Foundation both of Opinion and Conduct.[3]

Locke's critique of 'enthusiasm' is directed against the elevation of individual conscience above all other authorities as the final criterion for determining ethical principles and regulating political practice. The defining characteristics of 'enthusiasm' which Locke identified in this passage are the acceptance of subjective judgement beyond the testimony of experience, the elevation of revelation above reason and according ultimate authority to individual conscience in all cases of practical reasoning, even if this results in the denial of the sovereign authority of the civil magistrate. While in this chapter Locke was attempting to expose the irrationality of 'enthusiasts' and to undermine their intellectual pretensions, it can be argued that his political writings from the *Two Tracts* to the *Letters on Toleration* were intended to address the political consequences of religious 'enthusiasm'. The most obvious of these is the elevation of individual conscience and subjective opinion over the sovereign authority of the civil magistrate. The 'enthusiast's' absolute adherence to revelation even when this is contradicted by reason and experience entails the rejection of an objective public standard of reason. This rejection of reason also involves the abandonment of a public principle of right which determines the extent of the civil magistrate's jurisdiction. Consequently, the political problem posed by 'enthusiasm' is one of reconciling Christian liberty of conscience with the necessary sovereign authority of the civil magistrate.

In this essay I will argue that it is this problem of reconciling Christian liberty of conscience with the authority of the civil magistrate that provides the theoretical context within which Locke came to address the problem of toleration. Moreover, I will argue that this same problem underlies Locke's early 'conservative' writings, the *Two Tracts on Government* (1660–1).[4]

It has become a commonplace of Locke scholarship since Abrams's edition of the *Two Tracts* in 1967, to maintain a fundamental division between the early 'conservative' Locke, and the later, mature 'liberal' Locke of the *Two Treatises* and *Letters on Toleration*. Abrams is largely responsible for this interpretation of Locke as a conservative and authoritarian in his early works, but other distinguished Locke scholars have also come to similar conclusions. In his biography of Locke, Maurice Cranston claims that 'Locke in 1660 and 1661 was thus a man of the Right, an extreme authoritarian. Within a few years his political views were to be radically changed.'[5] And in a more recent lecture entitled 'John Locke and the case for toleration', he argues that:

> His earliest writings on the subject are directed against toleration. In his Oxford days, in 1661, he had written a pamphlet asserting that 'by appointment of the great sovereign of heaven and earth we are born subjects to the will and pleasure of another' – our earthly sovereign, who 'must necessarily have an absolute and arbitrary power over all indifferent actions of his people' including the forms and content of religious worship.[6]

It is clear that at one level there is an important change within Locke's political outlook, for from the mid-1660s when he wrote the unpublished 'Essay Concerning Toleration'[7] he favoured a policy of toleration rather than the imposition of an arbitrary uniformity of practice. However, underlying Abrams's claim that the young Locke was a conservative and an authoritarian is the argument that the concepts employed in the *Two Tracts* were derived from a world-view that he had abandoned by the time he wrote the *Two*

Treatises and the *Letters on Toleration*. In his introduction to the *Two Tracts*, Abrams writes:

> Locke in 1660 belongs, then, in the classical, pre-Lockeian tradition of political thought. The Tracts are a last statement of an old world-view. Both the problem involved and the categories used are backward-looking. The man himself had been trained in archaic skills and assumptions, the archaicism of which had not yet been quite acknowledged.[8]

The purpose of this essay is to contest the claim that Locke abandoned the categories that he employed in the *Two Tracts* when he wrote the *Letters on Toleration*, and suggest that the problem underlying these early works was the same problem that he addressed in his later writings on toleration. However, while showing that there is a philosophical continuity existing between the authoritarian *Two Tracts* and the liberal *Letters on Toleration*, I nevertheless reject the recent argument of R. P. Kraynak, who claims that the development of Locke's thought can be explained on the grounds that 'absolutism and toleration are the same in principle'.[9] This essay is intended to redirect attention from the policy prescriptions of these works to the form of argument within which these policy prescriptions arose. In this way it can be shown that there is not a fundamental change of argument and philosophical purpose between the early and the later writings on the relationship between the Christian liberty of conscience and the sovereign authority of the civil magistrate. And that Locke's 'conservatism', in so far as it can be given any determinate meaning, was not abandoned as he became involved in radical politics in his later life. Therefore, there is no necessary incompatibility between Cranston's claim that Locke was a 'conservative' and Richard Ashcraft's recent account of Locke as a political radical.[10] This is not, however, to maintain that historically religious toleration was unimportant for Locke. But it is to maintain that the question of whether a policy of toleration should be preferred to a policy of imposing an arbitrary uniformity of religious practice was necessarily subordinate to the primary task of reconciling Christian liberty of conscience with the authority of the civil magistrate. The main argument of this essay is that all of Locke's arguments are primarily directed towards justifying the civil magistrate's authority over the realm of indifferent things, that is those practices which are conventionally parts of religious practice, but which are not expressly prescribed by divine law revealed through scripture. The law of nature or divine law places formal limitations on the sovereign magistrate's power by marking out those spheres of personal interaction which were beyond his concern. However, within the limits imposed by natural and divine law the civil magistrate ought to adopt policies which have the best consequences, where the best consequences are those most conducive to civil peace and security. Consequently, the problem of toleration arose from the problem of reconciling Christian liberty of conscience with the authority of the sovereign legislator. All of the works considered in this essay are concerned with limiting the scope of conscience, by establishing an objective principle of right which delimits the respective spheres of judgement of the individual and the magistrate. Thus while Locke's political commitments changed, his perception of the danger of 'enthusiasm' remained, as did the basic concepts with which he drew the boundaries between individual conscience and civil authority. In the end the three works considered all tell different stories about how the magistrate should act, but each work presents the same framework of argument within which the legislator can make the choice between toleration and authoritarian impositions of uniformity. Locke neither came to reconcile authoritarian impositions with toleration as Kraynak argues,[11] nor did he abandon the epistemological framework within which he defended both authoritarian imposition and toleration, as Abrams argues.[12] In the last part of this essay I will argue that Locke's defence of toleration is based on consequentialist reasons and not rights-based arguments. Thus Locke's defence of toleration is markedly different from later liberal defences of toleration as a condition of scientific and social progress,[13] or as a virtue of liberal societies.[14]

I

In a letter to 'S.H.'[15] or Henry Stubbe, dated 1659, Locke expressed a cautious admiration for Stubbe, a notorious champion of toleration. This letter provides the earliest evidence of Locke's interest in the problem of toleration and the limits of civil authority with respect to Christian liberty. Yet only a year later Locke was to write the *First Tract on Government*, in which he set out to refute Edward Bagshaw's argument for the liberty of Christian conscience in matters of religious practice. In his *The Great Question Concerning Things Indifferent in Religious Worship* (Oxford 1660) Bagshaw argued that each Christian should be free to decide whether or not to observe certain forms of religious worship where these were indifferent matters, and not the subject of divine legislation. At first sight Bagshaw's argument does not appear to create serious problems, given that he was simply advocating toleration of individual conscience within the realm of indifferent things. However, Locke saw Bagshaw's argument as threatening the peace and security of society. In the *First Tract on Government*, he argued against Bagshaw that if the magistrate was denied the right to legislate over indifferent things then his authority was effectively denied. This was because it was precisely within the realm of indifferent things that the civil magistrate was empowered to legislate for the good of the community and to maintain civil peace and security. Even though Bagshaw only advocated the extension of Christian liberty of conscience to the realm of indifferent things in respect of religious worship, Locke maintained that the implications of his argument were much wider since: 'there is no action so indifferent which a scrupulous conscience will not fetch with some consequence from Scripture and make a spiritual concernment'.[16] If each Christian was entitled to follow his conscience in matters of indifferent things in religious worship, the authority of the magistrate was effectively undermined, unless it was possible to provide an objective determination of the necessary components of religious worship and practice.

The problem of reconciling Christian liberty of conscience with the authority of the civil magistrate was one consequence of the collapse of certainty following the Reformation.[17] The effects of the Reformation, considered as a series of events, and the epistemological crisis that they initiated are extremely varied and complex, differing from one country to another. Nevertheless, the search for a rational justification for religious and ethical beliefs was a major preoccupation of philosophical speculation in the generations following the English Reformation. And it is the political context of the English Reformation which provides the theoretical framework within which Locke addressed the philosophical problems of the foundation, justification and limits of civil authority. The debates to which Locke's *Two Tracts* were intended to serve as a practical contribution were debates between the dissenting Puritans and the Anglican authorities. However, beyond their immediate political significance, which is reconstructed in recent studies by Abrams[18] and Ashcraft,[19] these debates also manifest a crisis of authority which is a product of the Reformation challenge to the Roman Magisterium. The Protestant emphasis on individual responsibility for salvation created the conditions within which the individual conscience became the standard for determining the religious and ethical requirements of salvation. Once an individual's conscience became the ultimate standard for determining what was necessary for salvation, there arose the situation in which conscience posed a direct challenge to the authority of the civil magistrate. Personal responsibility for salvation implied that only authentically held beliefs would be sufficient to guarantee salvation. However, by placing the emphasis on the individual conscience as the guarantor of authentic beliefs, the Protestant dissenters ultimately raised subjective judgement above the authority of the civil magistrate.

The difficulty of distinguishing the dictates of individual conscience from mere subjective opinion is manifested most clearly in the works of two controversialists, William Ames and William Perkins. Ames's *Conscience With the Power and Cases Thereof* (London 1643) and Perkins's *The Whole Treatise of Cases of Conscience* (London 1651) both asserted that the correctly informed conscience was supreme above all political authority. Both authors accepted that part of the standard scholastic theory which identified conscience as the faculty by which an individual agent judged his actions to be in accordance with the precepts of divine law. However, they departed from scholasticism by arguing that the individual was the sole arbiter of the substance of those precepts. The abandonment of the objective framework of divine law, within which the scholastic account of conscience functioned, had the effect of collapsing judgements of conscience into subjective opinion. Ames and Perkins attempted to avoid the subjectivism that threatened their theories by arguing that the sincere believer was guided by the divine grace, which would guarantee that his conscience was correctly informed. This appeal to the inner guidance of divine grace as the means of authenticating the requirements of divine law was standard among Protestant writers. John Milton used exactly the same argument when he wrote that:

> Every believer has a right to interpret the Scripture for himself, in as much as he has the spirit for his guide, and the mind of Christ is in him; nay the expositions of the public interpreter can be of no use to him except so far as they are confirmed by his own experience.[20]

Locke's scepticism of the rationality of such arguments was expressed in his attack on 'enthusiasm' and in his assertion of a publicly accessible system of natural or divine law throughout his writings.

Both his political writings and *An Essay Concerning Human Understanding* can be seen as theoretical and practical attempts to undermine 'enthusiasm'.[21] The main criticism of appeals to the guidance of divine grace or the special epistemic qualification available to the regenerate following the conversion experience is that they were self-validating. The individual who is persuaded that his judgement was sanctioned by divine grace is the only judge of the veracity of his validating experience. Thus on this argument it is not possible to distinguish someone who is merely persuaded (falsely) that his judgements are consistent with the requirements of divine law, from someone who is correctly judging in accordance with divine law.

By combining conscience with a subjective criterion of the dictates of divine law, the Puritan dissenters such as Ames, Perkins, Bagshaw and Milton provided grounds for questioning the authority of the civil magistrate. The conscientious appreciation of the requirements of religious worship and practice had the effect of setting the boundaries to the magistrate's authority in accordance with the substance of each individual's judgement. This meant that where the requirements of religious worship and practice were interpreted extensively to include all aspects of private and public behaviour, the authority of the civil magistrate was effectively denied. Admittedly the debate to which the *Two Tracts* contributed was only concerned with sanctioning liberty of conscience over indifferent things in religious worship. However, Locke believed that if the magistrate was required to accommodate liberty of conscience over indifferent things in religious worship, then his authority was effectively undermined because each individual and sect could still claim to be the ultimate determinant of whether an action was objectively indifferent or whether it formed part of the necessary requirements of religious worship and practice.

Locke saw the dangers of unrestricted 'enthusiasm' as the main consequence of Bagshaw's pamphlet. Nevertheless, as a Puritan, he also acknowledged the importance of liberty of conscience in matters of belief. His acknowledgement that only authentically held beliefs could guarantee salvation entailed both liberty of belief and opinion and the irrationality of persecution to achieve religious conversion. Even in the 'authoritarian' English *Tract*, Locke argued that:

'Twould be tyranny in a father to whip a child, because his apprehensions were less quick, or his sight not so clear, or the

131

lineaments of his face perhaps not so like his own as the rest of his brethren, who yet with equity enough chastise his wilful disorders. To conclude, rigour which cannot work an internal persuasion may notwithstanding an outward conformity, all that is here required, and may be as necessary in the one as useless in the other.[22]

The magistrate is entitled to concern himself with the disobedience of his subjects, because he is only concerned with establishing an outward conformity of behaviour. But for him to punish a subject because he did not authentically believe certain doctrines would be like a father punishing his son because his sight was weak. Persecution for the sake of religious conversion can at best bring about an outward profession of belief, when what is required is authentic inner conviction. Authentic belief is the product of a real persuasion of the truth of the doctrines professed, and this is a propositional attitude based on the reasonableness of what is professed and not on any external considerations such as the threat of punishment. The argument for the irrationality of persecution reappears in Locke's later justification of toleration.[23] However, it is only effective against persecution for the sake of religious conversion. Consequently, it provides only an indirect justification for toleration of religious practice or other public behaviour.

Despite his Puritan commitment to liberty of conscience, at least in respect of belief, Locke attached greater importance in all of his writings to the peace and stability of the social order. His fear of anarchy and disorder, and his respect for authority is captured in the following quotation from the preface to the English *Tract*:

As for myself, there is no one can have a greater respect and veneration of authority than I. I no sooner perceived myself in the world but I found myself in a storm, which hath lasted almost hitherto, and therefore cannot but entertain the approaches of a calm with the greatest joy and satisfaction.[24]

Locke's 'respect and veneration for authority' was not simply a consequence of his early 'conservative' temperament. The maintenance of civil peace and stability is the most important political goal underlying all of his political writings from the *Two Tracts* to the *Two Treatises* and *Letters on Toleration*. This is because civil peace and stability are necessary conditions for the development and flourishing of man's two essential functions, rationality and agency. The successful flourishing of these two defining features of human nature is a condition not only of the successful and industrious life, but it is also a condition of realizing man's greatest goal, namely personal salvation. Thus, the assertion of the rule of law, and the subordination of the individual's subjective judgement to the authority of the civil magistrate underlies the early 'conservative' and later 'liberal' works of Locke. This can be seen most clearly in the early *Two Tracts*. However, Locke's use of the same conceptual framework in his defence of toleration in the later 'Essay' and *Letters on Toleration* entails the same concern for political stability and control, and the subordination of individual judgement before the legitimate authority of the civil magistrate.

II

In his brief discussion of the *Two Tracts* John Dunn argues that: 'both expound the single proposition that there does exist an area of religious duty which is not explicitly defined by divine positive law and which it lies within the authority of the magistrate to determine';[25] and that: 'It is claimed as axiomatic that the supreme power in any legitimate polity has the right of unrestricted legislative activity (in all religiously indifferent matters).'[26] While both of these claims contain an element of truth, both are also misleading. First, the whole thrust of the argument of the *Two Tracts* is to assert the civil magistrate's authority over the realm of indifferent things. And that while he might require a uniformity of practice, this can only be an arbitrary uniformity concerning indifferent things. The magistrate has no power or authority to legislate over the content of authentic religious worship, so it is misleading to argue that the arbitrary uniformity determines a part of religious duty, for its object is not to encourage authentic religious observance, but simply to maintain civil peace and security. Second, the fact that the supreme power has the right of unrestricted legislative activity only in the realm of religiously indifferent things shows that the supreme power is restricted by the requirements of divine law. It is clear from Locke's answer to Bagshaw that if the magistrate did not have the right to act in the realm of religiously indifferent things then he would have no sphere within which to exercise his jurisdiction, for precisely the reason that the realm of religiously indifferent things is an indeterminate category that can potentially extend right across the realm of public activity.

Dunn is right to argue that Locke does not develop an account of the criteria of legitimacy of the sovereign power in the *Two Tracts*, but such an argument is implicit. The adoption of the concepts of indifferent and necessary things presupposes an account of natural or divine law, which gives substance to this distinction. The substance of divine law also provides the conditions of legitimacy, for it sets the boundaries around the respective spheres of individual and legislative activity. Locke does not spell out the conditions of legitimacy of the civil magistrate until the *Two Treatises*, and he does not adequately develop the epistemology of natural law, although his *An Essay Concerning Human Understanding* was intended to contribute to that end.

In the *Latin Tract* Locke did suggest that some form of consent theory is the source of magisterial authority and the basis of legitimacy. He claimed that he only adopted a consent theory in order to accommodate his opponents. However, he used the consent argument in order to explain how the magistrate could have power over that which the divine law has left as the realm of individual liberty, as the following passage shows:

> That all things not comprehended in that law are perfectly indifferent and as to them man is naturally free, but yet so much master of his own liberty, that he may by compact convey it over to another and invest him with a power over his actions, there being no law of God forbidding a man to dispose of his liberty and obey another. But on the other side, there being a law of God enforcing fidelity and truth in all lawful contracts it obliges him after such a resignation and agreement to submit.[27]

Locke's concern in the *Two Tracts* wasn't with the source of legitimate power, but rather with the reasons for individuals limiting their freedom and submitting themselves to the authority of the magistrate to determine over the realm of indifferent things. The reason given is that in the absence of a sovereign magistrate with supreme authority over the realm of indifferent things, there would be anarchy and disorder. The anarchy that would result from each individual acting as his own legislator would destroy the conditions of peace and security within which each individual can secure his own material needs and pursue his salvation. Locke argued that: 'God wished there to be order, society and government among men. And this we call the commonwealth. In every commonwealth there must be some supreme power without which it cannot truly be a commonwealth.'[28] The sovereign legislator is necessary to determine the framework within which each individual can act, and in order to determine this framework he must be able to establish uniformities of behaviour. These uniformities are the magistrate's positive laws. However, he is only entitled to establish such a uniformity of behaviour in the realm of indifferent things. In respect of the dictates of divine law he is not empowered to interfere. He can give positive law sanctions to the divine law, as when he incorporates the prescription of the ten commandments into the criminal law. But his actions in this case add nothing to the status of the divine law. Also he cannot require what is contrary to the dictates of divine law, nor is he entitled to prohibit authentic worship and religious practice. It is in this context that Locke emphasizes the indifferent–necessary distinction in order to distinguish the imposition of an arbitrary uniformity of practice from any attempt to legislate in the realm of religious belief and authentic worship.

The category of indifferent things includes all actions and objects which are not expressly prescribed by divine law as part of religious worship and belief or the necessary components of morality. An action or object is objectively indifferent whatever significance any individual or sect may wish to attach to it. Consequently, Locke argues against Bagshaw that there is no category of indifferent things used in religious worship which the legislator should leave inviolable. Religious worship cannot require freedom to dispose of indifferent things otherwise these objects and practices would more properly fall within the requirements of divine law. Instead Locke maintained that the basic requirement of religious worship was the inner worship of the heart. But as he also acknowledges:

> this worship, wholly silent and secret as it is, completely hidden from the eyes and observation of men, is neither subject to human laws, nor indeed capable of such a subjection. God who lays bare the most secret of the mind and who can alone either know the private deliberations of the mind or pass judgement upon them, is the only examiner of men's hearts.[29]

The magistrate has no control nor authority over this inner worship of the heart. This is not simply because he has no special epistemic qualification which entitles him to determine the content of divine law. Rather, he lacks power in this area because authentic belief is a combination of a propositional attitude and the gift of grace. And the legislator can neither persuade someone of the truth of a proposition by physical sanction, nor can he authenticate a belief in the absence of grace. Therefore, the magistrate's task is not the imposition of a uniformity of belief and worship, but the creation of the conditions within which individuals can seek their own salvation in peace. This argument reappears throughout Locke's writings on the relationship between Christian liberty of conscience and the civil authority, and as I have already suggested it provides only indirectly for the most limited toleration. Dunn has argued that it is this argument which Locke uses in the 'Essay on Toleration' to justify the privileged position of religion in relation to political interference. While Locke undoubtedly uses this argument in his defence of prudential toleration in the 'Essay on Toleration', Dunn fails to acknowledge that Locke used the same argument in the *Two Tracts*. Thus while the policy prescriptions of the 'Essay' certainly differ from those of the *Two Tracts* there is a greater similarity of argument than Dunn allows for.[30]

However, more is required of authentic worship than the mere inner persuasion and acknowledgement of God. This inner persuasion must be manifested through certain public acts, and it is these which constitute religious worship. Yet Locke denied that the form of this outward worship was left free to each believer to determine. Instead certain minimal components such as public prayer and psalm singing and the participation in those sacraments explicitly prescribed by scripture were required by divine law, and these the magistrate must recognize and respect. However, the circumstances of these forms of worship are not prescribed by divine law, and here the magistrate can impose an arbitrary uniformity if this is necessary to maintain social peace and security. What the magistrate cannot do is impose a uniformity on the grounds that it is a requirement of divine law.

The effectiveness of the distinction between indifferent and necessary things is dependent on the accessibility of a criterion for determining the content of divine law. Locke did not provide such a criterion in the *Two Tracts*, and at the end of his life was unable to defend such a criterion, other than by pointing to the clear guide set out in scripture.[31] However, what is clear from this work, and crucial to his argument against 'enthusiasm', is the claim that the criterion of divine law was publicly accessible and objective, and not dependent on some private and self-validating inner experience. This assertion of the objective character of divine law enabled Locke to argue that the imposition of an arbitrary uniformity was not contrary to the Christian liberty of conscience of an 'enthusiast', as the following passage shows:

> Imposing on conscience seems to me to be, the pressing of doctrines or laws upon the belief or practice of men as of divine original, as necessary to salvation and in themselves obliging the conscience, when indeed they are no other but the ordinances of men and the products of their authority.[32]

Locke accepted the standard scholastic model of conscience, whereby it only became an authority when it was correctly judging in accordance with divine law. Thus in the *Latin Tract* he presented a hierarchy of laws based on a standard scholastic model, in which the claims of conscience were subordinated to the divine law. When conscience was removed from the context of an objective system of divine law it became: 'nothing but an opinion of the truth of any practical position, which may concern any actions as moral as well as religious, civil or ecclesiastical'.[33] The claims of conscience have no authority when they conflict with the requirements of divine law. And this entails that they have no purchase when they encroach upon the realm of the magistrate's authority.

Locke did make some small concession to the liberty of conscience of the 'enthusiast'. In the *Latin Tract* he distinguished between formal and material obligation. A formal obligation binds the will of an agent because it originates from a recognized authority. However, it does not require assent to the truth or necessity of what is prescribed. Thus when the magistrate imposed an arbitrary uniformity of dress in religious matters, the obligation created originates in his legitimate authority to legislate over indifferent things and not in any ability to judge the truth or necessity of a particular course of action. A formal obligation does not oblige the agent to judge in accordance with the magistrate's commands, but only to act in accordance with them. A material obligation such as that of divine law also binds the judgement, since it lays down the truth or necessity of the requirement. Thus when the magistrate legislates over indifferent things, he leaves the judgement of the 'enthusiast' free, and in that sense allows for liberty of conscience. Consequently, Locke wrote:

> hence I say that all the magistrate's laws, civil as well as ecclesiastical, those that concern divine worship as much as

137

those that concern civil life, are just and valid, obliging men to act but not to judge: and providing for both at the same time, unite a necessary obedience with a liberty of conscience.[34]

Locke's conservatism in the *Two Tracts* resides in his assertion of the importance of a sovereign authority who maintains peace and security. He asserts the rule of law above the judgement of individual conscience, and argues that this is necessary if each person is to be able to pursue their own salvation. Underlying this argument is the distinction between indifferent and necessary things, which enables the magistrate to impose an arbitrary uniformity of practice. However, interpreted in this way Locke's conservatism is uncontentious, at least in the sense that he retained his commitment to the rule of law as the condition of social organization throughout his later writings. What some commentators have intended by describing Locke as a conservative in his early writings is the claim that he advocated considerable legislative interference in religious matters. But is this necessarily the case? The answer really depends on the character of the claims that faced the legislator and the threat they pose to peace and security. All that Locke's argument entailed is that in order to maintain peace and security the magistrate can impose an arbitrary uniformity over indifferent things. It may well be that the Quaker practice of wearing hats during religious worship caused great offence and was likely to upset public peace. In this case the legislator would be entitled to require them to remove their hats as long as his action was in the interests of public security and not based on some religious argument. However, it is important that the magistrate is only entitled to act in such circumstances if there is a threat of civil disturbance as a result of the practice. Therefore, the amount of legislative interference in religious affairs will depend on the number of indifferent acts incorporated into religious practice which pose a threat to social peace and security. In the next section I will show that the same argument underlies the 'Essay' and *Letter on Toleration* despite the different policies advocated in those works.

III

The 'Essay on Toleration', written in 1667, during Locke's association with the Earl of Shaftesbury, is usually taken as the point in Locke's work where he abandoned his early 'conservatism' and adopted an increasingly liberal and radical political theory which culminated in the *Two Treatises*. However, while the 'Essay' and the *Two Tracts* undoubtedly differ in policy, in terms of argument there is a great similarity.

The most striking difference between the 'Essay' and the *Two Tracts* is that in the former Locke transforms the utilitarian justification of the magistrate's authority into a criterion for the legitimate exercise of that power. Thus he is not only empowered to maintain social peace and security, but his authority only extends to actions which serve that end. Locke advances this view in a passage that reflects some of his later 'liberal' writings:

> the whole trust, power and authority of the magistrate is vested in him for no other purpose but to be made use of for the good, preservation and peace of men in that society over which he is set, and therefore that this alone is and ought to be the standard and measure according to which he ought to square and proportion his laws, and model and frame his government.[35]

However, just as in the *Two Tracts*, the magistrate remains the judge of what constitutes a threat to peace and security. There is no right of resistance based on the breach of trust.

Having limited the magistrate's jurisdiction to the maintenance of security and peace, Locke then enquires what actions and beliefs would be tolerated as a matter of right. And here he identifies speculative opinions and matters of divine worship as beyond the concern of the civil magistrate. This appears to advance beyond the position of the *Two Tracts*, and some commentators have gone on to argue that the privileged status afforded religious belief and practice in the 'Essay' represents a theoretical departure from the argument of the *Two Tracts*.[36] Nevertheless, on a closer inspection there is a greater similarity of purpose. In the *Two Tracts* Locke had acknowledged that religious beliefs were beyond the power and authority of the civil magistrate, because he could neither effect the appropriate propositional attitude nor create authentic religious beliefs. Yet Locke did not even claim that all speculative opinions were beyond the scope of the magistrate's concern, for he wrote:

> There are some speculative opinions and actions which are in their natural tendency absolutely destructive to human society, as that faith may be broken with heretics, that if the magistrate

does not reform the religion the subjects may, that one is bound to broach and propagate any opinion he believes himself, and such like, and in actions, all manner of frauds and injustices, etc and these the magistrate ought not to tolerate.[37]

The magistrate cannot change the beliefs of Roman Catholics, atheists or enthusiasts simply by the exercise of his external physical sanctions. Nevertheless when any belief is necessarily destructive of the social order he can punish all who hold that belief.

In the case of religious worship, Locke also appears to have departed from the argument of the *Two Tracts*, for he included in this category the place, time and circumstances of worship, precisely the things he left the magistrate to determine in his earlier argument. This new position is justified on the grounds that the form of religious worship is solely the concern of the individual and God. This takes the form of religious worship out of the realm of the magistrate's jurisdiction. However, Locke immediately introduced a caveat which suggests that the argument is not so different from that of the *Two Tracts*. The magistrate can have no interest in religious worship if it concerns an indifferent act. Locke never even considered that what is prescribed by divine law could threaten social peace or violate the jurisdiction of the magistrate, or that the legislator could restrict what is prescribed by divine law. Underlying the toleration of religious worship is the notion of a class of indifferent acts over which the legislator has ultimate jurisdiction. The magistrate may have good reason to tolerate all manner of religious practices which are consistent with social peace and security, but once there is some threat to the social order, he is required to act just as he was in the *Two Tracts*. Locke still rejected the argument that the 'enthusiast' should be allowed liberty of conscience to determine the content of religious worship, because he still acknowledged a publicly accessible system of divine law against which the claims of conscience could be judged. Any judgement of conscience that claims more than divine law sanctioned was merely a subjective opinion, and had no special title to toleration. Thus in a passage which reflects the argument of the *Two Tracts* Locke maintained that:

> no such opinion has any right to toleration on this ground, that it is a matter of conscience and some men are persuaded that it is either a sin or a duty; because the conscience or the

persuasion of the subject cannot possibly be a measure by which the magistrate can or ought to frame his laws, which ought to be suited to the good of all his subjects, not the persuasions of a part, which often happening to be contrary one to another must produce contrary laws; and there being nothing so indifferent which the consciences of some or other do not check at, a toleration of men in all that which they pretend out of conscience they cannot submit to will wholly take away all civil laws and all the magistrate's powers, and so there will be no law nor government if you deny the magistrate's authority in indifferent things over which it is acknowledged on all hands he has jurisdiction.[38]

This re-emphasizes Locke's concern with limiting the claims of liberty of conscience and subordinating individual judgement to the authority of the magistrate. Thus the 'Essay on Toleration' reflects the same conservative commitment to the maintenance of social stability and peace, and the assertion of the rule of law as the means to that end, that is found in the *Two Tracts*. The reliance on the separation of necessary and indifferent acts in order to justify the magistrate's interference with religious worship and speculative opinions also reflects the same form of argument employed in the *Two Tracts*, despite the fact that the 'Essay on Toleration' defends limited religious toleration on prudential grounds. It remains to be seen whether the same form of argument underlies the later *Letter on Toleration*, which was published in 1689.

The *Letter on Toleration* was written in Latin in 1686, during Locke's exile in Holland, and was published along with the *Two Treatises of Government* on his return to England in 1689 following the Glorious Revolution. The chronological proximity of these two works has lent further support to the view that Locke's commitment to toleration in the 1680s was the result of his new liberal theory of the constitutionally limited sovereign expounded in the *Two Treatises*. And part of this view is that the *Letter on Toleration* employs a conceptual framework that differs from that of his early works. On the surface, there is much that can be said in support of this view, given that the main argument concerns the separation of the civil and ecclesiastical realm. However, underlying this separation, and the policies of toleration that are based on it, is the same conceptual framework that Locke employed in the *Two Tracts*.

Locke determines the realms appropriate to the civil and ecclesiastical power by defining their respective natures in the following manner: 'A church then I take to be a voluntary society of men joining themselves together of their own accord, in order to the public worshipping of God, in such manner as they judge acceptable to him.'[39] And a civil society is described as:

> a society of men constituted only for the procuring, preserving, and advancing of their own civil interests. Civil interests, I call life, liberty, health, and indolency of body; and the possession of outward things such as money, lands, houses, furniture, and the like.[40]

This account of the role and function of civil society and the consequent limitation of the magistrate's authority, is based on three reasons. First, as in the earlier works, Locke argued that the magistrate had no concern with the salvation of his subjects, because the responsibility for salvation is placed on each individual and it is inalienable. Second, any attempt by the magistrate to take on this responsibility would be irrational, because his physical sanctions only extend over external things, and they can have no effect in authenticating beliefs or persuading the judgement. Third, the magistrate has no special epistemic qualification to determine the correct path to salvation that is not already available to all men. Each component of the argument in favour of the limitation of the magistrate's authority to civil concernments is already implicit in the arguments of his previous works. More important, however, is the fact that the effective division of the ecclesiastical and civil realms depends on the distinction between indifferent and necessary things. This is most clearly borne out in Locke's description of churches as voluntary associations of individuals, each of whom chose to adopt certain forms and practices of worship. Locke's account of the role and nature of ecclesiastical authority rests on the view that the direct relationship between the individual and God contains all the necessary components of religious worship. The church only has authority to determine the form and circumstances of worship because the individual has authorized it to do so. Thus the form and circumstance of worship have significance only for those who give it significance: 'because whatsoever is practiced in the worship of God is only so far justifiable as it is believed by those that practice it to be acceptable to him'.[41] And this is because, although the adoption of certain practices can be given significance by those who adopt them, they nevertheless remain objectively indifferent. Locke emphasizes this in one of the few passages in the *Letter* which clearly states the distinction:

> Things in their own nature indifferent cannot, by any human authority, be made any part of the worship of God, for this very reason, because they are indifferent. For, since indifferent things are not capable, by any virtue of their own, to propitiate the Deity, no human power or authority can confer on them so much dignity and excellency as to enable them to do it.[42]

However, the ecclesiastical authority lasts only as long as the individual church members continue to give it their consent. Once one of its members withdraws his consent, the church has no power to impose orthodoxy on him because its authority only extends over those who consent to it. Furthermore, since ecclesiastical authority only extends over the form and circumstances of worship, which are indifferent things, any attempt to impose orthodoxy on an ex-member of the church becomes a political act. The attempt to impose orthodoxy on those who no longer recognize it results in an infringement of liberty and becomes a legitimate concern of the civil magistrate. Once again the claims of conscience of 'enthusiasts' and sects are subordinated to the civil authority.

The account of ecclesiastical authority in the *Letter* is only possible within the theoretical framework of indifferent and necessary things. If the ecclesiastical authority had a divine law sanction for a particular form of worship, then considerations of civil peace and security would not count against it. Thus while Locke argued that the magistrate can only interfere in religious matters in order to secure the civil interests of his subjects, and not to pursue some religious policy, the fact that he is able to interfere at all must be based on the objective indifference of the form and circumstances of religious worship. Although Locke favoured a policy of toleration in the *Letter*, as opposed to a policy of an imposed arbitrary uniformity of practice, he needed the same conceptual framework to justify either policy. Consequently, the concepts and language of the early *Two Tracts* were not abandoned by Locke in his later liberal writings as Abrams suggested.

IV

In each of the three works considered the prudential case for toleration varies. In the *Two Tracts* Locke suggested that toleration would invite anarchy and disorder, in the 'Essay' and *Letter* he argued that toleration of practices consistent with civil order was most likely to contribute to peace and stability. In each case what differs is the perception of the threat posed to the social order, and the policy most likely to remedy it. There is no attempt to advance a principled argument for toleration as a necessary component of the good society. Admittedly, in the *Letter* he did suggest that it should be the first virtue of a Christian society. Nevertheless he is sufficiently aware of human weakness and partiality to recognize that the virtue of an ideal Christian polity cannot be transformed into a right. As such Locke's arguments in these three works only appear to allow toleration of belief and speculative opinions, and this is only because the civil magistrate is unable to exercise any power over them. And even this concession to toleration is limited in the case of Roman Catholics, atheists and enthusiasts, whose beliefs are considered necessarily anti-social. Yet none of this is to deny that there are important differences between the three works. Although the conceptual framework employed in each is significantly similar, it is clear that Locke's perception of the complexity of the problem develops with changes in the historical circumstances. And this contributes an important insight into the justification of policies of toleration within Locke's work. The argument of this essay has emphasized the role of the indifferent–necessary distinction. This distinction is one manifestation of the foundational significance of divine or natural law in Locke's work. It determines the boundaries to the civil magistrate's sphere of influence, but within that realm it does not prescribe the particular policies which will secure the civil interests of his subjects. This practical question can only be answered, like all political questions, by an uneasy compromise between principle, experience and an understanding of human nature. It is this political balance which gives rise to the policies of toleration in Locke's later works. And the adoption of these policies undoubtedly reflects his own political experience. This insight further emphasizes the conservatism implicit in Locke's political outlook; a conservatism that underlies much liberal theory. This attitude is reflected in the belief that the basic framework of law will provide the conditions of ordered social interaction, but within that framework of law political problems have to be resolved which require more than an appeal to abstract principle.[43] It is this final lesson, derived from a lifetime's engagement in philosophical speculation and political practice, which the writings on authority, conscience and toleration still proclaim.

NOTES

1   This essay is a revised version of a dissertation, written for an MA degree in Political Philosophy (The Idea of Toleration) at the University of York, 1983–4.

2   J. Locke, *An Essay Concerning Human Understanding*, edited by P. H. Nidditch (Oxford 1975), book N, ch. xix.

3   ibid., IV, xix, 3.

4   P. Abrams (ed.), *John Locke: Two Tracts on Government* (Cambridge 1967).

5   M. Cranston, *John Locke: A Biography* (London 1957), p. 67.

6   M. Cranston, 'John Locke and the case for toleration'. See above p. 80.

7   J. Locke, 'An Essay Concerning Toleration', in H. R. Fox Bourne, *The Life of John Locke*, 2 vols (London 1876), vol. i, pp. 174–94.

8   Abrams, op cit., p. 80.

9   R. P. Kraynak, 'John Locke: from absolutism to toleration', *American Political Science Review*, 74 (1980), p. 53.

10   R. Ashcraft, *Revolutionary Politics and Locke's Two Treatises on Government* (Princeton 1986).

11   Kraynak, op cit.

12   Abrams, op cit.

13   The most famous defence of toleration as a condition of scientific and social progress is J. S. Mill's *On Liberty*, in J. S. Mill, *On Liberty and Other Writings*, ed. S. Collini (Cambridge 1989).

14   A recent defence of toleration as a virtue of the truly liberal society can be found in P. P. Nicholson, 'Toleration as a moral ideal', in J. Horton and S. Mendus (eds), *Aspects of Toleration: Philosophical Studies* (London 1985), pp. 158–73.

15   E. S. de Beer (ed.), *The Correspondence of John Locke*, 8 vols (Oxford 1976), vol. i, pp. 109–12. Locke had the curious habit of trying to disguise the identities of his correspondents by reversing their initials, so that Henry Stubbe became S.H.

16   Abrams, op cit., p. 140.

17   The role of the Reformation in the rise of scepticism and debates over the conditions of certainty are discussed in H. G. Van Leeuwan, *The Problem of Certainty in English Thought, 1630–1690* (The Hague 1963). See also R. H. Popkin, *The History of Scepticism: From Erasmus to Spinoza* (Berkeley 1979), pp. 1–17.

18   Abrams, op cit., pp. 3–111.

19   Ashcraft, op cit., pp. 39–74.

20   J. Milton, *De Doctrina Christiana*, in *The Works of John Milton*, 18 vols, gen. ed. F. A. Patterson (New York 1931–8), vol. xvi, p. 265.

21   For an original and interesting account of the relationship between Locke's moral theory and his *An Essay Concerning Human Understanding* see J. Colman, *John Locke's Moral Philosophy* (Edinburgh 1983). See also R. Ashcraft, 'Faith and knowledge in Locke's philosophy', in J. Yolton (ed.), *John Locke: Problems and Perspectives* (Cambridge 1969).

22   Abrams, op cit., p. 128.

23 See J. Waldron, 'Locke: toleration and the rationality of persecution', pp. 98–124.
24 Abrams, op cit., p. 119.
25 J. Dunn, *The Political Thought of John Locke* (Cambridge 1969), p. 13.
26 ibid., p. 13.
27 Abrams, op cit., pp. 124–5.
28 ibid., p. 231.
29 ibid., p. 214.
30 Dunn, op cit., p. 33.
31 Towards the end of his life, Locke was asked by William Molyneux to complete the task of *An Essay Concerning Human Understanding* by showing the demonstrability of ethics. In a letter to Molyneux, Locke refused the opportunity saying: 'the Gospels contain such a perfect body of Ethicks, that reason may be excused from that enquiry, since she may find man's duty clearer and easier in revelation than in herself' (*The Correspondence of John Locke*, op cit., vol. v, p. 595). This is not to suggest that Locke abandoned reason in favour of revelation. Instead Locke believed that the dictates of law were clearly discernible in scripture and in a manner accessible to all, thus removing the need for complex theology or theories of interpretation. He also believed that the clear precepts of divine law were consistent with reason. Therefore, any demonstration of the substance of ethics would only confirm what is already available to all men in scripture. This is not to concede everything to 'enthusiasm' because Locke still maintained that the demands of divine law were discoverable without the aid of any special qualification.
32 Abrams, op cit., p. 139.
33 ibid., p. 138.
34 ibid., p. 239.
35 Fox Bourne, op cit., vol. i, p. 174.
36 Dunn, op cit., p. 33.
37 Fox Bourne, op cit., vol. i, p. 174.
38 ibid., vol. i, pp. 178–9.
39 J. Locke, *A Letter Concerning Toleration*, see above p. 20.
40 ibid., p. 17.
41 ibid., p. 33.
42 ibid., p. 34.
43 It is this emphasis on the rule of law and the maintenance of authority within which political practice takes place, which allows Locke to be temperamentally a conservative, as Cranston suggests, while also being involved in radical politics in the way that Ashcraft has recently documented. All of the works considered in this essay emphasize the importance of establishing a stable social order against the claims of kings, bishops and Puritan zealots. However, this still leaves room for serious political debate over whether and how far toleration is to extend.

LOCKE: TOLERATION, MORALITY AND RATIONALITY

Susan Mendus

I begin with two quotations:

> For twentieth century liberals the problem of toleration is one that concerns the full liberty of belief and behaviour compatible with the necessary authority of a civil magistrate or power. How much does Locke contribute to our understanding of that problem? Locke says little if anything that is directly applicable . . . the essential role played by God in Locke's argument about liberty of conscience and toleration precludes any real contribution to contemporary debates about toleration.[1]

And:

> [Locke's argument] requires us to distinguish sharply between the grounds which he offers for his conclusions and the content of those conclusions themselves. And once we have drawn this rather obvious distinction it then underlines the yawning chasm between the implications of Locke's arguments for tolerating varieties of Christian belief and practice within a Christian state and society and the implications which they would bear for freedom of thought and expression more broadly within a secular state or a more intractably plural religious culture.[2]

The import of each of these quotations is to suggest that Locke's case for religious toleration, as given in his *Letter on Toleration*, is now well and truly dead and contains little, if anything, of lasting philosophical importance. However, where the former argument emphasizes Locke's own belief in God and the way in which that belief figures as an essential premise in his case against religious intolerance, the latter argument emphasizes the Christian belief of Locke's audience and the way in which that assumption restricts the scope of his case against religious intolerance. In other words, the first quotation dwells upon the kinds of arguments which philosophers may properly employ; the second argument dwells upon the kinds of people philosophers may properly hope to convince. On the first analysis, Locke's account is based on a false premise and is therefore invalid; on the second analysis, Locke's account is addressed only to Christian believers and is therefore incomplete. Either way, his case against religious intolerance is profoundly inadequate once the truth of Christianity is questioned. Here, then, are two cases against Locke's account of toleration.

A third case is made by Jeremy Waldron in his article (see above, pp. 98–124) 'Locke: toleration and the rationality of persecution'. Waldron accepts that much of Locke's argument is historically specific in that it depends crucially on Christian belief. Nevertheless, he hopes to salvage something by considering it as 'a practical intellectual resource that can be abstracted from the antiquity of its context and deployed in the modern debate about liberal theories of justice and political morality'.[3] Ultimately, however, this hope is dashed and Waldron concludes that once the Christian content of his case is removed, all Locke has to offer is the not wholly original idea that intolerance is irrational without any concomitant sense that it is morally wrong. The upshot of these three lines of thought is essentially the same: that Locke's case against religious intolerance is either invalid, because dependent on the now unacceptable premise that God exists, or incomplete, because addressed only to those who believe that God exists, or inadequate, because it misidentifies the wrong done by acts of religious intolerance, construing them as merely irrational, rather than morally wrong.

The aim of this paper will be to suggest that, *pace* these commentators, there is something in Locke's case against religious intolerance which survives the demise of Christian belief and which is of importance to modern political theory. In making this case I shall not, for the most part, deny the textual points made by the commentators quoted above. I shall accept that Locke's account is essentially Christian in both of the ways described. I shall also accept that, when stripped of its Christian background, it turns on the irrationality of persecution, not on moral wrongness, but I shall suggest that there is something deeper and more interesting in such a defence of toleration than is allowed for by many modern commentators. My main line of attack will therefore be on Waldron's claim that Locke's argument for the irrationality of persecution is fundamentally without interest.

When stripped of its Christian premises (if indeed it can be so stripped, and I shall not here comment on that vexed question), Locke's argument proceeds as follows: the state is to be defined in terms of the means at its disposal. These are 'to give orders by decree and compel with the sword': 'rods and axes', 'force and blood', 'fire and the sword' are the characteristic means available to the magistrate, yet these means are not simply inefficient, but incapable of inducing genuine religious belief. They operate on the will, but belief is not subject to the will and so those who would attempt to induce religious belief by applying the coercive means at the disposal of the state are engaged in fundamental irrationality. As Waldron remarks, there is nothing in this argument which so much as hints at any moral wrongness associated with religious persecution: the point against it is quite simply that it is, and can be seen to be, irrational and by showing that intolerance is irrational, Locke thinks himself excused from the messy business of indicating the reasons why it is wrong.[4]

Two further, associated points should be made here: first, that Locke's argument is an argument against certain kinds of *reasons* for religious intolerance. As we have seen, what is irrational is the attempt to induce genuine religious belief by coercive means. There is, however, nothing intrinsically irrational in religious intolerance engaged in for other purposes. Second, the argument against religious intolerance is addressed exclusively to the would-be perpetrators of intolerance, not to their victims. So where we might ask what is the morality of intolerance, Locke asks whether it is rational; where we might ask what are the consequences of intolerance, Locke asks what motivates it; where we might focus on the rights of the tolerated, Locke focuses on the rationality of the tolerators. These three areas – morality and rationality; consequences and reasons; tolerated and tolerators are the three areas where, it is suggested, Locke concentrates on wholly the wrong aspect of the problem. Something has already been said about the alleged inadequacy of concentrating on the irrationality of persecution rather than its immorality. What of the other two points – the emphasis on reasons rather than consequences, and the emphasis on tolerators rather than tolerated? In what ways are these thought to represent misdescriptions of the nature of the problem? And what are the consequences of concentrating on these features of the case?

The distinction between the reasons for intolerance and the consequences of intolerance highlights an important difference between Locke's case for toleration and the case made by John Stuart Mill, or by modern liberals generally. In Mill's *On Liberty* much is made of the importance of diversity and of the need to foster a society which contains a rich variety of styles of life. Mill sees such diversity as being a good in itself and as something which should be fostered for itself. In brief, Mill and modern liberals are concerned about the consequences of intolerance, namely that it will generate dull uniformity. By contrast, Locke has no commitment to the value of diversity as such and does not subscribe to the ideal of a good society as one which can accommodate a wide variety of different beliefs. The focus of his attention is therefore quite distinct from that of modern liberals. Similarly, his emphasis on the irrationality of would-be persecutors is wholly at odds with much modern thought on the subject of toleration: this is not only because ethical rationalism is no longer in vogue, but also because individual autonomy is a central concept of modern liberalism and, in consequence of that fact, the emphasis is thrown on to the rights of the victims of intolerance and away from the obligations of the perpetrators of intolerance. Where modern political theorists ask 'What are the rights of individuals to practise their own faith?' Locke asks, 'What are the reasons which should dissuade us from preventing them practising their own faith?'

These three areas, then, are all areas in which Locke adopts a standpoint on the problem of toleration quite distinct from that of modern philosophy. Many commentators have taken this bare fact as proof that Locke's theory of toleration is dead and that he has nothing interesting to say to us. Yet it is a large (and somewhat immodest) move from the claim that Locke focuses on different aspects of the problem to the claim that he has nothing interesting to say to us. (That the interest of his argument is less in so far as it assumes the existence of God is not something with which I would quarrel. My point here simply concerns the intrinsic interest of his philosophical points, abstracted from their theistic background.)

Nevertheless, it is undeniably true that the focus of Locke's argument is distinct from the modern focus in each of the ways described. The criticisms of this way of proceeding are: first that Locke says nothing about the moral wrong perpetrated by the intolerant; second that he says nothing against intolerance as such, but only against coercion or repression engaged in for certain specific reasons;

and third that he says nothing of the wrong done to the victims of intolerance. I want now to suggest that each of these criticisms is, in part, ill-founded and that Locke's account gestures towards important truths concerning the problem of toleration, which are standardly ignored in modern philosophy. To the extent that modern philosophy chooses to ignore these features of the case, it is, in my view, partial and impoverished.

MORALITY AND RATIONALITY

The criticism made of Locke here is that he fails to isolate the moral wrong involved in intolerance because he is so insistent on emphasizing its irrationality, at least as it affects religious belief. Locke's ethical rationalism certainly guarantees that his argument will be couched in terms of irrationality rather than moral wrongness and, with the demise of ethical rationalism, this strikes us as an odd approach. Nevertheless, this way of looking at the problem serves, I think, to highlight an important point about both moral and religious belief which is now often neglected. Ethical rationalism aside, the crucial feature of Locke's argument here concerns the impossibility of deploying the coercive means available to the state in order to bring about conformity of religious belief. 'Light is needed to change men's opinions and light can by no means accrue from corporeal suffering' he says. Commenting on this argument, Waldron perceives in it a fatal crack which, he claims, serves to undermine the case made for religious toleration. The crack appears when we consider not the state of belief itself and its immunity from interference, but rather the 'epistemic apparatus' that surrounds and supports belief.

> Suppose that the religious authorities know that there are certain books that would be sufficient, if read, to shake the faith of an otherwise orthodox population. Then, although again people's beliefs cannot be controlled directly by coercive means, those who wield political power can put it to work indirectly to reinforce belief by banning everyone on pain of death from reading or obtaining copies of these heretical tomes. Such means may well be efficacious even though they are intolerant and oppressive; and Locke, who is concerned only with the rationality of persecution, provides no argument against them.[5]

151

Waldron's case here seems to me to be impeccable: coercion cannot work directly on the will, but it can be employed so as to support and foster certain sorts of beliefs rather than others and this, properly understood, can constitute an indirect case of coercing belief. So Locke is wrong, and belief can in fact be coerced as every persecutor worth his salt has known all along. So much seems to me undeniably true and I would not even attempt to gainsay it. However, what worries me about this argument is its pretension to completeness. It seems to me that Locke's claim that religious belief cannot be coerced contains an important grain of truth, which is ignored by Waldron and neglected more generally in modern political and moral thought. What follows is a very partial and incomplete account of my concern, but I hope that it will be enough to suggest that there may be something alive and important in this aspect of Locke's philosophy.

The argument presented by Waldron to the effect that belief can be coerced overlooks two important features both of Locke's argument and of some of our own intuitions. The first is that religious belief may not count as genuine when it is coerced, even if the coercion is of the indirect and subtle kind mentioned above. This may be because the manner in which a belief is held or the causal story which explains how it came to be held, are crucial to determining whether it counts as a belief at all. In his article 'Deciding to Believe', Bernard Williams points to four conditions which are necessary for belief.[6] Among these is the 'acceptance' condition, which dictates that for full blown belief we need both the possibility of deliberate reticence (not saying what I believe) and the possibility of insincerity (saying something other than what I believe. The point of the acceptance condition is to indicate that sincere utterance is neither a necessary nor a sufficient condition of belief: not necessary, because we may choose to be reticent about our beliefs; not sufficient, because the possibility of insincere utterance must be available to the speaker if it is to be appropriate to call him a believer. Now, depending on how certain beliefs are induced, it may be that this acceptance condition is unsatisfied. Cases of hypnotism, for example, might be of this sort, as might cases of brainwashing. Of course, the scenario which Waldron envisages in which belief is indirectly coerced will not be of this dramatic sort, but these examples, and the acceptance condition, serve at least to cast doubt on the assumption that all that is required for genuine belief is sincere utterance plus a reputable causal story about how the belief was acquired. And it is this latter which Waldron assumes.

The notion of sincerity is also problematic in another way: people who have not been hypnotized or brainwashed, and who are not insincere in their utterances, may nevertheless be held not to believe that p despite the fact that they claim to believe that p. This is very often evident in professions of religious or moral belief, where an individual's deeds betray his 'genuine' beliefs more clearly than his professed beliefs. People who sincerely claim not to be racially prejudiced may nevertheless act out their true beliefs in such a way as to undermine the professed belief.

The point of these considerations is not, I repeat, to deny Waldron's claim that coercion may work on the epistemic apparatus that surrounds belief even if it cannot work on the state of belief itself. It is simply to resist the move from that claim to the claim that genuine belief is constituted only by sincere utterance plus a causal story. In hinting at a distinction between genuine belief and sincere belief, Locke is pointing to an important difficulty in the philosophy of mind, and one which has consequences for moral and political philosophy. This is quite simply that sincerity is not enough, whether in the expression of moral beliefs, or religious beliefs, or empirical propositions. There may, in all these cases, be a gap between the sincerity of the utterance and the genuineness of the belief. How exactly that distinction is to be analysed I do not know, but the above considerations suggest that it exists and Waldron's argument works only by denying that it exists.

A further point which arises here concerns the relationship between moral or religious beliefs and factual beliefs. The foregoing remarks have suggested that there is an important distinction between a belief's being sincerely uttered and its being genuine, and that this distinction applies equally to the case of religious belief and the case of factual belief. Modern moral and political philosophy have tended to exaggerate the distinction between these two kinds of belief, partly no doubt as a result of the demise of ethical realism. Relatedly, modern moral philosophy has exaggerated the sense in which it is possible to choose or decide upon one's moral beliefs, often construing these choices as a matter of rationality. One important feature of Locke's claim that belief is not subject to the will is its implied assertion that moral and religious belief are not proper objects of choice at all.

Again, Williams:

> There are points of resemblance between moral and factual convictions; and I suspect it to be true of moral, as it certainly is of factual convictions that we cannot take very seriously a profession of them if we are given to understand that the speaker has just decided to adopt them. We see a man's genuine convictions as coming from somewhere deeper in him than that.[7]

One point to be made here is that this way of talking about moral or religious beliefs assimilates them to factual beliefs (at least in part) and distances them from mere preferences or fancies. Even if we believe that God is dead, we still construe the religious believer as acknowledging something rather than opting for something in the expression of his religious faith. To the extent that this is so, it is also the case that we are realists, if not rationalists about moral and religious matters.

That this way of thinking is not completely unfamiliar to us can be seen by looking at a recent justification of the English law of blasphemy. There it is held that the reason religious beliefs deserve special protection, over and above the protection afforded to other kinds of beliefs, is that religious belief is 'ultimate and compelling'. Ultimate in the sense that in a profession of religious faith a person states the most powerful conviction that it is possible to make; compelling in the sense that here the sincere religious believer has no choice in the matter. He simply acknowledges what is, for him, an undeniable reality.[8] Given this view of the matter, which is prevalent now as well as being encapsulated in Locke's account, the irrationality of coercing belief, even indirectly, is akin to the irrationality of brainwashing: it can certainly be done but it does not generate the right kind of belief or, more precisely, it does not generate a belief which is held in the right kind of way.

Obviously, there are great difficulties here which I have not even touched upon. It may be said, for instance, that in a sense we are all brainwashed, since we all are subject to selective sensory or other input which is causally related to the beliefs we sincerely hold. But it is one thing to say that all belief must be causally explicable in some way, quite another to say that any way is as good as any other and that all sincerely expressed beliefs are equally genuine.

However, even if it is admitted that the brainwashing argument will not do, there is another consideration which may serve to cast doubt on the criticism advanced against Locke. Earlier I summed up Jeremy Waldron's argument as issuing in the conclusion that belief can be indirectly coerced and that therefore Locke was wrong. Persecutors have long known that while they cannot literally beat believers into submission, they can nevertheless use subtler means to induce the right beliefs. While this can be done, it is a strategy which looks most plausible when dealing with children, or with those who have no fully developed convictions. But Locke's argument precisely concerns the irrationality of such a strategy in a case where belief is strong. Here we should not underestimate the difficulty which will be involved in coercing belief, however subtly and indirectly. One of the points made earlier about religious belief is that it is not only compelling, but also ultimate. It is the most powerful conviction that it is possible to make. Implicit in this is the recognition that it is a conviction which affects very many (if not all) aspects of life for the believer, and that altering such beliefs will not simply be a matter of making the Bible inaccessible, for instance, or of implementing state subsidy of copies of Nietzsche. Religious belief will, and has, survived all that. That it has survived is in part because of the ultimate and all-embracing nature of religious belief.

Since religious belief and profoundly held moral belief will inform and guide virtually everything a believer does, virtually everything will have to be dismantled if religious belief is to be stamped out or radically transformed. This argument also indicates the differences between indirect coercion in the case of religious belief and indirect coercion in the case of preferences. It is a rational strategy for government to coerce healthier eating habits by, for example, subsidizing wholemeal bread or placing prohibitive taxes on refined sugar. But that is because eating habits do not, generally speaking, impinge upon and inform one's whole life. The task of coercing believers into a state of unbelief, however indirect and subtle, would be an altogether different enterprise and I guess, though I cannot prove, that it would be not merely a more complex version of the dietary case, but a qualitatively different case altogether.

REASONS AND CONSEQUENCES

The foregoing discussion suggests two senses in which Locke's insistence that belief is not subject to the will and not something which can be coercively induced is both important for and acknowledged by modern attitudes to religious toleration. First, it emphasizes the all-pervasive nature of religious belief. Second, it emphasizes the very misleading nature of speaking of belief as something which may be the object of choice at all. The appropriate terms here are sight-analogous terms: recognizing, seeing, etc., not choosing, opting or deciding. This in turn indicates the realism which is incorporated in our own institutional attitude to religious belief and highlights the danger of attempting, as we do, to combine this attitude with a smorgasbord view of the diversity of life.

This brings me to the second feature of Locke's account which is criticized by Waldron and others: the suggestion that Locke is not interested in consequences, but only in reasons. In other words, he concentrates on irrationality in *motivation* and is indifferent to whether or not members of religious sects are treated even-handedly or given equal opportunities within society. Thus, for example, he has nothing to say against political or economic reasons for suppressing certain sects, but these may serve just as effectively as religious reasons to restrict the power and effectiveness of those sects. An example of this might be the repression or repatriation of immigrant Jews, not on grounds of their religion, but on the economic ground that the country cannot afford to offer them hospitality. Similarly, Locke will have no argument based on toleration against the suppression of certain religious practices just as long as those practices are restricted on grounds which are not religious. He says:

> But if peradventure such were the state of things, that the Interest of the Commonwealth required all slaughter of Beasts should be forborn for some while, in order to the increasing of the stock of Cattel, that had been destroyed by some extraordinary Murrain; Who sees not that the Magistrate, in such a case, may forbid all his Subjects to kill any Calves for any use whatsoever? Only 'tis to be observed, that in this case the Law is not made about a Religious, but a Political matter: nor is the Sacrifice, but the Slaughter of Calves thereby prohibited.[9]

Waldron remarks:

> but of course the effect of the economic ban on anim.l slaughter may be exactly the same as a ban that was religiously inspired. Perhaps in both cases the religious sect will wither

and die out as its congregation, deprived of their favourite ceremony, drift off to other faiths.[10]

For reasons which I have already given, I doubt whether the decline of the sect would be quite as easily obtained as that, nor do I think it fair to describe the members of the religious sect as deprived of their favourite ceremony in much the same way as I might be deprived of my favourite television programme should the government think it necessary, for economic reasons, to impose power cuts. Nevertheless, the point remains that Locke is here advocating what has been called a 'principle of restraint', that is a principle which (in this case) defines religious liberty not by the actions permitted on the part of the person whose liberty is in question, but by the motivations it prohibits on the part of the person who is in a position to threaten liberty. Locke does not think that there is a right to freedom of worship as such, but only a right not to have one's worship interfered with for religious ends. He is, therefore, officially indifferent as to whether religious sects flourish or wither. This aspect of his account may be sharply distinguished from most modern liberalism and from Mill's views in *On Liberty*. Both Mill and modern liberals characteristically view diversity as a good in itself and urge a much more strenuous principle of restraint than does Locke.

Waldron remarks on this difference, not primarily as an objection, but more as an indication of the gulf which separates much modern liberalism from the political theory of Locke's *Letter*: Locke has no commitment to diversity, no belief in the inherent goodness of varieties of ways of life and no argument for the preservation, as such, of religious subgroups within the dominant culture of a society. Again, his point is simply that it would be irrational to suppress them, not that it would be morally wrong. In considering this point, I shall be brief – not because I think that there is nothing to say, but because I shall largely be parading my own prejudices against the prejudices of others, and because I have dwelt upon these sorts of considerations at length elsewhere.[11]

In brief, then, the first point to make is that Locke's argument is a quite specific argument for toleration, or against persecution (he takes the two to be identical). Unlike Mill, and many modern liberals, he is not providing an argument for liberty generally. This is not an unimportant point, for there are two distinct and separable questions here: the first is 'What rights do I have to pursue my own way of life and ideals?' The second is 'What obligations do others have to desist from preventing me from pursuing my own way of life and ideals?' That these two are separable will be argued for and explained in the next section; all I wish to do here is to draw attention to the fact that where Mill is arguing for liberty, Locke is arguing against persecution, and to suggest that that fact alone may make an important difference to our assessment of their respective theories.

The second point to be made is that Locke's insistence on neutrality about reasons is something which meshes in with our own practice in modern society in at least one area. This is the area of race relations. The race relations acts hold precisely that people must be neutral as regards the reasons they have for preventing people of other races from doing certain kinds of things – namely that those reasons must not include the reason that they belong to that particular race. The law does not require total even-handedness; it requires only neutrality with respect to reasons and it does this by reference to what racial discrimination definitionally is – i.e. treating one person less favourably than another on grounds of race. Similarly with religious intolerance or persecution. This is, by definition, treating one person less favourably than another on grounds of religion. Further laws, for example, laws requiring equal opportunities may well be (and in my view are) highly desirable, but they will not be laws whose rationale is primarily concern for toleration. It follows from this that the argument for specifically religious toleration presented in the *Letter on Toleration* need not require in Locke an indifference as to whether religious groups flourish or wither. It requires only that the demands of toleration lead so far and no further.

One final point to bear in mind before criticizing Locke's conception of neutrality is that modern liberalism has often manifested its own inconsistency, or even disingenuousness, in urging extensive neutrality or even-handedness. It is doubtful whether such complete agnosticism with respect to the good for man is a possible aim, and even more doubtful whether those modern liberals who purport to recognize it as an ideal are in fact true to their official aspirations.[12] By contrast, Locke, in the *Letter on Toleration*, is advocating reasonableness in the ordering of society. This is not, as Cranston points out, an ideal which we attain today in what we tolerate and what we don't.[13] Perhaps part of the reason for this is the excessive commitment to the unattainable ideal of neutrality. Another possible reason will be explored in the final section of this paper.

TOLERATORS AND TOLERATED

The final feature of Locke's account to which I shall draw attention is his bias towards considering not the rights of the tolerated (the rights of the victims of persecution), but the obligations of the would-be perpetrators of intolerance. The criticism made of this way of proceeding is that it fails properly to acknowledge what is most objectionable about instances of intolerance, namely that intolerance frequently constitutes a violation of individual rights. Much modern political theory proceeds by outlining the rights which people may properly be said to have and then urging that these rights not be violated. Locke, of course, is no stranger to the notion of individual rights, but in the *Letter on Toleration* he concentrates exclusively on the obligations of the magistrates and says little about the rights of the tolerated. Indeed, as has been mentioned already, the *Letter* contains no general argument for a right to freedom of worship at all.

In the previous section I referred to two distinct but related questions which we may ask in this area: the question 'What rights do I have to pursue my own way of life and ideals?' and the question 'What obligations do others have to desist from preventing me pursuing my own way of life and ideals?' Much the greater proportion of modern philosophy has concentrated on the former of the two questions, and it is Locke's failure to do this which makes him the target of criticism. Recently, however, Onora O'Neill has suggested that there is much to be said for reminding ourselves of the latter question.[14] The reasons for this are not wholly sympathetic to Locke's own case, but they do provide a warning of the dangers of pursuing rights theories too vigorously. Again, all I wish to do is to suggest that the assumption that everything can be explained if we concentrate on victims' rights is far too simplistic, and that in so far as this is the charge against Locke, it is ill-founded. It may be better to adopt Locke's general strategy and concentrate on the obligations we have, rather than on the rights others have.

The burden of O'Neill's claim is that when considering questions of toleration a difficulty arises if we concern ourselves only with rights. This difficulty is that if we allow only libertarian rights, then we are forced to the conclusion that so long as no right is violated, there is nothing wrong with the policy we are pursuing. Conversely, if we allow more extensive, welfare rights, then we encounter the difficulty that there is no way of identifying a unique, maximal set of mutually consistent rights. Since rights can be cashed out in terms of obligations, it follows that welfare rights theorists will, standardly, impose inconsistent obligations on people. By contrast, libertarian rights theorists retain consistency but the price is that they fail to say what is wrong with a whole range of actions which appear to be very wrong indeed. The remedy for this, O'Neill suggests, is to remind ourselves that the perspective of rights is only one perspective in liberal political theory and that the alternative perspective, that of obligation, may serve us better in discussions of toleration. What lies behind this thought is the belief that, while rights can be exhaustively analysed in terms of obligations, the converse is not the case, and therefore the perspective of obligation may enable us to explain why certain actions are wrong even though they do not constitute a violation of rights. The specific question of toleration: 'which actions are to be permitted even though they are wrong, and which actions are both wrong and impermissible?', is of course a separate and further one. All that is being pointed to here is that a motivation exists for us, and for Locke, to turn to the perspective of obligation when once we realize that neither libertarian rights nor welfare rights can serve adequately to explain our attitude to various forms of disagreeable behaviour.

This, I believe, is a difficulty which lies at the heart of Locke's discussion of toleration: there is no general right to freedom of worship, but still there is something very wrong with religious persecution. (That there is, for Locke, no right to freedom of worship as such is generally accepted by commentators and highlighted by the distinction between Popple's claims in his preface to the *Letter* and the doctrines of the *Letter* itself.) For reasons which have already been discussed, Locke pinpoints the wrongness as lying in the irrationality of attempting to coerce religious belief. All men have obligations to be rational, and persecution of this sort manifests a failure in that obligation. We, perhaps, would give a rather different account, but the general form of the argument, a form which throws emphasis away from the rights of the tolerated and on to the obligations of the tolerators, should not be despised simply for that reason. Unless and until we can provide a more acceptable account of the nature and scope of individual rights, we should be wary of dismissing, out of hand, alternative explanations such as this.

CONCLUSION

It has been the aim of this paper to suggest that there is at least something which is still alive (or which ought to be alive) in Locke's treatment of religious toleration. Specifically, his insistence that religious belief cannot be coerced points to a distinction between genuine and sincere belief which has some force even if it will not bear the weight Locke puts on it. It reminds us that for the religious believer, the assertion of faith is more akin to an assertion of factual belief, an acknowledgement of an inescapable truth, than to a choice or preference. His emphasis on reasons draws attention to the distinction between the concept of toleration and the concepts of liberty or equality. It likewise warns us against exaggerated optimism in our attempts to attain official neutrality. Finally, his move from the perspective of rights to the perspective of obligations is not thereby a denial of the wrongs done to the victims of intolerance, but a reminder of the difficulties attendant upon supposing both that we must aim for internal consistency in our moral theories, and that there are some wrongs which are not violations of rights. Locke's emphasis on rationality is greater than and different from that which is favoured in modern moral philosophy. But we should not suppose that consistency, rationality and reasonableness have no force, simply because we believe that they do not have quite the force Locke believed them to have.

NOTES

1 P. J. Kelly, 'John Locke: authority, conscience, and religious toleration', MA dissertation, University of York (1984). A shortened version of this piece appears above, pp. 125–46.
2 John Dunn, 'What is living and what is dead in the political theory of John Locke?', in his *Interpreting Political Responsibility* (Oxford 1990), p. 19.
3 Jeremy Waldron, 'Locke: toleration and the rationality of persecution', p. 98 above.
4 ibid., p. 120.
5 ibid., pp. 116–17.
6 Bernard Williams, 'Deciding to believe', in his *Problems of the Self* (Cambridge 1973), pp. 136–51.
7 Bernard Williams, 'Morality and the emotions', in his *Problems of the Self*, op cit., p. 227.
8 For a discussion of this argument see D. S. Edwards, 'Toleration and the English blasphemy law', in J. Horton and S. Mendus (eds), *Aspects of Toleration* (London 1985).

9   See above, pp. 36–7.
10 See above, p. 113.
11 See Susan Mendus, 'Liberty and autonomy', *Proceedings of the Aristotelian Society*, LXXXVII (1986–7), pp. 107–20.
12 ibid.
13 See above, p. 94.
14 Onora O'Neill, 'Practices of toleration', unpublished paper. For an account of the rationale behind moving from a perspective of rights to a perspective of obligation see Onora O'Neill, 'The maxims of justice and charity', in N. MacCormick and Z. Bankowski (eds), *Enlightenment, Rights and Revolution* (Aberdeen 1989).

JOHN LOCKE'S LATER LETTERS ON TOLERATION

Peter Nicholson

INTRODUCTION

The publication of the *Letter Concerning Toleration* in 1689 led Locke to undertake an extensive controversy with one of its critics, and write three further letters on toleration.

The year after its publication a short reply appeared, *The Argument of the Letter concerning Toleration, Briefly Consider'd and Answer'd.*[1] Like Locke's *Letter* it was totally anonymous, without even a pseudonym. Its author was Jonas Proast, 'an Oxford scholar and clergyman'.[2] Proast states his agreement with Locke on many points, but insists that none the less it could be the magistrate's duty to use 'moderate' force in 'matters of religion'. This is an outright rejection of Locke's central thesis: from Locke's perspective Proast advocates persecution. Within months Locke responded with *A Second Letter Concerning Toleration*, under the pseudonym of Philanthropus (Friend of Man).[3] Proast's initial pamphlet was twenty-eight pages of spacious print; in 1691 he gave his rejoinder to Philanthropus, again anonymously, in seventy-nine closely printed pages entitled *A Third Letter concerning Toleration.*[4] Little more than a year later Locke, still disguised as Philanthropus, countered with his hefty book *A Third Letter for Toleration.*[5] At first Proast did not react. He had ended his *Third Letter* by soliciting Philanthropus' reply, promising to consider it carefully and if he was convinced he was wrong to admit it publicly. But he concluded:

> if instead of satisfactory Reason, I meet with nothing but Sophistry and unfair dealing; I am apt to think I shall content my self with what I have already said: being now sufficiently sensible, that Cavils and Impertinences are endless, when a Man of Parts shall not disdain to make use of them.[6]

Clearly Proast intended his silence to be taken as contempt for his opponent's failure to provide relevant and sound arguments. Later he seems to have decided that this pre-emptive strike had miscarried, for in 1704 he published *A Second Letter to the Author of the Three Letters for Toleration*, signing himself Philochristus (Friend of Christ).[7] This signally fails to match the scale to which Philanthropus' book had escalated the controversy, being a mere twenty-four pages. It is also slight in content. Proast writes that he has returned to print only to repudiate the rumour that his silence means that he has retracted his contentions. He produces no new arguments; and he ignores most of Philanthropus' *Third Letter* with the excuse that he can spend his time better 'than in unravelling cobwebs, and detecting Sophistrie'.[8] When Locke died in October of the same year he left the beginning of a reply which was included in his *Posthumous Works* as *A Fourth Letter for Toleration*.[9] This too adds little. After rebuking his opponent for concern with his reputation instead of for the truth, Locke concentrates on showing the emptiness of Proast's latest pamphlet. (In what follows I shall ignore the pseudonyms, and dispense with the sometimes confusing titles which the participants chose. I shall refer simply to Locke's *First*, *Second*, *Third* and *Fourth Letter*, and Proast's First, Second and Third Reply.)

The sheer bulk of Locke's contributions in this debate is striking. In the 1823 ten volume edition of his *Works* the *Four Letters* fill the whole of the longest volume. The *First Letter* occupies little more than the first tenth of it. Yet today it is the *First Letter* alone which is famous, always in print and constantly read and interpreted. The existence of the three later *Letters* raises some obvious questions. What did Proast argue which caused Locke to expend such considerable effort in rebutting? Is Locke successful in meeting Proast's contentions? Do the later *Letters* simply repeat the arguments of the *First Letter*, or do they elaborate or supplement them with new material? Is Locke forced to modify, revise or even retract claims made in the *First Letter*?

Modern commentators have given little attention to these questions, and when they have opinion is divided. At one extreme is the view that Proast has no case and that Locke's answers to him are unnecessary and excessively drawn out.[10] Other writers feel that Proast is making substantial points which require an answer. Most of them consider that Locke does win the debate. In Mabbott's words, Locke's case 'though made at inordinate length and with endless repetitions, is complete and effective'.[11] However, some qualify this verdict; Cranston, as we shall see, thinks Locke is forced into a major concession, while Waldron argues that Locke is unable to answer Proast adequately.[12]

Thus there is a range of opinion about the significance of Proast's arguments and about the level of Locke's success in dealing with them. Consequently, there is no agreement on the importance of Locke's later *Letters on Toleration*, and on whether reading them enhances one's understanding of the acknowledged classic, the *First Letter*. My aim in this paper is to display enough of the flavour of what Proast and Locke wrote in their controversy to enable the reader to form his or her own judgement.

PROAST'S CASE

In his First Reply, Proast accepts Locke's points that there is but one true religion, that a man must believe it to be the true religion if he is to be saved and that 'this Belief is to be wrought in men by Reason and Argument, not by Outward Force and Compulsion'.[13] None the less, Proast argues, Locke's policy of toleration – however much trade and commerce would gain from it – would not serve the interests of true religion.[14] For Proast does not agree that outward force is useless for promoting true religion and the salvation of souls.

> If Force be used, not in stead of Reason and Arguments, i.e. not to convince by its own proper Efficacy (which it cannot do,) but onely to bring men to consider those Reasons and Arguments which are proper and sufficient to convince them, but which, without being forced, they would not consider: who can deny, but that *indirectly* and *at a distance*, it does some service toward the bringing men to embrace the Truth, which otherwise, either through Carelessness and Negligence they would never acquaint themselves with, or through Prejudice they would reject and condemn unheard, under the notion of Errour?[15]

If a man is brought in this way to embrace the true religion, Proast notes, 'the True Religion ... is not the less True, for being so embraced', nor does the man's embracing of it 'lose its *Acceptableness with God*, any more then that Obedience does, which God himself drives men to by chastening and afflicting them'.[16]

Proast concedes that the use of force to bring men to the true religion and salvation would be unnecessary, and therefore could not be justified, 'if all men were but so faithful to their own Souls, as to seek the way of Saving them, with such Care and Diligence as the Importance of the matter deserves, and with Minds free from Prejudice and Passion'.[17] It is plain to Proast, however, that this is not the case, since then there would be no other religion in the world but the true religion. The very existence of a great variety of religions 'is an evident demonstration, that all Men have not sought the Truth in this matter, with that application of mind, and that freedom of Judgment, which was requisite to assure their finding it'.[18]

False religions are the result of men searching too little, and allowing their judgement to be affected by lust and passion. Proast remarks:

'Tis strange indeed: but yet whoever looks abroad into the world must see, that in this affair, the Impressions of Education, the Reverence and Admiration of Persons, Worldly respects, and the like incompetent Motives determine far greater numbers, than Reason, or such Considerations as are apt and proper to manifest the Truth of things.[19]

Furthermore, 'whatever Religion men take up without Reason, they usually adhere to it likewise without Reason'.[20] Men's conceit causes them to value the religion they choose, because they have chosen it, and to be prejudiced against any other because it is not theirs. Of course they will not admit that they choose or persist in their religion without reason, nor do they want others to think that they do. They look around for reasons: but all they seek is how to defend their own religion and attack every other, and they merely confirm their prejudices. 'And so, studying onely their own side of the Controversy, they come to be the more confirm'd in the way they have chosen, and to think they can shew that they have Reason on their side.'[21] It is, writes Proast, 'matter of common observation' that most men are impervious to reason about religion. He continues:

What means is there left (besides the Grace of God) to reduce those [men] that are got into a wrong Way, but to lay Thorns and Briars in it? that since they are deaf to all Perswasions, the uneasiness they meet with may at least put them to a stand, and encline them to lend an ear to those who tell them they have mistaken their way, and offer to show them the right.[22]

The only method which Proast thinks is possible for forcing such people to consider their religion rationally is that of laying such Penalties upon them, as may balance the weight of those Prejudices which encline them to prefer a false Way before the True, and recover them to so much Sobriety and Reflexion, as seriously to put the question to themselves, whether it be really worth the while to undergo such Inconveniences, for adhering to a Religion, which, for any thing they know, may be false, or for rejecting another (if that be the case) which for any thing they know, may be true, till they have brought to the Bar of Reason, and given it a fair Tryal there.[23]

When those concerned have already refused to be instructed or persuaded, no other method but force remains; and being necessary it is justified. There is no reason to question the success of the method, if it is rightly used, with those who are 'not altogether incurable' (those who are, 'must be left to God').[24]

However, not every kind and degree of force is justified. The force applied must

be duly *proportioned* to the Design of it. For, though upon the Considerations here offer'd, I take it to be clear in the general, that outward force is neither *useless* nor *needless* for the bringing Men to do, what the saving of their Souls may require of them: yet I do not say, that all manner of Force, or all the Degrees of it are fit to be used for this purpose. But then to determine precisely the just Measures of it, and to say upon good grounds, Thus much may fitly and reasonably be applied for the purpose we speak of, and no more; This may perhaps require some consideration. And to me, I confess, this seems to be the onely Point concerning which there is any ground for Controversy, in this whole matter.[25]

Proast expresses his 'perfect agreement' with Locke's protests against maiming, starving, torturing and killing, and concurs in the view that such cruelty is usually counter-productive.[26] But Proast is never more specific about how much force he would permit, beyond venturing this:

It may suffice to say, That so much Force, or such Penalties as are ordinarily sufficient to prevail with men of common discretion, and not desperately perverse and obstinate, to weigh matters of Religion carefully and impartially; and without which ordinarily they will not do this; so much Force, or such

Penalties may fitly and reasonably be used for the promoting true Religion in the World, and the Salvation of Souls.[27]

Having shown that 'outward Force (duly temper'd and applied)' is useful and necessary – contrary to Locke's claim – Proast next points out that it follows that Locke is also mistaken in saying that no body can have a right to use force to bring men to the true religion.[28] For we cannot suppose without impiety 'that the Wise and Benign Disposer and Governour of all things has not furnish'd Mankind with competent Means for the promoting his own Honour in the World, and the Good of Souls'.[29] So some body must have the right to apply force to promote the true religion; and Proast claims that the right is principally with the civil sovereign (what Locke calls the civil magistrate). The right is also, 'in a lower degree, in Parents, Masters of Families, Tutors', and so forth, but is not possessed by any private person, nor by any ecclesiastical officer or any church.[30]

Locke, of course, had explicitly limited the civil magistrate to the promotion of civil interests.[31] Proast agrees that 'the extent of the Magistrate's Jurisdiction is to be measured by the End for which the Commonwealth is instituted'; however, he contends that it is instituted not for civil interests alone:

if the *Spiritual* and *Eternal* Interests of men may any way be procured or advanced by Political Government; the procuring and advancing those Interests must in all reason be reckon'd among the Ends of Civil Societies, and so, consequently, fall within the compass of the Magistrate's Jurisdiction.[32]

Locke correctly states that God gave no man authority to compel another to his religion.[33] Yet this is irrelevant: Proast does not seek to force men to a religion, but simply to 'make them *bethink* themselves, and put it out of the power of any foolish Humour, or unreasonable Prejudice, to alienate them from the Truth or their own Happiness'.[34] All the right that the sovereign has is

onely an Authority to procure all his Subjects the means of Discovering the Way of Salvation, and to procure withal, as much as in him lies, that none remain ignorant of it, or refuse to embrace it, either for want of using those means, or by reason of any such Prejudices as may render them ineffectual.[35]

That authority – though not the right to compel another to his religion – may certainly be committed to the sovereign by God.

Proast also challenges Locke's assertion that the power to compel in religious matters cannot be vested in the magistrate by the people's consent because no one can blindly leave his salvation to the choice of another. To this Proast objects that if, under his scheme, the people give the magistrate the power to bring men 'to take such care as they ought of their own Salvation', this does not mean that they are abandoning the care of their salvation but the opposite:

> For if men, in choosing their Religion, are so generally subject, as has been shewed, when left wholly to themselves, to be so much swayed by Prejudice and Passion, as either not at all, or not sufficiently to regard the Reasons and Motives which ought alone to determine their Choice: then it is every man's true Interest, not to be wholly left to himself in this matter, but that care should be taken, that in an affair of so vast Concernment to him, he may be brought even against his own inclination, if it cannot be done otherwise (which is ordinarily the case) to act according to Reason and sound Judgment. And then what better course can men take to provide for this, then by vesting the Power I have described, in him who bears the Sword?[36]

Locke says that the magistrate's power consists in outward force, and that the understanding cannot be compelled to belief by force; thus the magistrate cannot force a man to his religion. This is correct. And it establishes, Proast urges, that what the magistrate *can* do, and what in the end he alone can do exactly because it requires force, is to dispose men 'to submit to Instruction, and give a fair Hearing to the Reasons which are offer'd, for the enlightenment of their minds and discovering the Truth to them'.[37] To this extent the 'care of Souls' must fall within the magistrate's jurisdiction.

Next, Proast considers Locke's objection that different princes uphold different religions. If magistrates enforced their own religion men would be obliged to abandon what their own reason and conscience told them; and in most cases men would follow their princes in the ways that lead to destruction. Proast finds this irrelevant. He does not argue that men should quit their own religion for the religion of the prince under whom they happen to be born – he is certainly not advocating the promotion by force of false religion. He writes:

The Power I ascribe to the Magistrate, is given him, to bring men, not to his *own*, but to the *true* Religion: And tho' (as our Author puts us in mind) *the Religion of every Prince is Orthodox to himself*, yet if this Power keep within its bounds, it *can* serve the Interest of no other Religion but the true, among such as have any concern for their Eternal Salvation; (and those that have none, deserve not to be consider'd;) Because the penalties that it enables him that has it to inflict, are not such as may tempt such Persons either to renounce a Religion which they believe to be true, or to profess one which they do not believe to be so; but only such as are apt to put them upon a serious and impartial examination of the Controversy between the Magistrate and them: which is the way for them to come to the knowledge of the Truth. And if, upon such examination of the matter, they chance to find that the Truth does not lie on the Magistrate's side; they have gained thus much however, even by the Magistrate's misapplying his Power, that they know better than they did before, where the Truth does lie: And all the hurt that comes to them by it, is only the suffering some tolerable Inconveniences for their following *the Light of their own Reason, and the dictates of their own Consciences*: which certainly is no such Mischief to Mankind, as to make it more eligible that there should be no such Power vested in the Magistrate, but *the Care of every man's Soul should be left to himself alone*, (as this Authour demands it should be:) That is, that every man should be suffered, quietly, and without the least molestation, either to take no care at all of his Soul, if he be so pleased, or in doing it, to follow his own groundless Prejudices, or unaccountable Humour, or any crafty Seducer whom he may think fit to take for his Guid.[38]

Thus on balance it is far better that magistrates use moderate force, for men's own good, to bring them to think carefully about their religion. Even if a magistrate enforces a religion which is false – an abuse of his power for which he will answer to God, Proast emphasizes in his Second Reply – men with the true religion who suffer the penalties are compensated by being brought to a deeper knowledge of the truth of their religion.

Finally, Proast accuses Locke of a fundamental fallacy in his argument:

whereas his Design obliged him to shew, That all manner of outward Force is utterly useless to the purpose of bringing men to seek the Truth with that Care and Diligence, and that freedom of Judgment which they ought to use, that so they may find and embrace it, and attain Salvation by it: which would have been a good Foundation for his Conclusion: instead of attempting *that*, he has contented himself with making a good Declamation upon the Impossibility of doing that by outward Force, which can onely be done by Reason and Argument; and upon the Inhumanity, as well as Absurdity, of using *Fire and Sword* and Capital Punishments, *to convince mens minds of Errour, and inform them of the Truth*. Which was much more easie to be done. . . .[39]

Thus Proast's critique has a sharp sting in the tail.

LOCKE'S REJOINDERS AND THEIR SUCCESS

These, then, are the main points in Proast's First Reply, reaffirmed without much development in the Second Reply, and they provide the issues in contention. As their controversy proceeds, other disagreements surface, for example over the reasons for the success of Christianity in the early centuries, especially the role of miracles. However these are subsidiary and I shall ignore them in order to concentrate on the utility and legitimacy of the magistrate's use of force in religious matters. These are the central issues in dispute.

Locke had to take Proast's pamphlet seriously, as the summary of it should have begun to make clear. The Toleration Act had now been passed (May 1689), but without improving matters in key respects. It did not provide the full and equal toleration Locke sought; it only granted limited indulgence, with those indulged remaining under various disabilities and with indulgence denied to Unitarians (towards whom Locke showed particular sympathy) and to Deists. Moreover, Locke surely would have regarded the degree of toleration established as precarious, after his lifetime's experience of political upheaval and reversal (it is only with hindsight that the revolutionary settlement can be viewed as inaugurating stability). Although in such a case we can never know an author's motives completely, it is reasonable to suppose that Locke would think it still necessary to argue for toleration as strenuously as possible, both to secure what had been gained and to achieve the fuller toleration he wanted.

If these were Locke's hopes and intentions, then Proast's arguments threatened them. His clarity, reasonable tone and stress on moderation made his arguments dangerously appealing. Proast writes that he does not wish to argue against the toleration Locke espouses, only to enquire whether Locke is able to prove his case for that toleration.[40] However in the course of undermining Locke's case Proast provides a justification for withdrawing the recent indulgences; while his eschewal of the severities which had marred state enforcement of religion previously, removes one obstacle to accepting his policy. Proast appears to mean well. He is a concerned do-gooder, advocating the use of the law to encourage men to do something which is for their own good. He cannot bear to stand by and take no action, when the matter is so important and there is ready to hand this method of helping others to save their souls by getting them to think about it carefully. Proast's position is not wholly implausible or unconvincing. How, then, does Locke go about demolishing this obstacle to the toleration he himself recommends?

Locke opens the *Second Letter* by noting that Proast accepts that force 'is improper to convert men to any religion', and immediately adds: 'Toleration is but the removing that force.'[41] It follows, Locke claims, that by assigning to the magistrate the use of force, even in moderation, Proast favours 'some remains of persecution'.[42] Locke hopes to reason him out of this 'prejudice'. The correct approach to such questions, Locke declares, is 'to see how they will prove when they are reduced into practice'.[43] That is, we can assess the merits of a proposal when we have examined the consequences of implementing it. Now Locke concedes that force is not utterly useless for promoting true religion. It is possible, occasionally and by accident, that it may lead to a man saving his soul: God in his goodness has seen to that. However Locke's estimate of the rarity and unpredictability of such an occurrence is well-conveyed by one of his examples – 'running a man through may save his life, as it has done by chance, opening a lurking imposthume'.[44] Furthermore, the imposition of penalties by the magistrate will produce 'other effects, contrary effects . . . and so may serve to keep men from the truth and from salvation'; for we must consider 'not only what it may, but what it is likely to produce: and the greater good or harm like to come from it, ought to determine the use of it'.[45] Locke's overall contention is that when all the effects are calculated the bad far outweigh the good, so that it proves more reasonable on Proast's own criteria *not* to use force.

The 'contrary' effects which Locke identifies in the *Second* and *Third Letters*, which may be taken together, can be placed into three principal categories. Locke argues that Proast's proposal is impracticable, illegitimate and epistemologically unsound. This is my categorization, not Locke's; it produces some reordering of Locke's discussion but without, I think, distorting it. I shall look at each category in turn, selecting a prominent example or two. In both respects I am sacrificing the density and richness of Locke's treatment, because a simplified account helps to bring out its main features while sufficing to allow us to judge its success against Proast.

First, then, Locke contends that Proast's scheme for exacting moderate penalties to force men to consider the reasons for adopting the true religion is impracticable. How, for instance, could the magistrate decide whether a man had considered the reasons? Since Proast supposes the magistrate to have the true religion, and the true religion to be such that anyone who considers the reasons for it will be convinced, the only evidence of careful consideration would be acceptance of the magistrate's religion. Proast would end up penalizing any who dissented from the national religion. In effect, men would be punished not for lack of serious consideration of their religion but for dissent, for not reaching the same conclusion as the magistrate. Yet some dissenters might have considered very carefully; and some conformists might not have considered at all. Again, how much and how often would a man be punished? Proast cannot stop at moderate penalties, as he thinks. If the initial, mild penalty does not make a man conform, that shows that he has not considered carefully enough and a severer penalty becomes necessary and permissible. Locke charges: 'you having set no time, nor bounds to this consideration of arguments and reasons, short of being convinced; you, under another pretence, put into the magistrate's hands, as much power to force men to his religion, as any the openest persecutors can pretend to'; and tells Proast that he cannot assign any bounds to his penalties 'because your principles, whatever your words deny, will carry you to those degrees of severity, which in profession you condemn'.[46] In other words, the scheme of *moderate* penalties to make men *consider* their religion simply cannot be put into practice.

Second, Locke attacks the legitimacy of Proast's proposal. In particular, Locke stands by his argument that the magistrate can have no authority to use force in matters of religion. The scriptures give that to no one. They instruct us only to preach, and to leave if our words are rejected. Nor can Proast claim that enforcement is justified because it is necessary, since we do have the alternative of preaching. Moreover, even if force *were* indirectly useful for promoting religion, usefulness cannot make an unlawful act lawful. That would be a very dangerous argument, justifying too much. For instance, many men endanger their souls by abandoning themselves to lust, so castrating the lascivious to make them chaste might indirectly lead to their salvation. But, he asks Proast,

> will you say, from such an usefulness as this, because it may, indirectly and at a distance, conduce to the saving of any of his subjects' souls, that therefore the magistrate has a right to do it, and may by force make his subjects eunuchs for the kingdom of heaven? It is not for the magistrate, or any body else, upon an imagination of its usefulness, to make use of any other means for the salvation of men's souls than what the author and finisher of our faith hath directed. You may be mistaken in what you think useful.[47]

Finally, it is wrong to allege that the magistrate is given the authority to use force when civil society is instituted. Locke offers a series of reasons in the *Second* and *Third Letters*: being forced in matters of religion could never have been part of the *design* of civil society, since men could save their souls for themselves *without* civil society, and since any benefit from the magistrate's use of force would be gained *accidentally*; holding a different religion does no one else any real harm so its suppression by force could not be intended by those entering the commonwealth; and having a religion forced on one is 'an injury which in the state of nature every one would avoid', therefore since protection from such injuries is the aim of a commonwealth, 'every man has a right to toleration'.[48]

Let us pause to consider what Locke believes would be the results of implementing Proast's proposal, given the defects he has urged against it. Such improper use of force will turn not only the sufferers, but also the bystanders, against the religion of the magistrate. If, as Proast supposes, the magistrate is of the true religion, this will hinder the true religion. In addition, it is 'those who have nothing of religion at all', and 'the vicious, the ignorant, the worldling, and the hypocrite' who will most easily be driven into the magistrate's church, all for the wrong reasons.[49] For Locke can see no way of checking that dissenters who conform have done so from having considered and been rationally persuaded. Force cannot produce conviction: what it can produce is conformity, and that is no gain to true religion but a liability. Locke writes:

> This at least is certain, that where punishments pursue men, like outlying deer, only to the pale of the national church; and, when once they are within that, leave them free there and at ease; it can do no service to the true religion. . . . For there being no necessity that men should leave either their vices or corruption, or so much as their ignorance, to get within the pale of the church; force, your way applied, serves only to bring them . . . to the profession, not to the knowledge, belief, or practice, of the true religion.[50]

Proast's policy can only do harm, it could not succeed: is it not 'utterly impertinent so to lay penalties on men, to make them consider, when they can avoid those penalties without considering?'[51]

There is a further and crucial dimension to the evil effects of what Proast proposes. In this matter we must concern ourselves with all mankind, all men being God's creation, and with every state. We need a policy which holds everywhere, for that is 'a good mark of truth'. Locke continues:

> For I shall always suspect that neither to comport with the truth of religion nor the design of the Gospel, which is suited to only some one country, or party. What is true and good in England, will be true and good at Rome too, in China, or Geneva.[52]

Proast's policy fails this universalizability test. In the huge majority of cases force would be exercised by a magistrate whose religion was false, since it is those with a false religion who are more likely to resort to force, the true religion being tolerant; and since only one magistrate in ten or a hundred (in a thousand, by the *Fourth Letter*) is of the true religion. Yet every magistrate, believing that his religion is true, would be entitled to force men to conform – including those who had dissented because theirs really was the true religion. Even if Proast's policy benefited true religion where it was the national religion – which Locke denies it would, on balance – it would severely impede it everywhere else.

All of these are powerful lines of argument, but they are not conclusive. Proast always insists that minimum force is to be used, and never execution and other extremes. He always accuses Locke of exaggerating the drawbacks and grossly understating the benefits. Again, the aptness of Locke's examples is contestable: are running a man through and castration comparable to the small fines Proast seems to have in mind? At this level, the dispute is over the balance of good and harm which would be done by using force in the way suggested. This is an empirical question, involving the sizing up of probabilities in a very approximate way, and a definitive conclusion is unobtainable. In fact Locke's answer, that Proast's penalties would not have led men to change their beliefs, may well have been right; Dunn thinks that, 'in the historical context', Locke's stand was 'a plausible extrapolation from the religious and political history of England over the preceding thirty years'.[53] But how could Locke prove that? Nor are the protagonists in the debate going to be able to settle the legitimacy of the policy. Proast admits it lacks scriptural authority, but asserts that it is sanctioned by the law of nature which is God's law too.[54] Locke responds that the law of nature only commissions a magistrate to do what is good.[55] This objection begs the question since Proast is contending that forcing men to consider their religion *is* good. Further, it has been remarked by Gough that Proast could have reinforced his case by adding that even when forcing dissenters to conform to the true religion does not bring them to believe it, it prevents them from corrupting those who do believe.[56] In short, if we consider the first two categories of Locke's arguments, we do not find a knock-out blow (though we may feel he is ahead on points). For that, we have to turn to the third, epistemological category.

Locke thinks that Proast's whole case rests on a single implicit assumption: 'you build all you say, upon this lurking supposition, that the national religion now in England, backed by the public authority of the law, is the only true religion'.[57] In his Second Reply Proast gladly acknowledges that he knows that the religion of the Church of England is the sole true religion (and writes that Locke ought to acknowledge it too, since 'you own yourself of the Church of *England*').[58] To Locke's mind, making that assumption has two disastrous consequences. First, it leads Proast to think that, every other religion being false, no other religion deserves toleration; and again, Proast later admits to this view:

all who have sufficient means of Instruction provided for them, may justly be punish'd for not being of the *National Religion*, where the true, is the National Religion: because it is a fault in all such, not to be of that Religion.[59]

Second, as we mentioned, if the magistrate in England is justified in enforcing the national religion so is the magistrate in every other country, since every magistrate believes his to be the true religion. Thus Proast's case permits persecution not simply in England but throughout the entire world, always in Locke's opinion at the cost of true religion. Therefore it is crucial that Locke should show how groundless is Proast's confidence – shared, of course, by adherents of many different and opposed churches and sects – that his, and his alone, is the true religion. This Locke sets out to do in a number of passages in the *Third Letter*.

Locke insists that in order for a magistrate to be able to perform the duty Proast alleges he has, he would have to *know* that his religion is the one true religion. Otherwise, he could not be certain that he was not abusing his power, that he was providing dissenters with the reasons and arguments sufficient to convince them, or that men were at fault for not conforming. However, none of us, magistrates *not* excepted, can have such knowledge.

> To you and me the Christian religion is the true, and that is built, to mention no other articles of it, on this, that Jesus Christ was put to death at Jerusalem, and rose again from the dead. Now do you or I know this? I do not ask with what assurance we believe it, for that in the highest degree not being knowledge, is not what we now inquire after. Can any magistrate demonstrate to himself . . . not only all the articles of his church, but the fundamental ones of the Christian religion? For whatever is not capable of demonstration, as such remote matters of fact are not, is not, unless it be self-evident, capable to produce knowledge, how well grounded and great soever the assurance of faith may be wherewith it is received; but faith it is still, and not knowledge; persuasion, and not certainty. This is the highest the nature of the thing will permit us to go in matters of revealed religion, which are therefore called matters of faith: a persuasion of our own minds, short of knowledge, is the last result that determines us in such truths.[60]

Since it is impossible for the magistrate to have the kind of knowledge which Proast's scheme requires, the magistrate will never be in a condition to exercise the power Proast gives him.[61] Here is the final blow, an impracticability grounded in an epistemological argument, which finishes off Proast's case conclusively. The only rejoinder Proast makes is the unsubstantiated assertion that, although there cannot be 'demonstration', the magistrate can believe his religion to be true 'upon just and sufficient grounds', so that he has 'Knowledge' or 'Full Assurance'.[62]

Nevertheless, it might be objected that Locke has now done as much damage to his own case as to Proast's. For instance Cranston writes of Locke being 'forced . . . to acknowledge a more sceptical attitude towards religion as such than he had previously admitted', because religion is a matter of belief not knowledge and belief can be false.[63] How can Locke hope to destroy Proast's claim to have knowledge about which is the true religion, without weakening his own claim that there is a true religion? I think his solution lies in two moves: the old distinction between what is necessary for salvation and what is indifferent, and closely related to this, a distinction between the true religion and the churches which uphold it. Both distinctions are already prominent in the *First Letter*. Locke also implies there that men cannot know which is the true religion, but makes little of it.[64] I think this is simply because his case there emphasizes the magistrate's lack of any knowledge greater than the individual's, and particularly the impossibility of producing sincere belief by force anyway. Proast's proposal to some extent succeeds in its design of bypassing the second objection, so that in order to refute it Locke has to adjust his emphasis and make more of the underlying epistemological objection. If this is correct, one should not see Locke as driven into conceding greater scepticism but rather as reorganizing his defence of toleration to meet a specific attack from a new direction.

How exactly does the fresh defensive move work? How can Locke deny that there can be knowledge of the true religion, without enfeebling the very idea of a true religion? Locke distinguishes between what we must believe if we are to save our souls, and the specific ceremonies and institutions of particular churches. The first is revealed to us in the scriptures. Locke states this several times in the *Letters on Toleration* without giving details. In 1695 he published *The Reasonableness of Christianity* (again, anonymously) which sets out in full the 'doctrine of salvation' he finds in the scriptures.[65] It is sometimes said that Locke reduces Christianity to one tenet, belief that Jesus is the Messiah; and indeed in places Locke gives this as the 'single truth' we need to believe to be saved.[66] However, the meaning of this truth has to be spelt out in two respects. First, what must be accepted is a whole nest of connected beliefs: that Jesus is the Messiah, the Son of God, i.e. the Saviour who will remit our sins; that he worked miracles; and that he was resurrected. Further, a man must already believe that there is only one true God, and that he will perform his promises. Second, as well as belief, certain action is required. To gain remission of sins, one must repent; and then follow to the best of one's ability the moral rules laid down by the law of Moses, as clarified by Jesus, and by 'the law of nature, knowable by reason'.[67] Faith and repentance, that is, believing Jesus is the Messiah and all that entails, and living a good life, are the joint indispensable conditions of obtaining salvation.[68]

Now Proast can hardly challenge Locke's assumption that God has revealed the one road to heaven in the scriptures; this is not in dispute in their controversy, so Locke does not need to justify it. His own view is clearly stated elsewhere. In the *Essay Concerning Human Understanding* he argues that we can know God's existence with certainty because it can be rationally demonstrated.[69] On the other hand, we cannot have knowledge of what God reveals to us in the scriptures.[70] However, being the testimony of God, who 'cannot deceive, nor be deceived', it 'carries with it Assurance beyond Doubt, Evidence beyond Exception', and 'as absolutely determines our Minds, and as perfectly excludes all wavering as our Knowledge it self; and we may as well doubt of our own Being, as we can, whether any Revelation from GOD be true'.[71] Of course, 'we must be sure, that it be a divine Revelation, and that we understand it right'.[72] In the case of the scriptural prescription for salvation, Locke would be confident that it is a revelation from God; while he writes *The Reasonableness of Christianity* precisely to fix the right understanding of it by textual analysis.

In other words, in denying that the magistrate can *know* which is the true religion, Locke is not relinquishing or endangering any of his own beliefs in the essentials of Christianity. Next let us turn to the differing practices, the ceremonies and institutions, of the various churches and sects. There is no possibility of knowledge about such matters: nor can we have any assured faith based on revelation to substitute for the lack of knowledge. In his exhaustive search of the scriptures Locke finds that Jesus specifies no details of worship, and all we can conclude is that God should be worshipped 'in spirit and truth, with application of mind and sincerity of heart', and that public ceremonies should be decent, orderly and edifying.[73] For example, we are instructed to baptize, but not that it should be done with the signing of the cross.[74] The latter is the kind of detail which each church has established for itself: it is a 'ceremony of human institution' which 'could not be known' and which, because it is something in its own nature 'indifferent' (neither prescribed nor prohibited by the law of God), cannot 'be known necessary to salvation'.[75]

In these indifferent matters of ceremonial, Locke is happy to establish that there is no possibility of reaching firm and assured conclusions. That stance in no way weakens his claims concerning the core truths of religion. At the same time recognizing our ignorance in the area of things indifferent is an essential part of the foundation of his case for toleration.[76] For in many cases what divide churches and sects are no more than trivial disagreements over ceremonial, concerning 'things not necessary to salvation', matters where we should maintain 'charity and brotherly kindness with the diversity of opinion'.[77] Churches which disagree over indifferent matters may none the less agree upon the infinitely more important truths necessary for salvation.[78] Locke's crucial point here is that the true religion is not confined to one church: there is a plurality of churches with the true religion. Proast has fallen into the trap of thinking that his is the *only* church with the true religion, and consequently condemns every other church as having a false religion: in fact other churches too may have the true religion, linked with ceremonials which are different yet not inconsistent with salvation. Then their religions are as true as his.[79] Once Locke has established that there can be a plurality of churches with the true religion, he has shown that Proast's 'lurking supposition' that his church has exclusive possession of true religion is indefensible.[80]

Having argued in these various ways that Proast's proposal is impracticable, Locke believes he has completely vindicated his policy of toleration. However, I must not leave the impression that Locke thinks that nothing can be done about the extremely serious problem of men's neglect of their souls. He concurs with Proast's observation that the problem is common.[81] He himself writes elsewhere that great error arises because most men give their assent in matters of religious faith on the basis of 'the Opinion of others' and never examine their opinions, holding them all the more firmly for that.[82] He also points out how hard it is to shift some men,

'Enthusiasts', from what they adopt without thought as their 'principles', however erroneous and irrational.[83] Locke can hardly dissent from Proast's diagnosis, then: instead he has challenged the remedy proposed. Locke is convinced that force, exercised by the magistrate or anyone else, cannot on balance do good; but this does not mean that no good can be done. The clergy such as Proast should preach to all who pay insufficient attention to their salvation, whether dissenters or conformists. Nor should they rely on church sermons but should conduct 'friendly and Christian debates with them at their houses,' and use 'the gentle methods of the Gospel . . . in private conversation' – provided their attentions are not rejected, for they may not force themselves on anyone.[84] Men should be directed to the scriptures to find their beliefs for themselves.[85] None of this falls to the magistrate. But the magistrate does have a role. He can properly act to reduce the temptation to follow a false religion – attractive to corrupt men because it allows them to pursue their passions – by legislating against the depraved and pleasant life. He should act severely against drunkenness, lasciviousness, debauchery, fraud and injustice, and by punishment, administration and example

> reduce the irregularities of men's manners into order, and bring sobriety, peaceableness, industry, and honesty into fashion. This is their proper business every where; and for this they have a commission from God, both by the light of nature and revelation; and by this removing the great counterpoise, which lies in strictness of life, and is so strong a bias, with the greatest part, against the true religion, they would cast the balance on that side. For if men were forced by the magistrate to live sober, honest, and strict lives, whatever their religion were, would not the advantage be on the side of truth, when the gratifying of their lusts were not to be obtained by forsaking her? In men's lives lies the main obstacle to right opinions in religion. . . .[86]

So Locke himself thinks the magistrate should 'indirectly' promote religion. His keenness to legislate morality may be surprising. However, as Cranston points out, it is a mistake to class Locke, particularly Locke after 1688, as a minimal statist who confines the function of the state to the protection of life, liberty and estate, because he 'also thought it included the promotion of the public good'.[87]

CONCLUSION

At the end of the three later *Letters* Locke is as adamant as before that force should never be used in matters of religion. In the controversy he exhibits the same robust common sense and pragmatism as in the *First Letter*. Most of the arguments he uses are already present there. Locke's strategy in his initial *Letter* seems to be to amass as many arguments as possible so that he makes his position defensible against attack from any direction. If one argument fails, or fails to convince, he has a further argument ready. Proast mounts an assault which Locke had not anticipated.[88] Proast's proposal outflanks Locke's main line of defence, that it is impossible to force men to *believe*, by suggesting instead that one force men to *consider* their beliefs. Locke has to admit that this *is* possible. But he claims that it would be ineffective, and that the magistrate has no authority to attempt it. These counters are disputable. More powerful, indeed conclusive, is Locke's argument that no man can possess the kind of certain knowledge which would be necessary if Proast's scheme, by his own account of it, were to be effective and legitimate.

In order to provide this decisive refutation of Proast's case, Locke has to reorganize the defences set out in the *First Letter*. Accordingly some of its arguments receive less emphasis in the later *Letters* and some, notably the limits to our knowledge in this whole area, receive more. The later *Letters* are impressive for Locke's energy and ingenuity in his dogged pursuit of his opponent, but not for the introduction of major new arguments. Reading the later *Letters* makes one more familiar with Locke's case for toleration but does not fundamentally alter one's understanding of it.

Finally, I should like to comment on Locke's style. Modern commentators have unanimously condemned it.[89] To the modern reader from whom the topic of the dispute is distant, the discussion no doubt is protracted and tedious. Locke goes through his opponent's writing systematically and takes it point by every single point, scrutinizing each thoroughly for ambiguity, vagueness, equivocation or circularity. Every fault is noted in detail, and every correction or reply is elaborately supported and justified. Locke holds that *every* argument must be examined: not to do so is to answer 'by specimen'.[90] When he finds one of his arguments not dealt with by Proast, he does not merely mention that but prints the argument again for consideration, filling nearly eight pages on one occasion in the *Third Letter*. Always the arguments for and the arguments against must be set out, so that the reader must judge for himself: often Locke prints his own and Proast's words side by side in two columns. The objective is to decide in the light of what is rational, and for the author to give the reader reason to agree with him. The author may not act as if his judgement were infallible. He must try to reach a position which, being rational, will appeal to all men. Thus the argument, and every side of it, must be displayed in full. There is, I think, a very important general lesson to be learned from this. Questions of toleration are of vital importance and must always be treated rationally and at full length. They must be examined impartially, carefully and comprehensively, both in themselves and in the light of their probable outcomes. This must be done even if it is time-consuming and boring. It is the mark of philosophy to test every argument and to follow it to its conclusion. Locke deserves great credit for meeting this exacting standard so highly. He wields the weapons of philosophy to great effect in his *Letters on Toleration*. These weapons are still needed urgently in discussions of toleration and related public issues, and we can admire and learn from Locke's expertise and stamina in exercising them.[91]

NOTES

1   Oxford 1690; licensed 9 April 1690.
2   M. Cranston, *John Locke: A Biography* (London 1957), p. 331.
3   John Locke, *A Second Letter Concerning Toleration. To the Author of the Argument of the Letter concerning Toleration, briefly consider'd and answer'd* (London 1690; licensed 24 June 1690). Page references are to *The Works of John Locke. A New Edition, corrected*, vol. VI (London 1823).
4   Jonas Proast, *A Third Letter concerning Toleration: In Defense of The Argument of the Letter concerning Toleration, briefly Consider'd and Answer'd* (Oxford 1691; licensed 21 February 1691).
5   John Locke, *A Third Letter for Toleration. To the Author of the Third Letter concerning Toleration* (London 1692; licensed 20 June 1692). Page references are to *Works of John Locke*, op cit., vol. VI.
6   Proast, *A Third Letter concerning Toleration*, op cit., p. 78.
7   Jonas Proast, *A Second Letter to the Author of the Three Letters for Toleration. From the Author of the Argument of the Letter concerning Toleration, Briefly Consider'd and Answer'd. And of the Defence of it. With a Postscript, taking some Notice of the Two Passages in 'The Rights of the Protestant Dissenters'* (Oxford 1704; licensed 19 June 1704).
8   ibid., p. 18.
9   John Locke, *A Fourth Letter for Toleration*, in *Posthumous Works of Mr. John Locke* (London 1706). Two omitted pages were supplied from the

manuscript by Lord King, *Life of Locke*, 2 vols (London 1829), vol. ii, pp. 360–1, and incorporated by Alexander Murray, *Four Letters on Toleration by John Locke* (London 1870). Page references are to *Works of John Locke*, op cit., vol. VI.

10 J. F. Stephen, 'Locke on Toleration', in J. F. Stephen, *Horae Sabbaticae. Reprint of Articles Contributed to 'The Saturday Review'*. 2nd series (London 1892), pp. 158–9.

11 Cranston, op cit., p. 182. All the commentators agree that Locke's style is dull, repetitious and prolix: Stephen, *Horae Sabbaticae*, op cit., pp. 158–60; S. P. Lamprecht, *The Moral and Political Philosophy of John Locke* (New York 1918), p. 152; and Cranston, op cit., p. 368, who makes the drastic suggestion that the *Third Letter* 'would probably have been better if it had been a quarter of its length'.

12 For Waldron's account, see section VIII of 'Locke: toleration and the rationality of persecution', above, esp. pp. 98–124.

13 Proast, *The Argument of the Letter concerning Toleration*, op cit., p. 3.

14 ibid., p. 2.

15 ibid., p. 4.

16 ibid., pp. 5–6.

17 ibid., p. 6.

18 ibid., p. 7.

19 ibid., p. 8.

20 ibid., p. 8.

21 ibid., pp. 9–10.

22 ibid., pp. 10–11.

23 ibid., p. 11.

24 ibid., p. 12.

25 ibid., p. 12.

26 Proast (ibid., pp. 12–13) quotes approvingly Locke's attacks on persecution by fire and sword in *A Letter Concerning Toleration*.

27 Proast, *The Argument of the Letter concerning Toleration*, op cit., pp. 14–15. In *A Third Letter concerning Toleration* Proast reaffirms that he means only 'the lowest and most moderate [penalties] that can be assigned', op cit., pp. 1–2.

28 Proast, *The Argument of the Letter concerning Toleration*, op cit., p. 15.

29 ibid., p. 16.

30 ibid., pp. 16–17.

31 ibid., p. 17, citing *A Letter Concerning Toleration*, pp. 17–18.

32 Proast, *The Argument of the Letter concerning Toleration*, op cit., pp. 18–19.

33 ibid., p. 21, citing *A Letter Concerning Toleration*, p. 18.

34 Proast, *The Argument of the Letter concerning Toleration*, op cit., pp. 20–1.

35 ibid., p. 21.

36 ibid., pp. 22–3.

37 ibid., pp. 23–4, and quotation from p. 13.

38 ibid., pp. 26–7. Proast uses italics not only for emphasis but also, as on three occasions in this passage, to indicate verbatim or near-verbatim quotations (from the *Letter Concerning Toleration*, pp. 37, 19, 28 and 42).

39 Proast, *The Argument of the Letter concerning Toleration*, op cit., pp. 27–8. The quotations are from *A Letter Concerning Toleration*, p. 25.
40 Proast, *The Argument of the Letter concerning Toleration*, op cit., p. 3.
41 Locke, *Second Letter*, op cit., p. 62.
42 ibid., pp. 61–2.
43 ibid., p. 62.
44 ibid., p. 69. Locke actually uses this example to illustrate the point that usefulness cannot make an unlawful act lawful.
45 ibid., p. 70.
46 ibid., p. 77; Locke, *Third Letter* op cit., p. 281. Locke's most extensive discussion of the extent of penalties is in ibid., ch. iv.
47 Locke, *Second Letter*, op cit., p. 81. For Locke's response to Proast's reply on this point see Locke, *Third Letter*, op cit., pp. 486–7.
48 ibid., p. 212. See Locke, *Second Letter*, op cit., p. 119, and Locke, *Third Letter*, op cit., ch. II. Locke does not develop the idea of a *right* to toleration.
49 Locke, *Second Letter*, op cit., p. 115; and on the danger of producing conformity rather than conviction see generally Locke, *Third Letter*, op cit., ch. 7.
50 ibid., p. 379.
51 ibid., p. 383.
52 Locke, *Second Letter*, op cit., p. 95. Locke several times complains that Proast argues for a party – the Church of England – not the truth (e.g., p. 137, and Locke, *Third Letter*, op cit., pp. 542–4).
53 John Dunn, *The Political Thought of John Locke. An Historical Account of the Argument of the 'Two Treatises of Government'* (Cambridge 1969) p. 33, n. 1.
54 Proast, *A Third Letter concerning Toleration*, op cit., pp. 31, 35.
55 Locke, *Third Letter*, op cit., p. 495.
56 J. W. Gough, 'Introduction' to *John Locke, Epistola de Tolerantia. A Letter on Toleration*, edited by R. Klibansky, translation by J. W. Gough (Oxford 1968), p. 33.
57 Locke, *Second Letter*, op cit., p. 65.
58 Proast, *A Third Letter concerning Toleration*, op cit., p. 11.
59 ibid., p. 20. Proast reaffirms that he would punish dissenters not for the fault of dissent but for the purpose of convincing them (p. 24).
60 Locke, *Third Letter*, op cit., p. 144; note too p. 421:

> The articles of my religion, and of a great many such other short-sighted people as I am, are articles of faith, which we think there are so good grounds to believe, that we are persuaded to venture our eternal happiness on that belief. . . . But we neither think that God requires, nor has given us faculties capable of knowing in this world several of those truths which are to be believed to salvation.

Locke repeats brief descriptions of knowledge and faith in *Fourth Letter*, op cit., p. 558. There is no sustained analysis of the epistemological argument in the *Letters*: for that, one turns to John Locke, *An Essay Concerning Human Understanding* (London 1689; 4th edn 1700), edited by Peter H. Nidditch (Oxford 1975; corrected reprint 1979).

61 Locke, *Third Letter*, op cit., p. 180.
62 Proast, *A Second Letter to the Author of the Three Letters for Toleration*, op cit., pp. 4–6.
63 Cranston, op cit., p. 367; likewise Gough, 'Introduction' to Locke, *Epistola de Tolerantia*, op cit., p. 31.
64 *A Letter Concerning Toleration*, e.g. pp. 30–6 for the former, and p. 24 for the latter.
65 John Locke, *The Reasonableness of Christianity, as delivered in the Scriptures* (London 1695), p. 3. Page references are to *Works of John Locke*, op cit., vol. VII.
66 E.g. ibid., p. 26.
67 ibid., pp. 103, 105, 50; the quote is from p. 13. The moral precepts are listed, pp. 115–21.
68 ibid., e.g. pp. 105, 122–3.
69 For the demonstration see Locke, *Essay*, op cit., bk IV, ch. x. Demonstrative knowledge is less certain than 'intuitive' or self-evident knowledge but more certain than 'sensitive' or empirical knowledge: see ibid., bk IV, ch. ii and ch. ix, sect. 2.
70 It cannot be intuited (i.e. it is not self-evident), it cannot be demonstrated (as a mathematical proposition can be proved) and it cannot be empirically verified by the senses – these are the three kinds of knowledge Locke allows.
71 Locke, *Essay*, op cit., bk IV, ch. xvi, sect. 14, p. 667.
72 ibid., bk IV, ch. xvi, sect. 14, p. 667; see further chs xviii and xix on the problems involved.
73 Locke, *Reasonableness of Christianity*, op cit., p. 148; see too Locke, *Third Letter*, op cit., pp. 156–8.
74 ibid., pp. 154–6.
75 ibid., p. 145.
76 For a plea for intellectual humility in the light of the limits to our knowledge, and in effect for toleration of differences of opinion, see Locke, *Essay*, op cit., bk IV, ch. xvi, sect. 4.
77 Locke, *Third Letter*, op cit., pp. 238, 237, and note pp. 237–40; and *A Letter Concerning Toleration*, above, pp. 53–6 on heresy and schism.
78 Locke, *Third Letter*, op cit., p. 327.
79 ibid., p. 328; also p. 320. A church may also contain all that is necessary to salvation, yet add things *inconsistent* with salvation so that it has not true religion – for instance the Roman Catholic Church (pp. 122–3). This of course fits exactly with his grounds for refusing to extend toleration to Roman Catholics in the *First Letter* (pp. 45–7).
80 Locke, *Third Letter*, op cit., pp. 332–3.
81 Locke, *Second Letter*, op cit., pp. 93, 129.
82 Locke, *Essay*, op cit., bk IV, ch. xv, sect. 6, ch. xvi, sect. 3, ch. xx, sect. 18.
83 ibid., bk IV, ch. xix, esp. sects 8–10.
84 Locke, *Second Letter*, op cit., p. 86; see pp. 82, 85–6; and Locke, *Third Letter*, op cit. pp. 433–4.
85 Locke, *Second Letter*, op cit., p. 130.

86 Locke, *Third Letter*, op cit., p. 469. See too the passages quoted from the *Second* and *Third Letters* by Cranston, 'John Locke and the case for toleration', above pp. 78–97.

87 ibid., p. 94, instancing Locke's mercantilism.

88 He tells Proast at one point: 'The author [i.e. himself in the *First Letter*] was not writing against your new hypothesis before it was known in the world': *Second Letter*, op cit., p. 123.

89 See the references in n. 11 above.

90 Locke, *Fourth Letter*, op cit., pp. 550–1.

91 I am grateful to David Edwards, John Horton, Susan Mendus and Susan Nicholson for their comments on a draft of this essay.

SELECT BIBLIOGRAPHY

LOCKE'S PRINCIPAL WRITINGS ON TOLERATION

Letter to S.H. [Henry Stubbe] (1659), in E. S. de Beer (ed.), *The Correspondence of John Locke*, 8 vols (Oxford 1976–89), vol. i, 109–12.

Two Tracts concerning Government (1660–2), edited by Philip Abrams (Cambridge 1967).

'An Essay on Toleration' (1667), in C. A. Viano (ed.), *John Locke: Scritti Editi e Inediti sulla Tolleranza* (Turin 1961), 81–107.

A Letter on Toleration (1689).

A Second Letter Concerning Toleration. To the Author of the Argument of the Letter concerning Toleration, briefly considered and answered (1690), in *The Works of John Locke. A New edition, corrected* (London 1823), vol. vi, 61–137.

A Third Letter for Toleration. To the Author of the Third Letter concerning Toleration (1692), in *Works*, vol. vi, 411–540.

A Fourth Letter for Toleration (1704), in *Works*, vol. vi, 549–74.

COMMENTARIES*

Aaron, R. I. (1937) *John Locke*, Oxford; 3rd edn 1971.

Abrams, Philip (1967) 'Introduction', *John Locke: Two Tracts on Government*, Cambridge: 3–111.

Ashcraft, Richard (1969) 'Faith and knowledge in Locke's philosophy', in John W. Yolton (ed.), *John Locke: Problems and Perspectives. A Collection of New Essays*, Cambridge: 194–223.

—— (1986) *Revolutionary Politics & Locke's 'Two Treatises of Government'*, Princeton: esp. chs 1–3 and 10.

Biddle, John C. (1977) 'John Locke's Essay on Infallibility: introduction, text, and translation', *Journal of Church and State*, 19: 301–27.

Byrne, James W. (1965) 'John Locke's philosophy of religious toleration', *The Personalist*, 46: 245–52.

Colman, John (1983) *John Locke's Moral Philosophy*, Edinburgh: ch. I.

Cranston, Maurice (1957) *John Locke: A Biography*, London.

Dunn, John (1969) *The Political Thought of John Locke. An Historical Account of the 'Two Treatises of Government'*, Cambridge.

Eisenach, Eldon J. (1981) *Two Worlds of Liberalism: Religion and Politics in Hobbes, Locke, and Mill*, Chicago: part 2, ch. 7.

Gough, J. W. (1968) 'Introduction: Locke's theory of toleration', in John Locke, *'Epistola de Tolerantia'. A Letter on Toleration*, edited by R. Klibansky, translation with an introduction and notes by J. W. Gough, Oxford: 1–42.

Kessler, Sanford (1984–5) 'John Locke's legacy of religious freedom', *Polity*, 17: 484–503.

Kraynak, Robert P. (1980) 'John Locke: from absolutism to toleration', *American Political Science Review*, 74: 53–69.

Lamprecht, Sterling P. (1918) *The Moral and Political Philosophy of John Locke*, New York: 152–61.

Mabbott, J. D. (1973) *John Locke*, London: ch. 20.

Mendus, S. L. (1989) *Toleration and the Limits of Liberalism*, London.

Molyneux, W. E. (1957) 'The development of Locke's theory of toleration', dissertation, Oxford.

Montuori, Mario (1983) *John Locke on Toleration and the Unity of God*, Amsterdam.

Moore, J. T. (1978) 'Locke on assent and toleration', *Journal of Religion*, 58: 30–6.

—— (1979) 'Locke's development from conservative to liberal on toleration', *International Studies in Philosophy*, 11: 59–75.

Parry, Geraint (1978) *John Locke*, London.

Pearson, Samuel C. (1978) 'The religion of John Locke and the character of his thought', *Journal of Religion*, 58: 244–62.

Reventlow, Henning Graf (1984) *The Authority of the Bible and the Rise of the Modern World*, London: part 2, ch. 4.

Schochet, Gordon J. (forthcoming) *John Locke and the Politics of Religious Toleration*.

Seaton, A. A. (1911) *The Theory of Toleration under the Later Stuarts*, Cambridge.

Spellman, W. M. (1988) *John Locke and the Problem of Depravity*, Oxford.

Stephen, J. F. (1867) 'Locke on toleration', reprinted in J. F. Stephen, *Horae Sabbaticae. Reprint of Articles Contributed to 'The Saturday Review'*, 2nd series, London 1892: 157–73.

Tully, James H. (1983) 'Introduction' and 'Further reading', in *John Locke: A Letter Concerning Toleration*, edited and introduced by James H. Tully, Indianapolis: 1–18.

Windstrup, George (1982) 'Freedom and authority: the ancient faith of Locke's "Letter on Toleration"', *Review of Politics*, 44: 242–65.

* See further the indispensable bibliography by Roland Hall and R. S. Woolhouse (1983) *80 Years of Locke Scholarship. A Bibliographical Guide*, Edinburgh, and its continuations in *The Locke News Letter*.

189

INDEX

WHITMAN COLLEGE LIBRARY

WITHDRAWN BY
WHITMAN COLLEGE LIBRARY